Contents

Adobe® InDesign® CS

CLASSROOM
IN A BOOK®

www.adobepress.com

Getting Started

Welcome to Adobe® InDesign® CS. InDesign is a powerful design and production tool that offers precision, control, and seamless integration with other Adobe professional graphics software. Using InDesign, you can produce professional-quality, full-color documents on high-volume color printing presses, or print to a wide range of output devices and formats, such as desktop printers, PDF files, and HTML files.

Writers, artists, designers and publishers can communicate to a broader audience than ever before and through an unprecedented variety of media. The Adobe Network Publishing vision recognizes this with tools for creating visually rich content that is available anywhere, any time, and on any device. InDesign supports this view with its seamless integration with *Adobe Photoshop®*, *Adobe Illustrator®*, *Adobe Acrobat®*, and *Adobe GoLive®*. The *Adobe InDesign CS Classroom in a Book* introduces and describes new features, workflows, and techniques that support this new wave of publishing.

About Classroom in a Book

Adobe InDesign CS Classroom in a Book® is part of the official training series for Adobe graphics and publishing software from Adobe Systems, Inc.

The lessons are designed so that you can learn at your own pace. If you're new to Adobe InDesign, you'll learn the fundamentals you'll need to master to put the program to work. If you've already been using Adobe InDesign, you'll find that Classroom in a Book teaches many advanced features, including tips and techniques for using this exciting design tool.

Each lesson provides step-by-step instructions for creating a specific project. You can follow the book from start to finish, or do only the lessons that meet your interests and needs. Each lesson concludes with a review section summarizing what you've covered.

Prerequisites

Before beginning to use *Adobe InDesign CS Classroom in a Book*, you should have a working knowledge of your computer and its operating system. Make sure you know how to use the mouse and standard menus and commands, and also how to open, save, and close files. If you need to review these techniques, see the printed or online documentation included with your Windows or Mac OS documentation.

Installing the program

You must purchase the Adobe InDesign software separately. For complete instructions on installing the software, see the "How to Install" Readme file in the application CD.

Installing the Classroom in a Book fonts

The Classroom in a Book lesson files use the fonts that installed with Adobe InDesign CS. If it is necessary to reinstall these font files, you can perform a custom installation from your Adobe InDesign software CD to reinstall only the fonts. See the "How to Install" Readme file in the application CD.

Copying the Classroom in a Book files

The Classroom in a Book CD includes folders containing all the electronic files for the lessons. Each lesson has its own folder. You must install these folders on your hard disk to use the files for the lessons. To save room on your hard disk, you can install the folders for each lesson as you need them.

1 Insert the Adobe InDesign Classroom in a Book CD into your CD-ROM drive.

2 Create a folder on your hard disk and name it IDCIB.

3 Do one of the following:

• Copy the Lessons folder into the IDCIB folder.

• Copy only the single lesson folder you need.

Restoring default preferences

To ensure that the tools and palettes function exactly as described in this lesson, you must delete or deactivate (by renaming) the InDesign Defaults file and the InDesign SavedData file.

The InDesign Defaults file and the InDesign SavedData file control how palettes and command settings appear on your screen when you open the Adobe InDesign program. Each time you exit Adobe InDesign, the position of the palettes and certain command settings are recorded in these files. To ensure that the tools and palettes function exactly as described in this book, you can delete the current InDesign Defaults and InDesign SavedData files at the beginning of each lesson. If they don't already exist, Adobe

InDesign will create new versions of these files the next time you start the program and save a file.

To delete your preferences to reset to their original default values:

1 Start Adobe InDesign.

2 Immediately select Control+Alt+Shift (Windows) or Control+Option+Command+Shift (Mac OS).

3 Click Yes to delete the InDesign preference files.

Important: *If you want to save the current settings, rename the defaults files rather than deleting them. When you are ready to restore the settings, change the names back and make sure that the files are located in the InDesign CS folder (Windows®) or the Preferences folder (Mac OS). If you rename the default files, you will be able to revert to your default settings after completing your InDesign Classroom in a Book exercises.*

1 If InDesign is running, choose File > Exit (Windows) or File > Quit (Mac OS).

2 To locate the InDesign defaults files, do one of the following:

• (Windows) Double click to open your hard drive containing your operating system folder. Open the Documents and Settings folder and locate the folder for your user name that you created when you installed your computer. Open this folder and locate the Application Data folder and choose the Adobe Folder. Inside the Adobe folder locate the InDesign folder and open the Version 3 folder. The InDesign Defaults and InDesign SavedData files are stored in this folder. You may need to set your operating system to show hidden files to make them visible. To do this, Choose Tools > Folder Options and click the View tab then select the Show hidden files and folders radio button. The complete path to locate these files is typically c:\\Documents and Setttings\user name\ Application Data\Adobe\Indesign\Version 3.0. Rename these files by adding the word "backup" to their names. Do not delete or change the name of any other InDesign file.

• (Mac OS) Open the hard drive containing your operating system and locate your user folder that was created when you installed your operating system. Open this user folder and locate the Library folder. Inside the Library folder, open the Preferences folder and then locate the Adobe InDesign folder. Within the InDesign folder is the Version 3.0 folder. The InDesign Defaults and InDesign SavedData files are stored in this folder. Rename these files by adding the word "backup" to their names. Do not delete or change the name of any other InDesign file. The complete path to locate these files is typically c:\\Users\user name\Library\Preferences\Adobe InDesign\Version 3.0.

If you renamed the defaults files to preserve them, you can return to your previous settings by first deleting the newest copies of the InDesign Defaults and InDesign SavedData files. Then restore the original names of the files you renamed in the steps above.

Additional resources

Adobe InDesign CS Classroom in a Book is not meant to replace documentation that comes with the program. Only the commands and options used in the lessons are explained in this book. For comprehensive information about program features, refer to these resources:

• Online Help, which you can view by choosing Help > Contents. (For more information, see Lesson 1, "Getting to Know the Work Area.")

• Training and support resources on the Adobe Web site (www.adobe.com), which you can view by choosing Help > Adobe Online if you have a connection to the World Wide Web.

Adobe Certification

The Adobe Training and Certification Programs are designed to help Adobe customers improve and promote their product-proficiency skills. The Adobe Certified Expert (ACE) program is designed to recognize the high-level skills of expert users. Adobe Certified Training Providers (ACTP) use only Adobe Certified Experts to teach Adobe software classes. Available in either ACTP classrooms or on site, the ACE program is the best way to master Adobe products. For Adobe Certified Training Programs information, visit the Partnering with Adobe Web site at http://partners.adobe.com.

A Quick Tour of Adobe InDesign

This interactive demonstration of Adobe InDesign provides an overview of key features of the program. It should take you approximately 30 minutes to complete.

Getting started

You'll start the tour by opening a partially completed document. You'll add the finishing touches to this 6-page article on Mexican folk art written for an imaginary travel magazine. Before you start Adobe InDesign, you should restore the default preferences for InDesign if you have not already done so in this session. Restoring default preferences ensures that the tools and palettes function exactly as described in this lesson. After you learn how to use InDesign, this step is no longer necessary.

1 Delete or deactivate the InDesign Defaults file and the InDesign SavedData file, following the procedure in "Restoring default preferences" on page 2.

2 Start Adobe InDesign.

3 Choose File > Open, and locate the ID_00 folder in the IDCIB folder you copied from the InDesign Classroom in a Book CD to your hard disk.

4 In the ID_00 folder, double-click ID_01.indd.

Note: Your extensions may be hidden based upon your computer system preferences. If this is so, the file appears without the .indd added to its name. So it will appear as ID_01 (not ID_01.indd) in the Open a File dialog box.

5 Choose File > Save As, and rename the file **Tour** in the ID_00 folder.

Viewing the document

The first spread (pages 2 and 3) appears on your screen. You'll now look at the rest of the 6-page article using several navigation methods. First, you'll use the Navigator palette, which is useful for changing the view magnification. As in Adobe Illustrator and Adobe Photoshop, palettes are often grouped with other palettes. However, you can move, separate, and combine these palettes any way you like. A check mark indicates this view is selected. The Fit Spread in Window option displays all of the adjoining pages in a spread.

1 Choose View > Fit Spread in Window.

2 Choose Window > Navigator to have the palette appear on your screen.

3 Position the pointer and click on the palette-menu button (⊙) on the right side of the palette window, and choose View All Spreads from the Navigator palette menu. If you can't see the three spreads well, drag the lower right corner of the palette down to resize it.

Like many palettes, the Navigator palette has a menu that displays additional options.

Notice that the red view box in the Navigator palette determines which area of the document is displayed.

4 In the Navigator palette, click the center of the middle spread to view pages 4 and 5. If necessary, drag the red box so that you can see pages 4 and 5.

5 Choose View > Fit Page in Window. You can see how the magnification displayed in the Navigator palette is automatically updated.

Now we'll look at the Pages palette, which is another useful tool for turning pages. You'll be using the Pages palette throughout this tour, so you'll separate the Pages palette from the other two palettes.

6 Click the Pages palette tab, and then drag the Pages tab away from the other palettes.

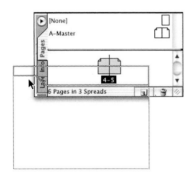

Feel free to move and rearrange palettes in this Quick Tour as needed. You can move a palette by dragging its title bar. You can place a palette in the docking area on the right side of the document window by dragging a palette by its tab, to this portion of the window. You can also click the minimize button or close button on the top bar.

When you need to use the palette again, click the palette name if it is in the docking area or use the restore button or choose the appropriate menu command (such as Window > Pages to display the Pages palette).

7 In the Pages palette, double-click the numbers 6-7 below the page icons to view the last spread in the document.

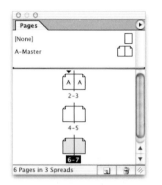

Double-clicking the numbers below the page icons centers the full spread in the document window. Double-clicking a page icon centers the page in the document window.

Now that you've seen all three spreads, let's go back to page 3 and start working.

8 In the Pages palette, double-click the page 3 icon to move to page 3.

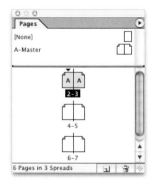

Turning on guides

In this document, the guides are hidden. You'll turn on the guides to make it easy to see your layout grid and snap objects into place. The guides do not print and do not limit the print area. They are for your reference only.

• Choose View > Show Guides.

Before and after turning on guides.

Adding text

You can import text created in separate word processing programs or create text using InDesign. In this exercise you are going to add a secondary headline to page 3.

1   Using the Type tool (**T**) click and drag to create a box for this headline between the two guides below the word Mexico in the right column of the page.

If the text box is not aligned exactly to the size of the guides, use the Selection tool (**▶**) to click on the corners of the box and enlarge or reduce them as necessary.

2 Enter the text **Exploring Mexican Folk Art** in the text box.

InDesign placed the text insertion point in the frame after it was created because it was built using the Type tool. For frames created with other tools, you will first need to click within the frame before entering text.

3 Select the frame with the Selection tool (↖).

4 Choose Type > Character.

5 Select the font Adobe Garamond Pro Regular and the size of 18 points in the Character Palette.

You can apply attributes to all the text within a box by selecting the box.

Threading text in frames

As a general rule, text is placed inside frames with InDesign. You can either add text to a frame that has already been created, or you can create the frame while you import text.

Placing and flowing text

An article describing Judith and Clyde's trip to Oaxaca has been saved in a word-processor file. You'll place this file on page 3 and then thread it throughout your document.

1 Make sure that no objects are selected, and then choose File > Place. In the Place dialog box, go to the ID_00 folder in the Lessons folder and double-click the 01_a.doc file.

The pointer takes the shape of a loaded text icon (⊞). With a loaded text icon, you have several choices: You can drag to create a text frame, click inside an existing frame, or click to create a frame within a column. You'll add this text to a column in the lower half of page 3.

2 Position the loaded text icon just below the fourth guide from the bottom margin and just to the right of the left margin, and click.

3 The text flows into a new frame in the lower half of the first column on page 3. When a text frame has more text than can fit, the frame is said to have overset text. Overset text is indicated by a red plus symbol in the out port of the frame (the small square just above the lower right corner of the frame). You can link overset text to another frame or create a new frame into which the overset text will flow, or expand the size of the frame.

If the text box is not placed in the left column, click the Selection tool (▸) and drag the sizing handles to move it to the proper location.

4 Click the out port in the selected frame.

5 The pointer becomes a loaded text icon. Now you'll add a column of text to the lower half of the second column.

6 Position the loaded text icon just below the fourth guide from the bottom margin and just to the right of the second column guide, and click. Text now fills the lower part of the right column.

You can also set the number of columns in a single text box by selecting the box and setting the number of columns for the box in the control palette. This allows you to create multiple columns of type without flowing text.

Threading text

Clicking the out port to flow text is called manual threading.

1 Click the out port in the second column (on page 3).

This prepares InDesign to flow the overset text from this text frame to another frame.

2 In the Pages palette, double-click the page 4 icon to center page 4 in the document window.

3 Holding down Alt (Windows) or Option (Mac OS), position the loaded text icon in the upper left corner of the first column, and click. Release the Alt/Option key.

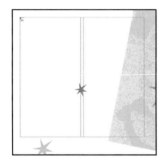

Note: After clicking on the out port, you can hold down Shift to thread text automatically so that all the overset text is flowed into the columns through a document. But you don't want to do that in this document because the text frames should not appear on every page. Alternatively, you can hold down Alt (Windows) or Option (Mac OS) to thread text one frame at a time without having to click the out port in each frame with overset text.

The text flows into the left column. Because you held down Alt/Option, the pointer is still a loaded text icon and you do not need to click in the out port before flowing text from this frame.

4 Position the loaded text icon in the upper left corner of the second column on page 4, and click.

💡 *Whenever the pointer is a loaded text icon, you can click any tool in the toolbox to cancel the operation. No text will be lost but any overset text will still need to be linked to another box or edited.*

Now you'll flow the text into the bottom of the two columns on page 7.

5 Click the out port in the second column of page 4, and then double-click the page 7 icon in the Pages palette to center page 7 in the document window.

6 Holding down Alt/Option, position the loaded text icon in the left column below the guide on page 7, and click. Release the Alt/Option key.

7 Position the loaded text icon in the second column below the guide, and click.

You have just finished threading text frames. A threaded set of frames is called a story.

8 Choose File > Save.

Adding a pull quote

To enhance the design on page 4 of your document, you'll add a pull quote. We copied text from the article and placed it into a frame on the pasteboard which is the area outside of the page. You will position this pull-quote text frame in the middle of page 4 and finish formatting it.

1 Choose View > Fit Page in Window. Then choose File > Save.

2 In the lower left corner of the document window, select page 4 from the list of available pages. If you cannot see the pull-quote text frame to the left of page 4, locate the scroll box on the horizontal scroll bar and drag it to the left.

3 Using the Selection tool (⬆), select the text frame on the pasteboard that contains the quote.

4 Click in the Control palette located just below the menus at the top of the page, entering an X value of **4 in** and a Y offset of **3 in**.

The pull quote should now be centered between the columns of text on page 4. If necessary, use the arrow keys to nudge the frames location. The bottom of the frame should pass through the middle of the red star.

💡 *It is important to include the "in" after each number to identify the units of measurement being used (inches). With Adobe InDesign you can use most forms of measurement throughout the program, including palettes and dialog boxes, as long as you identify them with standard abbreviations, such as pt for point or cm for centimeter.*

Wrapping text around an object

The text in the pull quote is difficult to read because the main story text does not wrap around the text frame. You'll wrap the main story text around the edges of the pull-quote text frame.

1 Make sure the pull-quote frame is selected.

2 Choose Window > Type & Tables > Text Wrap.

3 In the Text Wrap palette, click the third wrap option (▣) to wrap text around the object's shape.

4 Click the Close button to close the Text Wrap palette.

5 Choose File > Save.

Adding a stroke to the frame

Now you'll change the color of the text frame so that the stroke (border) matches the color of the red star. When you apply colors in InDesign, it's a good idea to use the Swatches palette instead of the Colors palette. Using the Swatches palette to name colors makes it easy to apply, edit, and update colors efficiently for all objects in a document.

This magazine article is intended for printing at a commercial press, so it uses CMYK process colors. We've already added the set of necessary colors to the Swatches palette.

1 Choose Window > Swatches.

2 With the text frame still selected, click the Stroke box (⬚) in the top of the Swatches palette and then select PANTONE Warm Red CVC in the Swatches palette. Selecting the Stroke box will allow the frame of the image to be affected by the color you select.

3 To change the weight of the stroke, right-click on the frame (Windows) or Ctrl+click on the frame (Mac OS) and select Stroke Weight > 0.5 pt. The context menus are an easy way to change many attributes of a selected object, including the stroke weight.

4 Choose Edit > Deselect All.

The text frame now has a thin red stroke.

Choose File > Save.

Changing the frame and text position

The text in the pull-quote frame is too close to the edge, making it unattractive and difficult to read. You'll now change the position of the text within the frame and change the type of frame style.

1 Using the Selection tool (▶), click the pull-quote text frame to select it, and then choose the Align center option from the Control palette.

2 With the frame still selected, choose the Thick-Thin stroke type from the control palette.

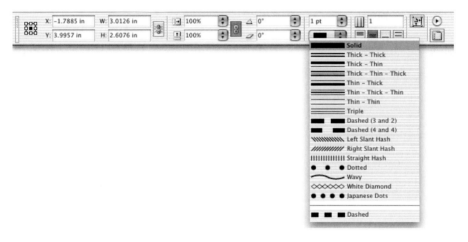

3 Use the control palette to increase the stroke weight to 4 pt.

You can also use the control palette to easily adjust important attributes for objects on your page.

Adjusting the size of an image

Next we will adjust the size of the picture of the moon on the adjacent page.

1 If necessary, select page 5 in the lower left hand corner of the document window to move to this page.

2 Using the Selection tool (↖) select the picture of the moon.

3 Using the Control palette choose 50% from the X Scale %, which is the top of the two scaling values in the Control palette.

Both the vertical and horizontal sizes adjust proportionally. This is because the Constrain proportions for scaling button is selected to the right of the scaling percentages. You can deselect this button if you wish to adjust one value independent of the other. As a general rule, bitmap images such as those scanned or taken with a digital camera, should not be scaled disproportionately and should not be scaled beyond 120% of their original size due to the possible loss of quality. In this case, we were reducing the size of the image, which generally has no adverse impact on its quality.

4 Choose File > Save.

Working with styles

InDesign includes two kinds of styles: paragraph and character. A paragraph style includes formatting attributes that apply to all text within a paragraph. You do not need to select text to apply a paragraph style, as it applies to all text in the paragraph where your cursor is located. A character style includes only character attributes, making it useful for formatting words and phrases within a paragraph. Text must be selected to apply a character style.

Applying paragraph styles

To save time, we created paragraph styles that you'll apply to the text. These styles will help you format the body text in the article.

1 In the Pages palette, double-click the page 3 icon to center page 3 in the document window.

2 Select the Type tool (T), and then click anywhere in the columns of text that you previously placed on this page.

3 Choose Edit > Select All to select the text in all the frames of the story.

4 Choose Type > Paragraph Styles to display the Paragraph Styles palette.

5 In the Paragraph Styles palette, click Body Text to format the entire story with the Body Text style.

6 Choose Edit > Deselect All to deselect the text.

Now you'll apply a different paragraph style to the first paragraph of the story.

7 Using the Type tool (**T**), click anywhere in the first paragraph on page 3.

8 In the Paragraph Styles palette, select Body Text / Drop Cap.

Like other options in the Paragraph and Character palettes, drop caps can be part of a style.

9 Choose File > Save.

Formatting text for the character style

Now you'll create and apply a character style to emphasize page references within paragraphs. Before you create this character style, you'll use the Character palette to italicize the text and make it one point smaller. You'll then base the character style on this formatted text.

1 In the Pages palette, double-click the page 7 icon to center page 7 in the document window. To make sure that you can read the text at the bottom of this page, press Ctrl+= (Windows) or Command+= (Mac OS) and use the scroll bars as necessary.

You should be able to see three references to other pages: (page 7), (page 2), and (page 5).

2 Using the Type tool (**T**), select the "(page 7)" reference.

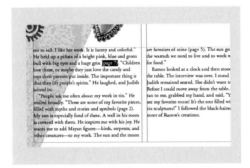

3 Choose Type > Character to display the Character palette.

4 Select Italic from the Type Style menu. For font size (𝐓T), select 11 pt.

The page reference is now formatted.

5 Choose File > Save.

Creating and applying a character style

Now that you have formatted the text, you are ready to create a character style.

1 Make sure that the text you formatted is still selected, and choose Type > Character Styles to display the Character Styles palette.

2 Click the New Style button (⊠) at the bottom of the Character Styles palette.

A new character style named Character Style 1 is created. This new style includes the characteristics of the selected text.

3 In the Character Styles palette, double-click Character Style 1 to open the Modify Character Style Options dialog box.

4 For Style Name, type **Emphasis** and click OK.

5 Using the Type tool (**T**), select the text "(page 2)" in the next paragraph, and then click Emphasis in the Character Styles palette to apply the style.

6 Apply the character style to the text "(page 5)" in the same paragraph.

Because you used a character style instead of a paragraph style, the style you applied affected only the selected text, not the entire paragraph.

7 Choose File > Save.

Working with graphics

Graphics used in an InDesign document are placed inside of frames. When working with placed graphics, you should become familiar with the two Selection tools.

The Selection tool (▶) is used for general layout tasks, such as positioning and moving objects on a page. The Direct Selection tool (▷) is used for tasks involving the content of the frame or drawing and editing paths; for example, to select frame contents or to move an anchor point on a path. The Direct Selection tool is also used for selecting objects within groups.

Note: While learning about the difference between frames and their content, you may want to make frame edges visible by selecting View > Show Frame edges.

Positioning graphics within a frame

Two of the pictures on the first spread need to have their frames resized or the pictures within them repositioned.

1 Select page 2 in the lower left corner of the document window to navigate to page 2.

2 Using the Direct Selection tool (▷) click and hold on the picture of the sun. Drag the picture to the center of the frame so that the entire sun is visible.

With the Direct Selection tool you can reposition graphics within their frame.

3 Using the Selection tool (▶) click on the picture of the blue hand.

4 Click and drag the center handle upward to expand the size of the frame.

💡 *You can preview the picture as you move or resize the frame if you pause briefly before resizing or moving the picture.*

5 Choose File > Save.

Working with grouped objects

The three stars on page 5 are grouped together. You'll select the rightmost star so that you can change its color.

1 In the Pages palette, double-click the page 5 icon to center page 5 in the document window. Choose View > Fit Page in Window.

2 Using the Selection tool (⬉), click the black star on page 5 to select it.

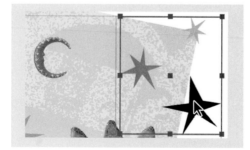

Notice that the star is part of a group. Instead of having to ungroup the objects to select only the black star, you can use the Direct Selection tool (⬉) to select the object within a group.

3 Click the Direct Selection tool (↖), and then click the black star.

The anchor points of the selected object appear.

4 To change the fill color to purple, choose Window > Swatches, and then select the Fill box (■) in the top of the palette.

5 Select PANTONE 265 in the Swatches palette.

Using the Pen tool to reshape an object

The purple star you selected needs another ray to match the other stars. You'll use the Pen tool to add anchor points so that you can create a new ray in the star.

1 Position the pointer over the Pen tool in the toolbox, and then click and hold down the mouse button to display additional tools. Select the Add Anchor Point Tool.

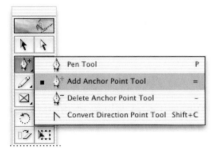

2 Click the edge of the star twice to add two anchor points.

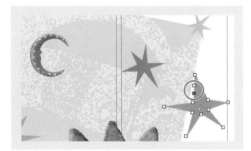

3 Select the Direct Selection tool ( ), and then drag the lower of the two anchor points away from the star to create another ray.

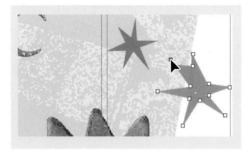

Note: You can select and drag more than one point. Shift-click to select multiple points; click the center point to select all points; click outside the shape to deselect all points. You can also click between two points and drag the segment.

4 Use the Direct Selection tool ( ) to drag anchor points as needed to reshape the star.

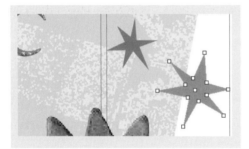

5 Choose File > Save.

Targeting layers when placing

Like Illustrator and Photoshop, InDesign lets you place objects on different layers. Think of layers as sheets of transparent film that are stacked on top of each other. By using layers, you can create and edit objects on one layer without affecting—or being affected by—objects on other layers. Layers also determine the stacking position of objects.

Before you place a photograph of an armadillo, you'll make sure that you add the frame to the appropriate layer.

1 In the Pages palette, double-click the page 3 icon to center page 3 in the document window.

2 Choose Window > Layers to display the Layers palette.

3 Click the word "Photos" in the Layers palette to target the Photos layer. (Do not click the boxes to the left of the Photos layer, or you'll hide or lock the layer.)

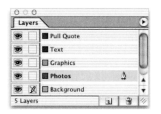

4 Select the Selection tool (⬆).

5 Choose File > Place, and double-click the 01_b.tif file located in the ID_00 folder.

6 With the loaded graphics icon (⬛), click in the white area above the top margin to place the armadillo at the top of the page. You'll move the graphic later, after you rotate and crop it.

Notice that the armadillo frame is the same color as the Photos layer in the Layers palette. An object's frame color tells you which layer it belongs to.

7 In the Layers palette, click the box next to the Text layer name so that the lock icon (🔏) appears.

Locking this layer prevents you from selecting or making any changes to the Text layer or any objects on that layer. With the Text layer locked, you can edit the frame containing the armadillo without accidentally selecting the frame containing "Hecho en Mexico."

Cropping and moving the photograph

You'll now use the Selection tool to crop and move the photograph.

1 Choose Edit > Deselect All.

2 Select the Selection tool (▶) in the toolbox, and then click the armadillo.

3 Position the pointer over the middle handle on the right side of the armadillo frame and hold down the mouse button. Drag the frame toward the center of the armadillo to crop it.

4 Using the Selection tool (▶), position the pointer over the center of the armadillo frame and drag the object so that it snaps to the right edge of the page.

Notice that the edge of the armadillo is behind the decorative border. This is because the Photos layer is below the Graphics layer in the Layers palette.

5 Choose File > Save.

On your own

Congratulations! You've completed the InDesign tour. You're now ready to create your own InDesign documents. To learn more about InDesign, you may want to try the following:

• Continue experimenting with the travel document. Add new pages, edit the master pages, move items among the layers, create text frames, and adjust the graphics using the tools in the toolbox.

• Choose Help > InDesign Help to use online Help.

• Go through the lessons in the rest of this book.

1 Getting to Know the Work Area

To make the best use of the extensive drawing, layout, and editing capabilities in Adobe InDesign, it's important to learn how to navigate in the work area. The work area consists of the document window, the pasteboard, the toolbox, and the floating palettes.

In this lesson, you'll learn how to do the following:

• Work with tools, document windows, the pasteboard, and palettes.

• Change the magnification of the document.

• Navigate through a document.

• Work with layers.

• Manage palettes and save your workspace.

• Use context menus and online help.

• Use Adobe online services.

Note: This lesson covers tasks that are common to Adobe products such as Photoshop®, Illustrator®, and Acrobat®. If you are familiar with these Adobe products, you may want to skim through this lesson and move ahead to the next lesson.

Getting started

In this lesson, you'll practice using the work area and navigating through pages of the Exploring the Library booklet. This is the final version of the document—you won't be changing or adding text or graphics, only checking to make sure everything is ready for print. Before you begin, you'll need to restore the default preferences for Adobe InDesign.

1 To ensure that the tools and palettes function exactly as described in this lesson, delete or deactivate (by renaming) the InDesign Defaults file and the InDesign SavedData file. See "Restoring default preferences" on page 2.

2 Start Adobe InDesign.

To begin working, you'll open an existing InDesign document.

Note: If you have not already copied the resource files for this lesson onto your hard disk from the ID_01 folder from the Adobe InDesign CS Classroom in a Book CD, do so now. See "Copying the Classroom in a Book files" on page 2

3 Choose File > Open, and open the 01_a.indd file in the ID_01 folder, located inside the Lessons folder within the IDCIB folder on your hard disk. If an alert message appears that asks which dictionary file you want to use, click No (Windows) or Document (Mac OS).

4 Choose File > Save As, rename the file **01_Library.indd**, and save it in the ID_01 folder.

Note: This document was saved with the frame edges hidden (View > Hide Frame Edges). By default, frame edges are visible in all documents.

Looking at the work area

The InDesign work area encompasses everything you see when you first open or create a document: the toolbox, document window, pasteboard, and palettes. You can customize and save the work area to suit your work style. For example, you can display only the palettes you frequently use, minimize and rearrange palette groups, resize windows, add additional document windows, and so on.

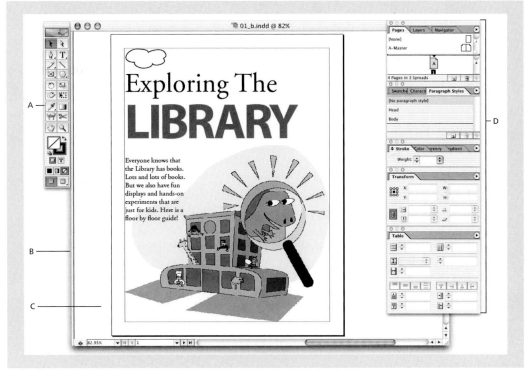

A. Toolbox. B. Document window. C. Pasteboard. D. Palettes.

Toolbox

The InDesign toolbox contains tools for selecting objects, working with type, drawing, and viewing, as well as controls for applying and changing color fills, strokes, and gradients.

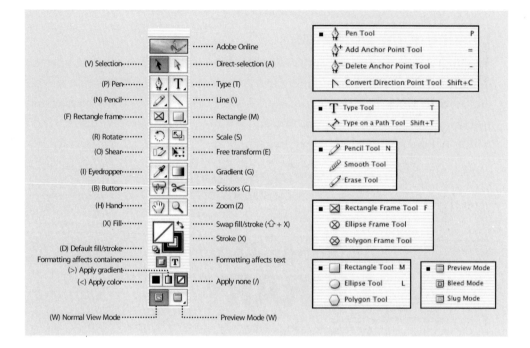

As you work through the lessons, you'll learn about each tool's specific function. Here you'll familiarize yourself with the toolbox and the tools.

1 Position the pointer over the Selection tool (▶) in the toolbox. Notice the name and shortcut are displayed.

You can select a tool by either clicking the tool in the toolbox or pressing the tool's keyboard shortcut. Because the default keyboard shortcuts only work when you do not have a text insertion point, you can add an additional key command. To do this, use the Keyboard Shortcuts command which is covered in the next chapter and in Adobe InDesign online Help.

2 Position the pointer over the Pen tool and hold down the mouse button—additional Pen tools appear. Drag to the right and release the mouse button over one of the additional tools to select it. Any tool that displays a small black triangle at the bottom right corner contains additional tools.

3 Select the Selection tool (✸) again; then click the edge of the little cloud in the top left corner of page 1 to select it.

Now you'll use the color controls, which are located on the bottom half of the toolbox.

4 Select the Fill box () to make sure that any changes you make affect the center portion of the object and not its stroke.

5 Click the Color box (■) in the toolbox. The object becomes filled with solid black. Click the Gradient box (▣). The object becomes filled with a white-to-black gradient. Click the None box (⊘) to return the object to its original unfilled state.

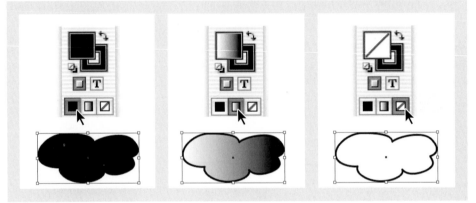

Object filled with black (left), filled with a gradient (center), and reset to no fill (right).

Note: *If you accidentally double-click a Fill or Gradient box, the Color or Gradient palette will open. Close the palette to continue with the lesson.*

When you start InDesign, several groups of palettes are collapsed into tabs at the side of the application window (Windows) or screen (Mac OS). You can move collapsed palettes into windows of their own or collapse other palettes into side tabs. Palettes collapsed into side tabs can be grouped and rearranged.

- *To display a collapsed palette: Click the palette's tab to display or hide it.*

- *To convert a collapsed palette to a floating palette: Drag a palette's tab away from the side of the application window (Windows) or of the screen (Mac OS).*

- *To collapse a palette into a side tab: Select the palette's tab and drag it to the left or right side of the application window (Windows) or of the screen (Mac OS).*

- From Adobe InDesign CS online Help

6 Now select the Stroke box ( ) so that any changes you make affect the object's stroke.

7 Click the Gradient box ( ) in the toolbox. The solid stroke becomes a gradient stroke. Click the Color box ( ) to return the object to its original stroke. Then click a blank area of the page or pasteboard to deselect the cloud.

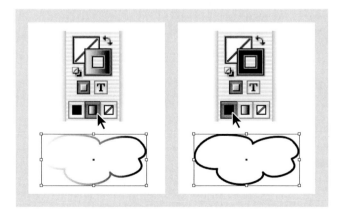

To learn how to change the color of a fill, stroke, or gradient, see Lesson 6, "Working with Color."

Document window

The document window contains your document pages. You can have more than one document window open at a time. Here, you'll open a second window so that as you work you can see two different views of the document at the same time.

1 Choose Window > Arrange > New Window. A new window titled 01_Library.indd:2 opens. Notice that the original window is now titled 01_Library.indd.1.

2 To view both windows simultaneously, choose Window > Arrange > Tile.

3 Now select the Zoom tool in the toolbox (🔍) and click twice on the dinosaur in the rightmost document window. Notice that the original document window remains at the original magnification. This arrangement lets you work closely on details and see the overall results on the rest of the page.

4 Close the 01_Library.indd:2 document window, by clicking the close window button at the top of the document window. Windows users, be careful not to close the program, as the close window and close program buttons are located adjacent to each other. Be sure to only close the second document window. Then resize and reposition the remaining window by clicking the Maximize button on the top of your document window.

The Maximize (Windows) button is in the middle box in the upper right corner of any window. In Mac OS, this is the green button in the upper left corner of the window.

Pasteboard

Each page or spread in your document has its own pasteboard surrounding it, where you can store objects relating to your document as you create your layout. The pasteboard also provides additional space along the edges of the document for extending objects past the page edge. Extending objects past the edge of a page is called a bleed, and is used when an object must print entirely to the edge of a page.

1 To see the full size of the pasteboard for the pages in this document, choose View > Entire Pasteboard.

Note: *If you cannot see the graphic of a book on the pasteboard, it may be hidden behind one of the palettes. Move the palettes or reduce the size of the document window so that you can see all these objects.*

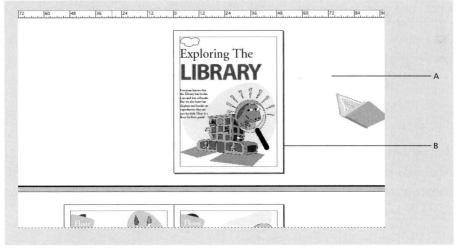

A. Pasteboard. B. Document.

Notice the book graphic on the pasteboard for page 1. This graphic was originally placed in the document, but then moved to the pasteboard in anticipation that it would be used somewhere else in the document. It is no longer necessary to keep this image with the document.

2 Using the Selection tool (↖), select the book image on the pasteboard and press Delete.

3 Choose View > Fit Page in Window to restore the window to its previous size.

4 Choose File > Save.

🔆 *Use the pasteboard as an extension of your working area. You can import multiple placed images or text files and hold them on the pasteboard until you are ready to use them.*

Viewing and arranging palettes

Palettes provide quick access to commonly used tools and features in InDesign. By default, palettes appear in stacked groups, which you can reorganize in various ways. Here you'll experiment with hiding, closing, and opening palettes.

1 Choose Window > Workspace > Default to reset the palettes to their original location.

2 Click the Layers palette tab to make this palette appear or choose Window > Layers.

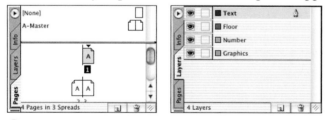

🔆 *To find a hidden palette, choose the palette name on the Window menu. If the palette name already has a check mark, then the palette is already open and in front of any other palettes in its palette group. If you choose a checked palette name on the Window menu, the palette will close.*

Now you'll reorganize the palette group.

3 Drag the Layers palette tab outside the group to create a new palette window.

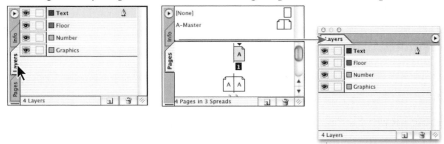

Palettes are grouped (left). Drag the palette tab to separate a palette from the group (right).

You can also move palettes from one palette group to another to create custom palette groups of the palettes you use most often.

 Press Tab to hide all open palettes and the toolbox. Press Tab again to display them all again. You can hide or display just the palettes (not the toolbox) by pressing Shift+Tab.

Docking palettes

Dock palettes by connecting the lower edge of one palette to the top edge of another palette, so that both palettes move together and are shown and hidden together. When you dock palettes, both palettes remain fully visible. In contrast, when you group palettes, only the frontmost palette is visible.

You can dock one palette to another single palette or to a group of palettes. However, you can't dock a group of palettes unless you dock each of them individually, because docking involves dragging an individual palette's tab and not the title bar.

–From Adobe InDesign CS online Help.

To dock palettes, drag a palette's tab to the bottom edge of another palette. When the bottom edge of the other palette is highlighted, release the mouse.

4 If the Paragraph palette is not visible, open it by selecting Type > Paragraph. Then drag the Layers palette tab into the center of the Paragraph palette group. Then drag the tab back to the Pages palette group.

Note: *To add a palette to a group, make sure you drag its tab into the middle of the palette. If you drag a palette tab to the bottom of another palette, you will dock the palette instead of adding it. See the "Docking palettes" sidebar above.*

Now you'll organize the palettes to create more space in your work area.

5 After dragging a palette from the docking area, you can double-click the tab containing the name of the palette to reduce the size of the palette. Double-click the tab again to minimize the palette.

Note: You can double-click a third time to return to the full size view of the palette. These clicking options work only after the palette has been pulled out from the docking area.

Customizing your workspace

You can save the position of palettes and easily open a group of related palettes by creating a workspace. Next we will create a workspace that brings up a group of commonly used palettes.

1 Select Window > Pages then select Window > Navigator and also select Window > Transform.

2 Position the three palettes so they are all visible on the side of the screen.

3 Select Window > Workspace > Save Workspace and name the workspace Navigation.

4 Switch to the default palette layout by selecting Window > Workspace > Default. Note that the palettes return to their default positions. Toggle between the two workspaces using the Window > Workspace command and selecting the workspace you wish to use but switch back to the Default Workspace before going on to the next exercise.

Using palette menus

Most palettes have a palette-menu button in the upper right corner of the palette window when the palette is not collapsed into the side window. This menu appears in the upper left corner of a docked palette. Clicking this arrow-shaped button opens a menu with additional commands and options for the selected palette. You can use this to change options for the palette display or access additional commands relating to the palette. Next we will change the display of one of the palettes used to create and save color, called the Swatches palette.

1 Click the Swatches palette tab in the docking area on the right side of the window. You can also choose Window > Swatches to display this palette. Drag the palette to the left, separating it from the docking area. Note that the palette menu has moved to the upper right corner of the palette. The palette menu changes position if a palette is in the docking area or if it is on the page in its own window.

2 Position the pointer on the palette-menu button in the upper right corner of the Swatches palette, and click the mouse button to display the palette menu.

3 Choose Small Name. This command affects the Swatches palette rows, but not the other paletts visible on the screen. The commands in the palette menu apply only to the active palette.

4 On the Swatches palette menu, choose Name to return the swatches names to their original size.

Changing the magnification of your document

You can reduce or enlarge the view of the document to any magnification level from 5% to 4000%. When you are viewing a document, InDesign displays the percentage of the document's actual size in the lower left corner of the document window and also at the top of the document in the title bar of the window, next to the filename.

Using the view commands and magnification menu

You can easily enlarge or reduce the view of a document by doing one of the following:

• Choose a percentage from the magnification menu at the lower left corner of the document window to enlarge or reduce the display by any preset increment.

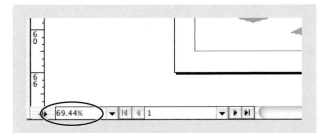

• Type a percentage in the magnification menu by positioning your cursor over this area and clicking to obtain an insertion point, entering the desired viewing percent and then using the return key to enter the value.

• Choose View > Zoom In to enlarge the display by one preset increment.

• Choose View > Zoom Out to reduce the display by one preset increment.

Note: Preset sizes are those listed in the magnification menu.

• Choose View > Actual Size to display the document at 100%. (Depending on the dimensions of your document and your screen resolution, you may or may not see the entire document on-screen.)

• Choose View > Fit Page in Window to display the targeted page in the window.

• Choose View > Fit Spread in Window to display the targeted spread in the window.

Using the Zoom tool

In addition to the view commands, you can use the Zoom tool to magnify and reduce the view of a document.

1 Select the Zoom tool (🔍) in the toolbox and position it over the dinosaur on page 1. Notice that a plus sign appears in the center of the Zoom tool (🔍).

2 Click once. The view changes to the next preset magnification, centered on the point where you clicked. Now you'll reduce the view.

3 Position the Zoom tool pointer over the dinosaur and hold down Alt (Windows) or Option (Mac OS). A minus sign appears in the center of the Zoom tool (🔍).

4 With Alt/Option still held down, click twice over the dinosaur; the view is reduced.

You can also use the Zoom tool to drag a marquee around a portion of a document to magnify a specific area.

5 With the Zoom tool still selected, hold down the mouse button and drag a marquee around the dinosaur; then release the mouse.

The percentage by which the area is magnified depends on the size of the marquee: the smaller the marquee, the larger the degree of magnification.

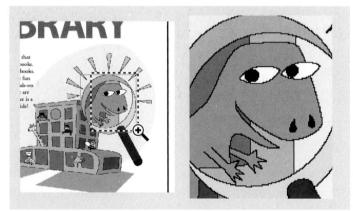

Dragging a marquee with the Zoom tool (left) and the resulting view (right).

6 In the toolbox, double-click the icon for the Zoom tool to return to a 100% view.

Because the Zoom tool is used frequently during the editing process to enlarge and reduce the view of your document, you can temporarily select it from the keyboard at any time without deselecting any other tool you may be using. You'll do that now.

7 Click the Selection tool in the toolbox and position it in the document window.

8 Hold down Ctrl+spacebar (Windows) or Command+spacebar (Mac OS) so that the Selection tool icon becomes the Zoom tool icon, and then click on the dinosaur to magnify the view. When you release the keys, the pointer again appears as the Selection tool icon.

9 Hold down Ctrl+Alt+spacebar (Windows) or Command+Option+spacebar (Mac OS) and click to zoom out, returning to a 100% view.

10 Choose View > Fit Spread in Window to center the page.

You can also change your magnification using key commands. Use Ctrl+= (Windows) or Command+= (Mac OS) to increase the magnification and Ctrl+- (Windows) or Command+- (Mac OS) to decrease the magnification.

Navigating through your document

InDesign provides several options for viewing and navigating through a document, including the Pages and Navigator palettes, and the scroll bars.

Turning pages

You can turn pages using the Pages palette, the page buttons at the bottom of the document window, the scroll bars, or a variety of commands.

The Pages palette provides page icons for all the pages in your document. Double-clicking on any page icon or page number brings that page or spread into view.

Targeting and selecting spreads or pages

You can target or select spreads, depending on the task at hand:

• *Target a spread where the next new object should appear. This is helpful when, for example, several spreads are visible in the document window and you want to paste an object on a specific spread. Only one spread can be the target at any time. By default, the target spread occupies the center of the document window. It is indicated by the highlighted page numbers (not highlighted page icons) in the Pages palette.*

• *Select a page or spread when your next action will affect a page or spread rather than objects, as when you're setting margin and column options for a specific page only. When all pages of a spread are highlighted in the Pages palette, that spread is selected. You can select multiple spreads in a document. The selected spread is indicated by the highlighted page icons (not highlighted page numbers) in the Pages palette.*

–From Adobe InDesign CS online Help.

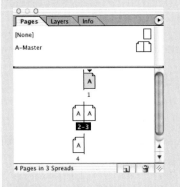

Page 1 selected; pages 2 and 3 targeted.

1 Make sure that the Selection tool (✦) is still selected and select Window > Pages if the Pages palette is not already open.

2 In the Pages palette, double-click the 2–3 page numbers below the page icons to target and view the spread on pages 2 and 3. You may need to scroll in the Pages palette to see pages 2 and 3. Choose View > Fit Spread in Window to view both pages of the spread.

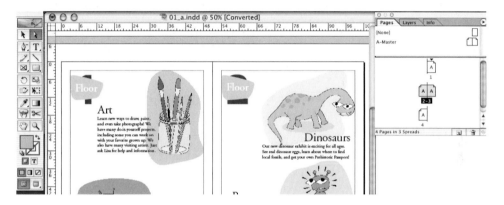

3 Double-click the page 3 icon to select and center only that page in the document window.

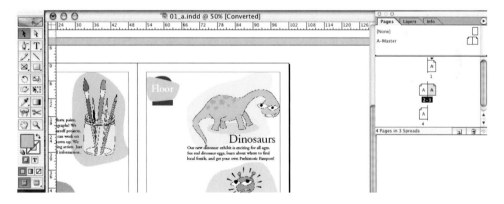

Now you'll use the page buttons at the bottom of the document window to change pages.

4 Click the next-page button (▶) at the lower left corner of the document window to go to page 4. This is located to the right of the magnification percentage.

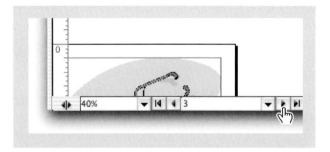

You can also turn to a specific page number by typing the number in the page box. Use the Enter or Return key after entering the page number.

5 Select 4 in the page box at the lower left of the document window, type **1**, and press Enter or Return.

Now you'll change pages using a menu command.

6 Choose Layout > Go Back to return to page 4.

7 Choose Layout > Previous Page to turn to page 3.

You can also turn to a specific page number by selecting the page number from the Page pop-up menu in the bottom of the document window.

8 Click the downward facing arrow (▼) to the right of the page box, and select 2 from the Page pop-up menu that appears.

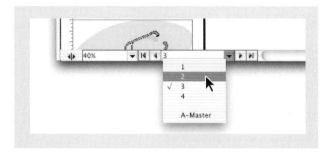

You can experiment with all the different methods for navigating through a document. For a full list of commands used for turning pages, see "Turning pages" in online Help.

Scrolling through a document

You can also use the Hand tool, or the scroll bars along the side of the document window, to move to different areas or pages of a document. Here you'll use both methods to navigate through the document.

1 Drag the scrollbar along the right side of the document window all the way to the top to view page 1. If necessary, drag the horizontal scroll bar across the bottom of the window until you can see page 1.

2 With the Selection tool (▶) selected in the toolbox and the pointer positioned over the document, hold down the spacebar on the keyboard. Notice that the Selection tool icon changes to the Hand tool (✋). You can use this shortcut when you don't want to change tools while moving through the document. You can also select the Hand tool (✋) in the toolbox.

3 With the spacebar still held down, click and drag upward in the document window until the page 2–3 spread appears on-screen. As you drag, the document moves with the hand. The Hand tool lets you scroll both vertically and horizontally within your documents without using the scroll bars.

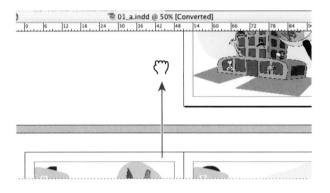

You can also use the Hand tool as a shortcut to fit the page or spread in the window.

4 In the toolbox, double-click the icon for the Hand tool to fit the spread in the window.

5 Using the Hand tool, click on or near the bug in the lower right corner and drag to center it in the window.

Using the Navigator palette

The Navigator palette provides several navigation and view tools in one location, so you can quickly and easily magnify and scroll to a desired location.

1 Choose Window > Navigator to access the Navigator palette.

2 In the bottom of the Navigator palette, drag the slider to the right to increase the magnification of the document on your monitor. As you drag the slider to increase the level of magnification, the red outline in the Navigator window decreases in size, showing you the area that is visible on your monitor.

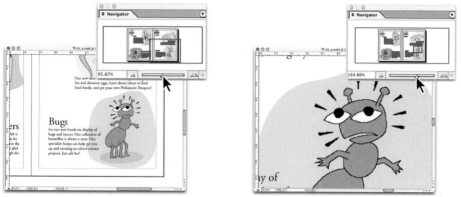

Increasing the magnification using the Navigator palette.

3 In the Navigator palette, position the pointer inside the red outline. The pointer becomes a hand, which you can use to scroll to different areas of the page or spread.

4 From within the red box, drag the hand to scroll to the upper left corner of page 2 to change the page that is visible within the document window.

5 Close the Navigator palette and save the file.

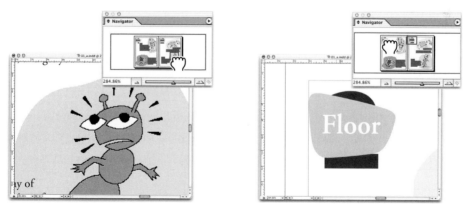

Scrolling to a different area using the Navigator palette.

Working with layers

By default, a new document contains just one layer (named Layer 1). You can rename the layer and add more layers at any time as you create your document. Placing objects on different layers lets you organize them for easy selection and editing. Using the Layers palette, you can select, display, edit, and print different layers individually, in groups, or all together.

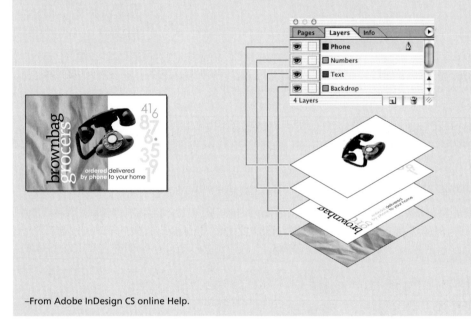

What are layers?

Think of layers as transparent sheets of film stacked on top of each other. If a layer doesn't have objects on it, you can see through it to any objects on the layers behind it.

–From Adobe InDesign CS online Help.

The 01_Library.indd document has four layers. You'll experiment with these layers to learn how the order of the layers and the placement of objects on layers can greatly affect the design of your document.

1 Click the Layers palette tab to activate the palette, or choose Window > Layers.

2 In the Layers palette, click the Number layer. Notice that a pen icon (✒) appears to the right of the layer name. This icon indicates that this layer is the target layer and anything you import or create will belong to this layer. The highlight indicates that the layer is selected.

3   Position the pointer in the Layers palette then click and drag the Number layer between the Floor layer and the Graphics layer. When you see a black line appearing where you would like to move the layer, release the mouse. Notice how the objects now appear in a different stacking order in your document, as some objects are now positioned on top of others.

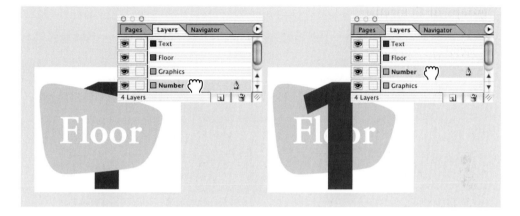

4   Click the empty square to the left of the Number layer name. This square lets you lock a layer so it cannot be edited. When you lock a layer, the palette displays a crossed-out pencil icon (✗) in the square.

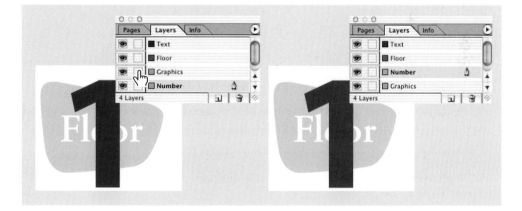

5   Using the Selection tool (↖), click the word "Floor" in the document window. Notice in the Layers palette that the Graphics layer is selected and a dot appears to the right of the layer name. This indicates that the selected object belongs to this layer. You can move objects from one layer to another layer by dragging this dot between the layers in the palette.

6 In the Layers palette, drag the dot from the Graphics layer to the Floor layer. The word "Floor" now belongs to the Floor layer and appears in the stacking order in the document accordingly.

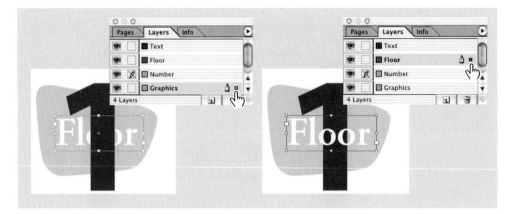

7 Now that you're done editing the layers, you can click the crossed-out pencil icon for the Number layer to unlock this layer.

8 Save the file.

Using context menus

In addition to the menus at the top of your screen, you can use context-sensitive menus to display commands relevant to the active tool or selection.

To display context-sensitive menus, position the pointer over an object or anywhere in the document window, and click with the right mouse button (Windows) or press Control and hold down the mouse button (Mac OS).

1 Make sure that the word "Floor" is still selected.

2 With the Selection tool (⬆), right-click (Windows) or Ctrl-click (Mac OS) the word "Floor." Options for the text under the tool are displayed in the context-sensitive menu. These same options are also in the Object menu. Being careful not to select any of the commands on the context menu, click a blank area of the page to close the menu.

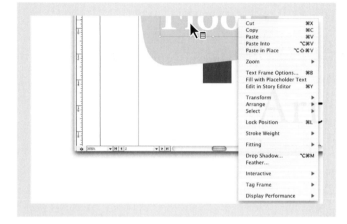

3 Click in the pasteboard area to deselect all objects, then right-click (Windows) or Ctrl-click (Mac OS) the pasteboard. Notice that the options listed on the context menu have changed so that they relate to the area of the page where you right-click or Ctrl-click.

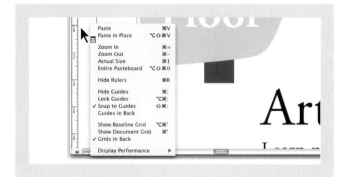

Selecting Objects

InDesign lets you know which objects will be selected when you move your Selection tool over an object by highlighting the object frame. You can then use commands to help select objects that are placed behind other items on your page.

1 Choose the Selection tool (▸). If necessary, navigate to page 2.

2 Move the cursor over various blocks of text and graphics on the page and notice how the cursor changes to include a point (▸.) as the cursor passes over them. This signals that an object will be selected if you click.

3 Click between the two o's in the word Floor where it overlaps the number 1. The text box containing the word Floor is selected.

4 Right-click (Windows) or Control-click (Mac OS) and choose Select > Next object below. Repeat this process until you have cycled through the three separate objects. You can also hold down your Ctrl key (Windows) or Command key (Mac OS) and click to cycle through stacked objects.

Using online Help

You can use online Help to find in-depth information about Adobe InDesign CS. InDesign online Help appears in a browser window. If you do not have a browser installed on your machine, you can use an Adobe Acrobat® version of Help that is included on your InDesign application CD. Adobe Reader® is also included on the application CD.

InDesign online Help includes its own complete set of instructions on how to use the Help system, which may be slightly different from other online Help systems you may have used.

1 Choose Help > InDesign Help.

Your browser application opens and displays the InDesign Help home page. You can click any underlined text, called a link, to jump to another topic. Your pointer turns into a pointing-finger icon (🖑) when you move it over any link or hotspot.

2 In the upper left corner of the left side of the Help page, click Using Help.

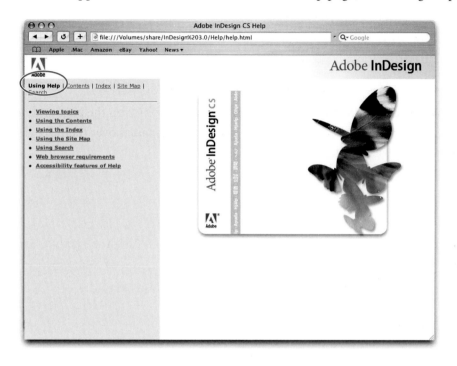

3 Click the Viewing topics link on the left side of the page. The topic "Viewing topics" opens on the right side of the page.

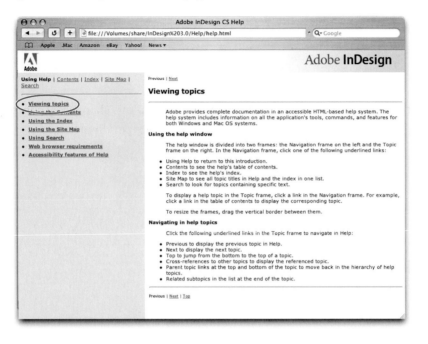

4 When you finish reading the "Viewing topics" page, do one of the following to open the next Help page:

• At the bottom of the topic page, click the linked word Next if you want to open the next topic, "Using the Contents."

• Click the linked word Top, also at the bottom of the page, if you want to jump back to the top of the "Viewing topics" page.

• On the left side of the Help window, click the title of the topic you want to read, such as "Using the Index" or "Using Search."

5 Continue exploring each of the "Using Help" topics until you are comfortable using InDesign online Help.

6 When you are finished using Help, you can close or minimize the Help window, or you can leave it open and switch back to InDesign.

On your own

Now that you have explored the work area, try some of the following tasks using either the Library_01.indd document or your own document.

1 Choose Window > Info to display the info palette. Notice the information provided about the document or click to select individual items and see how it changes as you select them.

2 Learn more about existing key commands and how you can change key commands by exploring the Keyboard Shortcuts window (Edit > Keyboard Shortcuts).

3 After you've been working on a document and using multiple palettes, choose Window > Workspace > Default to reset your palettes to their default location. Try organizing your palettes to meet your needs, and creating your own workspace by choosing Window > Workspace > Save Workspace.

Review questions

1 Describe two ways to change your view of a document.

2 How do you select tools in InDesign?

3 Describe three ways to change the palette display.

4 Describe two ways to get more information about the InDesign program.

Review answers

1 You can select commands from the View menu to zoom in or out of a document, or fit it to your screen; you can also use the Zoom tools in the toolbox, and click or drag over a document to enlarge or reduce the view. In addition, you can use keyboard shortcuts to magnify or reduce the display. You can also use the Navigator palette to scroll through a document or change its magnification without using the document window.

2 To select a tool, you can either click the tool in the toolbox or you can press the tool's keyboard shortcut. For example, you can press V to select the Selection tool from the keyboard. You select hidden tools by clicking the triangle on a tool in the toolbox and dragging to select from the additional tools that appear.

3 To make a palette appear, you can click its tab or choose its name on either the Window menu or the Type menu, for example, Window > Align. You can drag a palette's tab to separate the palette from its group and create a new group, or drag the palette into another group. You can drag a palette group's title bar to move the entire group. Double-click a palette's tab to display palette titles only. You can also press Shift+Tab to hide or display all palettes.

4 Adobe InDesign contains online Help, which includes keyboard shortcuts and full-color illustrations. InDesign also has links to training and support resources on the Adobe Systems Web site, www.adobe.com.

2 | Setting Up Your Document

By taking advantage of the tools that help you set up your document, you can ensure a consistent page layout and simplify your work. In this lesson, you'll learn how to create master pages and set columns and guides.

In this introduction to setting up your document, you'll learn how to do the following:

- Start a new document.
- Create, edit and apply master pages.
- Set document defaults.
- Adjust pasteboard size and bleed area.
- Add sections to change page numbering.
- Override master-page items on document pages.
- Add graphics and text to document pages.

Getting started

In this lesson, you'll set up a 12-page magazine article about origami, and then you will place text and graphics on one of the spreads. Before you begin, you'll need to restore the default preferences for Adobe InDesign, to ensure that the tools and palettes function exactly as described in this lesson. Then you'll open the finished document for this lesson to see what you'll be creating.

Note: If you have not already copied the resource files for this lesson onto your hard disk from the ID_02 folder from the Adobe InDesign CS Classroom in a Book CD, do so now. See "Copying the Classroom in a Book files" on page 2.

1 Delete or deactivate (by renaming) the InDesign Defaults file and the InDesign SavedData file. See "Restoring default preferences" on page 2.

2 Start Adobe InDesign.

3 To see what the finished document will look like, open the 02_b.indd file in the ID_02 folder, located inside the Lessons folder within the IDCIB folder on your hard disk. You can leave this document open to act as a guide as you work.

The document window shows several spreads, including pages 2–3, which is the only spread that you'll complete in this lesson. You can refer to this document throughout this lesson.

Note: *As you work, feel free to move palettes or change the magnification to meet your needs. See "Changing the magnification of your document" on page 53.*

Creating and saving a custom page size

InDesign lets you save your common page defaults, including page size, number of pages and margins. This lets you quickly build new documents using a saved document size.

1 Choose File > Document Presets and click Define.

2 Click New in the Document Presets dialog box that follows.

3 In the New Document Preset dialog box, set the following:

• For Document Preset Name, type **Magazine**.

• For Number of Pages, type **12**.

• Make sure that the Facing Pages option is selected.

• For Width, type **50p3** (the abbreviation for 50 picas and 3 points).

• For Height, type **65p3**.

• Under Columns, type **5** for Number.

• Under Margins, type **4** for Bottom and leave the Top, Inside, and Outside margins at 3 picas (3p0).

4 Click More Options, which will expand the dialog box and enter **.25 in** for the Bleed on all four sides of the document.

This creates an area outside the page that will print and is used when you have items that extend off the page area, such as a picture or a colored background on a page.

*You can use any form of measurement in any dialog box or palette. If you are using a value other than the default form of measurement, simply type the indicator for the unit you want to use, such as **p** for picas, **pt** for points, and either **in** or " (quotation marks) for inches. After you type a value, either press Tab, or click another option, the measurement is automatically converted to the default unit of measurement which is set in your preferences.*

5 Click OK in both dialog boxes to save the document preset.

Starting a new document

When you first start a new document, the Document Setup dialog box appears. You can use a document preset to build the document or use this dialog box to specify the number of pages, the page size, and the number of columns. You'll use the magazine preset that you just created.

1 Choose File > New > Document.

2 In the New Document dialog box, select the Magazine document preset.

3 Click OK.

4 Open the Pages palette by selecting Window > Pages, if it is not already open.

The document window appears, displaying page 1, as indicated in the Pages palette. The Pages palette is divided into two sections. The top section displays icons for the master pages. The bottom half displays icons for document pages in your document. In this document, the master consists of a two-page spread for facing pages.

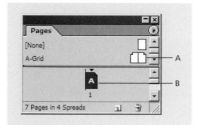

A. Master-pages icon.
B. Document-page icon.

5 Choose File > Save As, name the file **02_Setup.indd** in the ID_02 folder, and then click Save.

Editing master pages

Before you add graphics and text frames to the document, you'll set up the master pages. A master page is like a template that you can apply to pages in your document. Any object that you add to a master page will appear on document pages to which the master page is applied.

In this document, you'll use three sets of master pages. One contains a grid, another contains footer information, and a third contains placeholder frames. By creating several types of master pages, you allow for variation of pages in a document while ensuring a consistent design.

Adding guides to the master

You'll start by adding guides to the document. Guides are non-printing lines that help you lay out your design precisely. Guides that you place on master pages appear on any document pages to which the master is applied. For this document, you'll add a series of guides that, along with the column guides, act as a grid to which you can snap graphics and text frames to place.

1 In the upper section of the Pages palette, double-click A-Master.

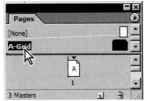

Double-clicking the name of the master page displays both pages of the A-Master.

The left and right master pages appear centered in the document window.

2 Choose Layout > Create Guides.

3 Under Rows, type **8** for Number, and type **0** for Gutter.

4 For Fit Guides to, select Margins.

```
Create Guides
┌─ Rows ───────────────┐  ┌─ Columns ──────────────┐   ┌──────────────┐
│  Number: ▲▼ 8        │  │  Number: ▲▼ 0          │   │      OK      │
│                      │  │                        │   └──────────────┘
│  Gutter: ▲▼ 0p0      │  │  Gutter: ▲▼ 1p0        │   ┌──────────────┐
└──────────────────────┘  └────────────────────────┘   │    Cancel    │
                                                        └──────────────┘
                                                         ☑ Preview
┌─ Options ─────────────────────────────────────────┐
│   Fit Guides to:  ⊙ Margins                        │
│                   ○ Page                           │
│   ☐ Remove Existing Ruler Guides                   │
└────────────────────────────────────────────────────┘
```

Selecting Margins instead of Page causes the guides to fit within the margin boundaries rather than the page boundaries. You won't add column guides because column lines already appear in your document.

5 Select Preview to see how the horizontal guides will appear on your master pages.

6 Click OK.

 Grids can also be added to individual document pages using the same command.

Renaming the master page

You will rename this first master page "Grid." In documents that contain several master pages, you may want to rename each master page to give them more descriptive names.

1 Click the palette-menu button (⊚) on the right of the Pages palette, and choose Master Options for "A-Master." If your Pages palette is still docked in its default location to the right of your working area, the palette-menu button is located in the upper left hand corner of the Pages palette.

Note: *If the Master Options for "A-Master" is dimmed on the Pages palette menu, double-click A-Master again to make sure the master pages are open in the document window.*

2 For Name, type **Grid,** and then click OK.

Note: *In addition to changing the name of master pages, you can also use the Master Options dialog box to change other properties of existing master pages.*

Creating a master for footers

The grid you added to the master is necessary for most of the pages in the document. In addition to the common grid, most document pages will require consistent text along their top (a header) or consistent text along their bottom (a footer). Some of these document pages will also require consistent placement of text and graphics. To accommodate these different designs, you'll create a separate master for pages that require footers, and another master that contains placeholder frames for text and graphics.

You can build each master page independently or you can base master pages on other master pages. In this document, the footer master will be based on the Grids master, and the Placeholder master will be based on the Footer master. By basing master pages on other masters, any change to the parent master will appear on the child masters.

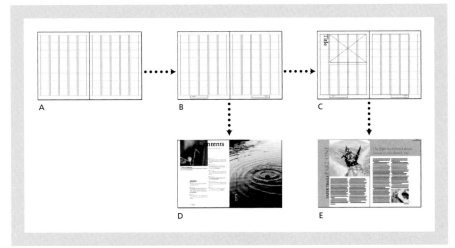

*A. A-Grid master. **B**. B-Footer master. **C**. C-Placeholder master. **D**. Document pages based on B-Footer. **E**. Document pages based on C-Placeholder.*

1 In the Pages palette, choose New Master from the Pages palette menu.

2 For Name, type **Footer**.

3 For Based on Master, choose A-Grid, and then click OK.

You're now working on a separate master-page spread, as indicated by the selected B-Footer icons that appear in the upper section of the Pages palette. You can also confirm the current page in the lower left corner of the document window. The grid you added to the A-Grid master appears on the new master spread.

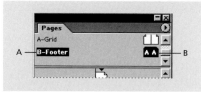

A. *Name of Master.* **B.** *The A's indicate that the B-Master is based on the A-Master.*

Dragging guides from rulers

Footers are often below the lower margin of the page, where there are no column guides. To position the footers accurately, you will add a horizontal ruler guide and two vertical ruler guides. This is easily done by dragging from the document rulers on the top and left sides of the window.

Note: You can create page ruler guides, which apply only to the page on which you drag, or a spread ruler guide, which applies across all pages in the spread and across the pasteboard.

1 Make sure that the B-Footer master pages are still in view. The page box near the bottom left corner of the document window indicates which page is displayed.

2 If the Transform palette is not open, choose Window > Transform.

3 Without clicking in your document, move the pointer around the document window and watch the horizontal and vertical rulers as the pointer moves. Notice how the hairline indicators in the rulers correspond to the pointer's position. Also notice that the dimmed X and Y values in the Transform palette also indicate the position of the pointer.

4 Holding down Ctrl (Windows) or Command (Mac OS), position the pointer in the horizontal ruler and drag down to the 62 pica marker to create a ruler guide. Don't worry about placing the guide exactly at 62 picas—you'll do that in the next step. (You can look in the Transform palette to see the current position.)

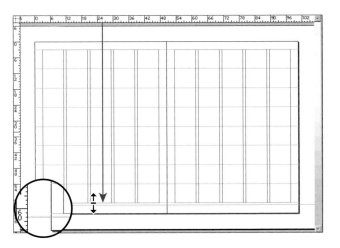

Holding down Ctrl (Windows) or Command (Mac OS), while dragging a guide, applies the guide to the spread instead of the individual page.

You can also drag the ruler guide without the Ctrl or Command keys and release the guide over the pasteboard to have a guide appear across all pages in a spread as well as the pasteboard.

5 To make sure the guide is at the 62 pica location, select the Selection tool (✸) in the toolbox, hold down Ctrl (Windows) or Command (Mac OS) and click the guide to select it. When selected, the guide changes color. In the Transform palette, the Y value is no longer dimmed because the guide is selected. In that Y box, type **62p**, and then press Return or Enter.

6 Drag a ruler guide from the vertical ruler to the 12p0.6 marker. The ruler guide will snap to the column guide at that location. Refer to the X value in the Transform palette as you drag.

7 Drag another guide from the vertical ruler to the 88p5.4 marker.

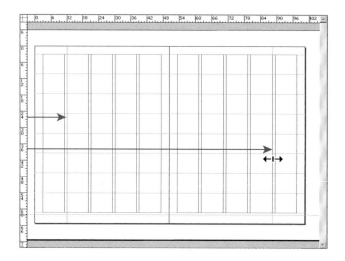

8 Choose File > Save.

Creating a footer text frame in the master

Any text or graphics that you place on the master page will appear on pages to which the master is applied. To create a footer, you'll add a publication title ("Origami") and a page-number marker to the bottom of both master pages.

1 Make sure that you can see the bottom of the left master page. If necessary, zoom in and use the scroll bars or Hand tool (✋).

2 Select the Type tool (T) in the toolbox. On the left master page, drag to create a text frame below the second column where the guides intersect, as shown. Don't worry about drawing the frame in exactly the right location—you'll snap it into place later.

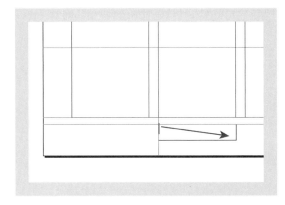

Note: When drawing a frame with the Type tool, the frame starts where the horizontal baseline intersects the I beam in the cursor—not the upper corner of cursor.

3 With the text insertion point blinking in the new text frame, choose Type > Insert Special Character > AutoPage Number.

The letter B, which represents the B-Footer master, appears in your text frame. This character will reflect the current page number in your document pages, such as "2" on page 2.

4 To add an em space after the page number, right-click (Windows) or Control-click (Mac OS) with your cursor blinking in the text frame to display a context menu, and then choose Insert White Space > Em Space. You can also choose this same command under the Type menu if you prefer.

5 Type **Origami** after the em space.

Next, you'll change the font and size of the text in the frame.

6 In the tool box, select the Selection tool (▶) and click on the text frame containing the footer.

7 In the Character palette, on the font family pop-up menu, scroll to the g's on the alphabetical list and select Adobe Garamond Pro. For Size (𝐓T), select **10 pt**.

Note: You can edit the attributes of all text in a frame by selecting the frame with the Selection tool (▸). To change the attributes of a portion of text, select the Type tool (T).

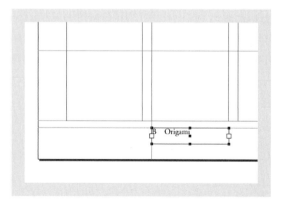

Note: It's easy to confuse the Size menu (𝐓T) with the Leading menu (ᴬIA). Make sure that you change the font size, not the leading.

💡 *Changes made in the Character palette or other palettes when no items are selected become your default settings. To avoid modifying your defaults, be certain an object is selected before making changes in a palette.*

8 In the toolbox, select the Selection tool (▸). If necessary, drag the footer frame so that it snaps to the horizontal and vertical guides, as shown.

9 Click a blank area of your document window or choose Edit > Deselect All to deselect the footer frame.

Duplicating to create a second footer

You have created a footer text frame on the left master page. Unless you insert a similar footer on the right master page, only the left-facing pages in your document will have page numbers. You'll copy the text frame to the right master page, and edit it from there.

1 Choose View > Fit Spread in Window to show both master pages.

2 Using the Selection tool (▶), select the footer frame, and then hold down the Alt key (Windows) or Option key (Mac OS) and drag the text frame to the right master page so that it snaps to the guides, mirroring the right master page as shown.

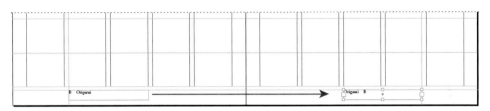

3 Make sure that you can see the bottom of the right master page. If necessary, zoom in and use the scroll bars or Hand tool.

4 Select the Type tool (**T**), and then click anywhere inside the text frame on the right master page to place an insertion point.

5 Click the Paragraph palette tab (or choose Type > Paragraph), and then click Align Right (≣).

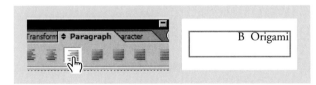

The text is now right-aligned within the footer frame on the right master page. Now you will improve the mirror effect by placing the page number after "Origami" on the right master page.

6 Delete the em space and page number at the beginning of the footer.

7 Place the insertion point at the end of the word "Origami," and then choose Type > Insert Special Character > Auto Page Number.

8 Place the insertion point between "Origami" and the page number; right-click (Windows) or Control-click (Mac OS), and then choose Insert White Space > Em Space.

Left footer and right footer.

9 Choose Edit > Deselect All and then choose File > Save.

Creating a placeholder master

Next, you'll create a third master page for placeholders for the text and graphics that will appear in your articles. By creating placeholders on the master pages, you can ensure a consistent layout among articles, and you won't need to create text frames for each page in your document.

1 In the Pages palette, choose New Master from the Pages palette menu.

2 For Name, type **Placeholder.**

3 For Based on Master, choose B-Footer, and then click OK.

Notice that the C-Placeholder icons display a B in each page in the Pages palette. This letter indicates that the C-Placeholder master is based on the B-Footer master. If you were to change either the A-Grid master or the B-Footer master, the changes would be reflected in the C-Placeholder master. You may also notice that you cannot select objects, such as the footers, from other master pages unless you override those objects. You'll learn about overriding master-page objects later in this lesson.

Adding a title placeholder frame

The first placeholder will contain the title of the article in a rotated text box.

1 To center the left page in the document window, double-click the left page icon of the C-Placeholder master in the Pages palette.

2 Select the Type tool (T). Drag to create a text frame that is slightly wider than the page and approximately as tall as one of the grid blocks. You'll position and resize this text frame later.

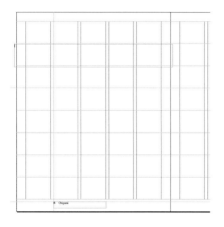

3 Type **title part xxx.**

4 Triple-click the text you typed in step 3 to select all the characters in the frame.

5 Click the Character palette tab (or choose Type > Character). Select Trajan Pro.

The Trajan font family has only capital letters, so now the text you type appears in all capitals.

6 Double-click to select the word "TITLE." Then, in the Character palette, for Size, select 36 pt from the pop-up menu. Then select the words "PART XXX" and select 60 pt.

7 Select the Paragraph palette tab and click the Align Center option.

8 Select the Selection tool (▲). If necessary, click the new text frame to select it. Then drag the text frame by the lower center handle until the frame is just tall enough to hold the text. If the text disappears, just drag the handle down again to make it taller. When you finish, choose View > Fit Spread in Window to zoom out.

9 In the Transform palette, select the upper left handle in the proxy icon (▦). Then open the palette menu and select Rotate 90° CW, to rotate the object clockwise, 90 degrees.

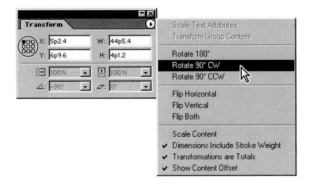

10 Drag the rotated text frame down so that it snaps to the top of the right column guide in the far left column. Then drag the center handle on the bottom of the frame to stretch the frame to the lower margin of the page.

11 Click a blank area of the page or pasteboard to deselect, and then save the document.

Adding a placeholder frame for graphics

You have now created the placeholder text frame for the title of your article. Next, you'll add two graphics frames to the master pages. Similar to the text frames, these graphics frames act as placeholders for the document pages, helping you to maintain a consistent design.

Note: While you are creating placeholder frames for text and graphics in this exercise, it is not necessary to build placeholder frames on every document you create. For some smaller documents, you may not need to create master pages and placeholder frames.

Two tools can create rectangles: the Rectangle tool and the Rectangle Frame tool. Although they are more or less interchangeable, the Rectangle Frame tool—which includes a non-printing X—is commonly used for creating placeholders for graphics.

Creating a guide before you draw makes it easy to position the graphics frames.

1 On the View menu, make sure that the Snap to Guides command is checked, or choose it now.

2 Drag a ruler guide from the horizontal ruler to the marker at 36 picas on the left master page.

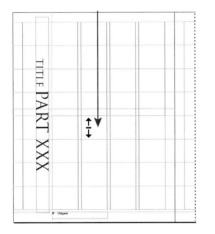

3 To make sure that the guide is at the 36-pica location, select the Selection tool (↖) in the toolbox and click the guide to select it (the guide changes color). Then type **36p** in the Y box of the Transform palette, and press Enter or Return.

4 Select the rectangle Frame tool (⊠) in the toolbox.

5 Draw a frame in the upper area of the left page, so that the frame covers the area from the top edge of the page down to the horizontal guide you set at the 36-pica mark and spreads across the page from the vertical guide at the 12p0.6-mark to the center of the spread.

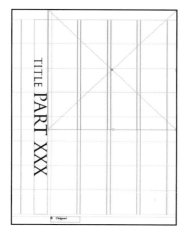

6 Choose File > Save.

Drawing a colored shape

You'll now add a colored background for the title bar and another one across the top of the right master. These elements will then appear on any pages that you assign to the C-Placeholder master. This time, you'll use the Rectangle tool instead of the Rectangle Frame tool because you'll give the frame a fill.

1 Choose Edit > Deselect All.

2 In the Pages palette, double-click the right page of the C-Placeholder master page or scroll horizontally so that the right page is centered in the document window.

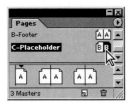

3 In the toolbox, select the Selection tool (↖) and drag from the horizontal ruler to the 16 pica mark to create a new ruler guide. Then click a blank area to deselect the guide.

💡 *Hold down the shift key while creating ruler guides to have them positioned at the increments shown on the ruler.*

When you are selecting and dragging frames, it's common to drag guides accidentally. To prevent guides from being dragged, you'll lock guides.

4 Choose View > Lock Guides.

💡 *The Lock Guides command is also available from the context menus when right-clicking (Windows) or Ctrl-clicking (Mac OS) on a blank area of the page or pasteboard.*

5 Choose Window > Swatches to open the Swatches palette.

6 In the upper left corner of the palette, click the Stroke box (▣) to activate it, and then click None in the list of Swatches. This eliminates the outline around the edge of the shape you are going to draw.

Notice that the Stroke box is also in front of the Fill box in the toolbox.

7 In the same area of the Stroke palette, click the Fill box (◼) to make it active. Then click [Paper] in the list of swatches, to set Paper as a placeholder color for the objects you draw next.

8 Select the Rectangle tool (▢) in the toolbox, and draw a frame in the right page from the top edge of the paper to the guide at 16 picas, and stretching from one edge of the page to the other. Leave the frame selected for the next step.

Notice that the Paper fill now hides the column guides and margins that are behind the rectangle.

Note: If this did not cover your guides, you may need to set your preferences to place guides behind all objects. You can do this by selecting Edit > Preferences > Guides & Pasteboard (Windows) or InDesign > Preferences > Guides & Pasteboard (Mac OS), then placing a checkmark next to "Guides in Back" in the Guides Options area.

9 In the Pages palette, double-click the left page icon for C-Placeholder, to center the left master page in the document window.

10   Still using the Rectangle tool (□), draw a frame covering the left margin of the page along with the first column and extending from the top to the bottom of the page. Notice that the new frame blocks the title placeholder text from view.

11   With the new rectangle frame still selected, choose Object > Arrange > Send to Back.

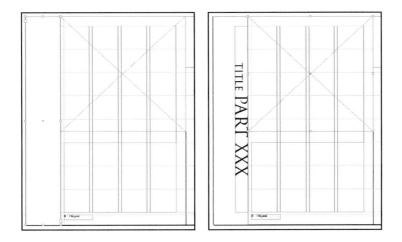

12   Save your file.

Creating text frames with columns

You have added placeholders for the title, graphic, and two background blocks for the C-Placeholder master pages. To finish the C-Placeholder master, you'll create the text frames for the story text.

1 Select the Type tool (**T**), and then drag to create a text frame on the left master page, snapping the frame to the guides so that it is three rows tall and four columns wide in the empty area at the bottom of the left master page.

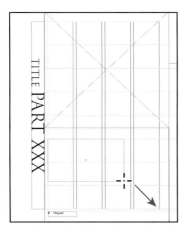

2 Choose View > Fit Spread in Window. On the right master page, drag to create a text frame four columns wide and six rows tall, snapping to the guides as shown.

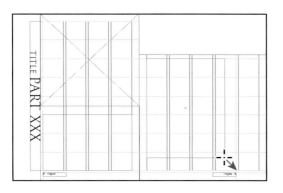

Next, you'll make sure that each of the main-story text frames has two columns.

3 Select the Selection tool (**↖**). Shift-click to select both text frames.

4 Choose Object > Text Frame Options. Under Columns, type **2** for Number, and then click OK.

Each of the main-story text frames will include two columns of text. To make the text flow from one text frame to the next, you will thread the frames.

5 Click the out port in the lower half of the text frame on the left master page. Hold the pointer over the text frame on the right master page so that it changes from a loaded text icon (⬚) to a link icon (⬚), and then click.

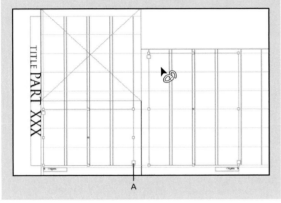

A. Out port.

6 Save the document.

Applying the masters to document pages

Now that you have created all your master pages, it's time to apply them to the pages in your layout. All the document pages are formatted with the A-Grid master by default. However, you will apply the B-Footer master and the C-Placeholder master to the appropriate pages. You can apply master pages by dragging the master-page icons onto the document-page icons or by using a palette-menu option.

In large documents, you may find it easier to display the page icons horizontally in the Pages palette.

1 In the Pages palette, choose Palette Options from the Pages palette menu (opened by clicking the palette-menu button in the upper right corner of the palette group window).

Note: Palette menus may be located in the top left corner if a palette is docked.

2 Under Pages, turn off Show Vertically, and then click OK.

3 Drag the bar down below the master pages so that you can see all the master pages. Then drag the lower right corner of the Pages palette down until you can see all the spreads.

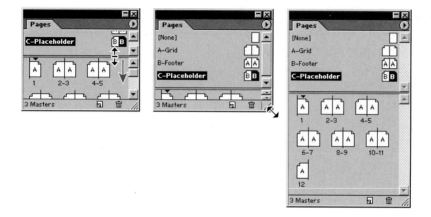

First, you'll use the drag-and-drop technique to apply the C-Placeholder master to pages in the document that will contain articles.

4 Drag the C-Placeholder name immediately to the left of the number 6 or immediately to the right of the number 7 below the page icons (not over the page icons themselves). When a box appears around both page icons in the spread, release the mouse button.

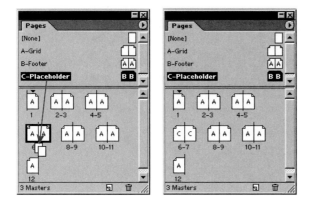

The C-Placeholder master pages are applied to pages 6 and 7, as indicated by the letter C in the page icons. Instead of dragging the C-Placeholder master to the remaining spreads, you'll use a different method to apply master pages.

5 Choose Apply Master to Pages from the Pages palette menu. For Apply Master, choose C-Placeholder. For To Pages, type **8-11**. Click OK.

Notice that pages 6–11 in the Pages palette are now formatted with the C-Placeholder master. Now you'll format pages 2–5 with the B-Footer master. Pages 2–5 will contain introductory material that requires a footer without placeholder frames.

6 Choose Apply Master to Pages from the Pages palette menu. For Apply Master, choose B-Footer. For To Pages, type **2-5**. Click OK.

Page 12 will require individual formatting without page numbering, so no master page is desired.

7 Drag the None master to page 12.

Make sure that the A-Grid master is assigned to page 1, the B-Footer master is assigned to pages 2–5, and the C-Placeholder master is assigned to pages 6–11; page 12 should not have a master page assigned to it.

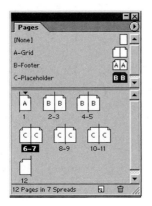

8 Choose File > Save.

Adding sections to change page numbering

The magazine you're working on requires introductory material that should be numbered with lowercase Roman numerals (i, ii, iii, and so on). You can change the page number by adding a section. You'll start a new section on page 2 to create Roman-numeral page numbering, and then you'll start another section on page 6 to revert to Arabic numerals and restart numbering.

1 In the Pages palette, double-click the page 2 icon to select it within the palette and view page 2 in the document window.

Notice that because the B-Footer master is assigned to page 2, the page includes the guides and footer information, but it does not include any of the placeholder frames that you added to the C-Placeholder master.

2 In the Pages palette menu, choose Numbering & Section Options. Then, in the New Section dialog box, make sure that Start Section and Automatic Page Numbering are selected, or select them now.

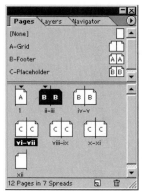

3 For Style, choose i, ii, iii, iv (lowercase) from the pop-up menu. Then click OK and notice the page icons in the Pages palette. Starting with page 2, the page numbering is now set to appear in Roman numerals in the footers of the pages.

The triangle above page ii in the Pages palette indicates the start of a section.

Now you'll specify Arabic numbers for the pages from 6 through the rest of the document.

4 Click page 6 (vi) in the Pages palette to select it.

Note: Single clicking a page targets the page for editing purposes. If you want to navigate to a page, double-click the page in the pages palette.

5 Click the Pages palette menu (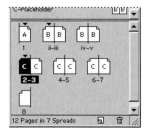) in the upper right corner of the Pages palette and choose Numbering & Section Options.

6 In the New Section dialog box, make sure that the Start Section is selected or select it now.

7 Select Start Page Numbering At, press Tab and type **2** to start the section numbering with page 2.

8 For Style, select 1, 2, 3, 4 on the pop-up menu, and then click OK. Save your file.

Now your pages are properly renumbered. Notice that a black triangle appears above pages 1, ii, and 2 in the Pages palette. These triangles indicate the start of a new section.

Adding New Pages

You can also add new pages to your existing document. We are going to add two additional pages.

1 In the Pages palette menu (▶) select the Insert Pages command.

2 Enter 2 for the number of pages, choose At End of Document from the drop down menu and then select C-Placeholder for the Master page.

3 Click OK. The document now has two more pages.

Deleting and Arranging Pages

With the pages palette you can also arrange the sequence of pages and delete extra pages.

1 In the Pages palette, click and hold down on the page 9 icon and drag it to the left of the page 8 icon and let go. Page 9 is moved to the position of page 8, and page 8 is moved back one page to the position previously held by page 9.

2 Double-click the hyphen beneath the spread containing the icons for pages 8 and 9 to select both pages.

3 Click the trash icon at the bottom of the palette. Both pages 8 and 9 have been deleted from the document.

Placing text and graphics on the document pages

Now that the framework of the 12-page publication is in place, you're ready to format the individual articles. To see how the changes you made to the master pages affect document pages, you'll add text and graphics to the spread on pages 2 and 3.

1 In the Pages palette, double-click the page 2 icon (not page ii) to center the page in the document window.

Notice that because the C-Placeholder master is assigned to page 2, the page includes the grid, the footers, and the placeholder frames.

When you want to import text and graphics from other applications, you can copy and paste, or you can use the Place command. You'll use the Place command to insert text in the frame.

2 Make sure that nothing is selected, or choose Edit > Deselect All. Then choose File > Place. Open the ID_02 folder in your IDCIB folder, and double-click 02_c.doc to open it.

The pointer takes the shape of a loaded text icon (▦). With a loaded text icon, you can drag to create a text frame or click inside an existing text frame. When you hold the loaded text icon over an existing text frame, the icon appears in parentheses (▦). You can click to insert the text into the individual frame, or you can Shift-click to autoflow the text into the threaded frames.

3 Holding down Shift, the loaded text icon (▦) changes to the automatic flow icon (▦). Click anywhere inside the text frame on the bottom of page 2. Release the Shift key.

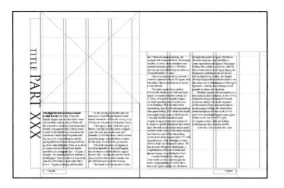

The text flowed into the text frames on pages 2 and 3. Now you'll add a graphic to the placeholder frame.

4 Choose Edit > Deselect All to make sure that no frames are selected.

If a frame is selected when you place a file, the contents of the file will be added to the selected frame. You can avoid this by either deselecting objects prior to importing or by deselecting "Replace Selected Content" in the Place dialog box when importing text or graphics.

5 Choose File > Place. Double-click 02_d.tif in the ID_02 folder. The pointer takes the shape of a loaded graphics icon (▨).

6 Position the loaded graphics icon over the graphics-frame placeholder on page 2 so that the pointer appears in parentheses (▨), and click.

The parentheses appear when InDesign recognizes a pre-existing frame beneath the cursor when importing. InDesign will use that frame rather than creating a new text or graphic frame.

7 To position the image correctly, choose Object > Fitting > Center Content. Then click on an empty portion of the page to deselect all objects.

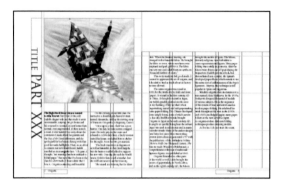

8 Select File > Save.

Overriding master-page items on document pages

The placeholders you added to the master pages appear on the document pages, but you cannot select them simply by clicking them. InDesign works this way so that you won't accidentally remove or edit master-page objects. However, you can override items on a master page to customize individual document pages. You'll now replace the word "Title" with "History of Origami."

1 To make sure you're on page 2, select Sec2:2 from the Pages pop-up list in the status bar at the bottom of the document window.

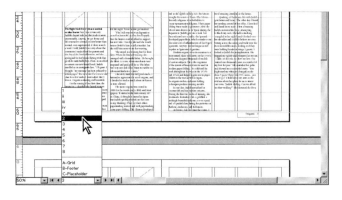

2 If necessary, adjust your view so that you can see the "TITLE PART XXX" text on page 2. Click it to try to select it—nothing happens.

You cannot select master-page items on the document pages simply by clicking. However, you can select a master-page item if you use the correct keyboard shortcut.

3 Holding down Shift+Ctrl (Windows) or Shift+Command (Mac OS), click the title placeholder frame on the left side of page 2 to select it.

4 Using the Type tool (**T**), double-click the word "TITLE" to select it, and then type **paper trails.** Then select the "XXX," and type **one.** (Remember that this text is set in the Trajan font, which has no lowercase characters, so all text appears uppercase.)

The text is now replaced on the document page. Now you will use the Eyedropper tool (✎) to color the text.

5 Triple-click the Type tool in "PAPER TRAILS PART ONE" to select all the text.

6 In the toolbox, select the Zoom tool (🔍) and then drag a marquee around the image of the origami crane to magnify the image, so that the area you drag fills the window.

7 In the toolbox, make sure that the text Fill box (▇) is selected, and then select the Eyedropper tool (🖊). Move the tip of the eyedropper over one of the deep red stripes on the crane and click to select it.

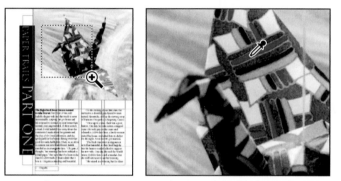

A. Dragging a zoom marquee. **B.** *Selecting color with the eyedropper tool.*

8 Choose View > Fit Spread in Window. Notice that even though you've used other tools, the text is still selected. Choose Edit > Deselect All to see the text now filled with the red color you selected.

9 Using the Selection tool (▸), hold down Ctrl+Shift (Windows) or Command+Shift (Mac OS) and click to select the two rectangles you created on the placeholder master pages.

Note: *While you created these rectangles on a master page, they appear on the document page you are currently formatting because the master page is applied to this document page.*

10 Repeat steps 6 and 7, but this time select a mustard yellow color from the crane paper to fill the rectangles. Do not deselect the rectangle frames.

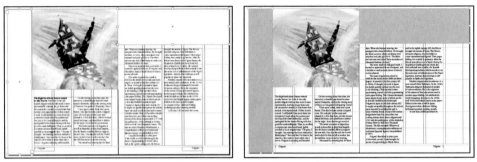

The document with the frames selected (left) and after color is applied to the frames (right).

11 Choose View > Fit Spread in Window, and choose Object > Arrange > Send to Back so that the yellow rectangles do not hide the title text. Then deselect all and save your file.

Editing master pages

You can make changes to master pages even after you apply them. To try this, you'll change the master page to reverse the direction of the vertical text and see how that affects the rest of the document.

1 In the Pages palette, double-click C-Placeholder to display those master pages.

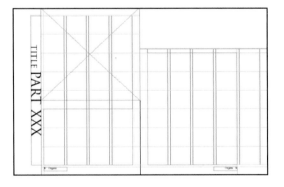

2 Select the Selection tool (↖), and then click the "TITLE PART XXX" text frame.

The proxy icon (▦) in both the Control and Transform palettes determines the point of rotation. In this case, we want the object to rotate around its center so that it stays in place.

3 In the Transform palette, select the center point in the proxy icon.

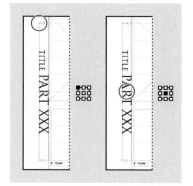

4 In the Transform palette menu, select Rotate 180°. The text block now reads up from the bottom of the column. Choose Edit > Deselect All.

5 In the Pages palette, double-click page 2 (not page ii) to switch views from the master pages to the page with the origami story.

Notice that the settings you applied (local overrides) to the title text on the document page remain in effect—that is, that the text is still red and still says "PAPER TRAILS" instead of "TITLE" and "PART ONE" instead of "XXX."

Rotating the frame on the master page affected all the pages to which the master was applied, including the page containing the local override. When you override a master-page item on a document page, you override only the set of attributes that you change. In this case, you changed the text and the color of text on the document page. If you were to change the text or color of text on the master page, those changes would not affect this overridden object.

Viewing the completed spread

Now you'll hide guides and frames to see what the completed spread looks like.

1 Choose View > Fit Spread in Window, if necessary.

2 In the toolbox, click the Preview Mode button (▣,) to hide all guides, grids, frame edges, and the pasteboard.

You have formatted enough of the 12-page document to see how adding objects to the master pages will help you maintain a consistent design throughout your document.

3 Choose File > Save.

Congratulations. You have finished the lesson.

On your own

A good way to reinforce the skills you've learned in this lesson is to experiment with them. Try some of the following exercises that give you more practice with InDesign techniques.

1 Place another photograph at the bottom of the second column of text on page 3. Use the 02_e.jpg image that is inside the Extras folder within the ID_02 folder.

2 Add a read-in pull quote: Using the Type tool (**T**), select the opening phrase of the story, from "The flight..." through "...take forever." Choose Edit > Cut. Then use the Type tool to drag a frame in the yellow panel across the top of page 3, and choose Edit > Paste. Triple-click the text you pasted and use the Character palette to format it using the font, size, style, and color of your choice.

3 Try rotating the "title" text block using different corners or edges of the proxy icon as the center of rotation, and notice the difference in the results.

4 Create a new pair of master pages for a spread that you could use for the continuation of this story. Name the new master page **D-Next** and select B-Footer for the Based On option. Then create placeholder frames for the text and graphics, giving the spread a different arrangement from C-Placeholder master pages. When you finish, apply the D-Next master pages to pages 4–5 of your document.

Review questions

1 What are the advantages of adding objects to master pages?

2 How do you change the page-numbering scheme?

3 How do you override a master-page item on a document page?

Review answers

1 By adding objects such as guides, footers, and placeholder frames to master pages, you can maintain a consistent layout on the pages to which the master is applied.

2 In the Pages palette, select the page icon where you want new page numbering to begin. Then choose Section Options from the Pages palette menu and specify the new page-numbering scheme.

3 Hold down Shift+Ctrl (Windows) or Shift+Command (Mac OS), and then click the object to select it. You can then edit, delete, or otherwise manipulate the object.

3 | Working with Frames

InDesign frames may contain either text or graphics. As you work with frames, you'll notice that InDesign provides a great amount of flexibility and control over your design.

In this introduction to working with frames, you'll learn how to do the following:

- Use the Selection and Direct Selection tools to modify frames and their contents.
- Resize and reshape text and graphic frames.
- Distinguish between bounding boxes and their frames.
- Crop a graphic.
- Scale an image contained in a graphics frame.
- Move a graphic within its frame.
- Convert a graphics frame to a text frame.
- Wrap text around an object.
- Create and rotate a polygon frame.
- Align graphic objects to each other.
- Center and scale an object within a frame.

Getting started

In this lesson, you'll work on a two-page article for a magazine about origami paper folding. Before you begin, you'll need to restore the default preferences for Adobe InDesign to ensure that the tools and palettes function exactly as described in this lesson. Then you'll open the finished document for this lesson to see what you'll be creating.

1 Delete or deactivate (by renaming) the InDesign Defaults file and the InDesign SavedData file, as described in "Restoring default preferences" on page 2.

2 Start Adobe InDesign. To begin working, you'll open an InDesign document that is already partially completed.

3 Choose File > Open, and open the 03_a.indd file in the ID_03 folder, located inside the Lessons folder within the IDCIB folder on your hard disk.

Note: If you have not already copied the resource files for this lesson onto your hard disk from the ID_03 folder from the Adobe InDesign CS Classroom in a Book CD, do so now. See "Copying the Classroom in a Book files" on page 2.

4 Choose File > Save As, rename the file **03_frames.indd**, and save it in the ID_03 folder.

5 To see what the finished document will look like, open the 03_b.indd file in the same folder. You can leave this document open to act as a guide as you work. When you're ready to resume working on the lesson document, choose Window > 03_frames.indd.

Note: *As you work through the lesson, feel free to move palettes around or change the magnification to a level that works best for you.*

Modifying text frames

In most cases, text must be placed inside of a frame. The size and location of a frame determine how the text appears on a page.

Resizing text frames

You'll resize a text frame using the Selection tool. The size of the text characters inside the frame remain unchanged, but when you resize a frame, the text flow will wrap differently or display more or less text after you change the frame size.

This document includes two layers: Art and Text. You'll confirm that the objects on the Art layer are locked so that you won't accidentally select the shapes while you resize the text frames.

1 Click the Layers palette tab (or choose Window > Layers if you do not see the Layers palette), and do the following:

• If necessary, click the lock box to the left of the Art layer to lock the layer.

• Using the Selection tool (↖), click to select the text frame on the left page. Notice that the text frame has eight hollow handles and a solid center point.

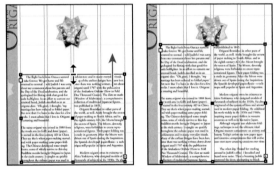

2 Drag the center top handle upwards to resize the height of the frame until it snaps to the horizontal guide immediately above the frame (near 22 picas on the vertical ruler). When you release the mouse, text reflows throughout the entire frame.

Before and after resizing text frame.

💡 *When you want to simultaneously resize a text frame and the text characters inside it, use the Scale tool (⬚).*

About frames, paths, and selections

When you select an object on an InDesign page, various color-coded lines and small squares appear around the object. These items represent different things, including the bounding box, handles, path, anchor points, and center point. The colors defined in the Layer palette determine how these attributes appear on screen.

- *The frame is a container for text, graphics, or colored fills, or it can be empty. The frame is independent of its contents, so the edges of the frame may hide part of its graphic contents or the contents may not entirely fill the frame. A frame with no content can serve as a placeholder for text, images, or fills that you add later.*

- *A bounding box is always rectangular, enclosing the maximum horizontal and vertical extensions of the selected item. The bounding boxes for a frame and for the graphic inside it can be different sizes.*

- *The path and the shape of a frame are identical and do not have to be rectangular. A path is a vector graphic. You can use InDesign drawing tools to create paths and then do all the things you can do to any closed paths, such as add fills, specify stroke attributes, and edit the paths with the Pen tool ( ).*

- *There are eight handles and a center point for a bounding box, appearing as small squares in the corners, at the midpoints of sides, and in the center. Dragging a handle modifies the bounding box.*

- *The path is defined by anchor points, which look like smaller handles. You drag anchor points to alter the shape of the path. When the anchor points are visible, you can also see the center point for the frame. When the path is visible, you can click the center point to select all anchor points in the path.*

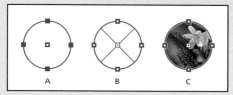

A. *Path.* **B.** *Frame as a graphic container.*
C. *Frame with a placed graphic.*

The tool you use to select an object determines how you can change it.

- *Use the Type tool (T) to type text and to select and edit text within a text frame.*

- *Use the Selection tool ( ) to move or resize a frame.*

- *Use the Direct Selection tool ( ) to reshape the path by selecting and working with anchor points. Also use this tool to set path characteristics and to resize, reshape, and move the graphic within a graphics frame without altering the frame itself.*

Using anchor points to reshape a text frame

So far, you've dragged a handle to resize the text frame, using the Selection tool. Now, you'll use an anchor point to reshape the frame, using the Direct Selection tool.

1 If the text frame on the left page is not selected, use the Selection tool (✦) to select it now.

2 In the toolbox, click the Direct Selection tool (✦). Four very small anchor points now appear at the corners of the selected text frame. The anchor points are hollow, indicating that none of them are selected.

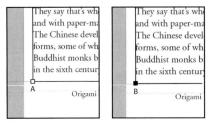

A. *Unselected anchor point.*
B. *Selected anchor point.*

3 Select the anchor point in the upper left corner of the text frame and drag it downward until it snaps to the horizontal guide below it. (After you start dragging, you can hold down Shift to restrict any horizontal movement.)

Make sure you drag only the anchor point—if you drag just below the anchor point, you'll move the text frame.

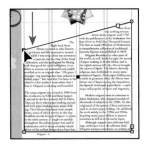

4 Press **V** on your keyboard to switch to the Selection tool (✦).

To see both the bounding box and the path, choose View > Show Frame Edges. To turn frame edges off again, choose View > Hide Frame Edges.

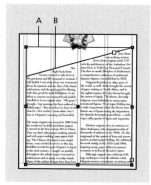

A. Bounding box. B. Frame.

Next, you'll change the text frame on the right page of the spread so that it mirrors the text frame on the left page.

5 Click a blank area of your document to deselect the text frame, or choose Edit > Deselect All.

6 Press **A** on your keyboard to switch back to the Direct Selection tool (↖) and click the large text block on page 5. Select the upper left anchor point of the text frame and drag it up to the same horizontal guide you used to reshape text on the left page. You can hold down Shift as you drag to ensure that the change is only vertical.

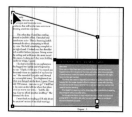

7 Deselect all objects and then choose File > Save.

*Pressing the **A** and **V** keys to toggle between the Selection and Direct Selection tools are just two of many keyboard shortcuts available in InDesign. For more shortcuts, refer to "Keyboard shortcuts" in online Help.*

Modifying graphics frames

In this section, you'll focus on different techniques for modifying frames and frame contents. To start, you'll import an image and place it in your document spread. Because you'll be working on graphics rather than text, your first step is to make sure that the graphics appear on the Art layer rather than on the Text layer. Isolating items on different layers helps your work process so that it's easier to find and edit elements of your design.

1 In the Layers palette, click the second-column box to unlock the Art layer. Lock the Text layer by clicking in the second column box. Then select the Art layer by clicking on the name of the layer so that new elements will be assigned to this layer.

2 To center page 4 in the document window, choose 4 from the Pages pop-up menu at the bottom of the document window.

3 Choose File > Place and in the Place dialog box deselect "Replace Selected Item" and then double-click 03_c.tif in the ID_03 folder.

The pointer changes to a loaded graphics icon ( ).

Note: If the pointer appears with a line through it ( ), the current layer is selected but still locked. You cannot add objects to a locked layer. Make sure that the Art layer in the Layers palette is both unlocked and selected. The pointer should then appear as a loaded graphics icon so that you can proceed with this step.

4 Click near the top left corner of page 4 to place the graphic. It doesn't matter exactly where you place it or that the purple image may cover some of the story text. You'll fix that later.

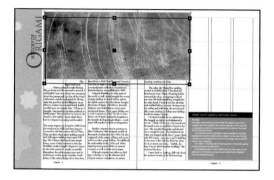

5 Press **V** to select the Selection tool (↖). Then drag the image so that it snaps into place at the top of the page and on the left side of the column gutter. The left edge of the graphic should fit snugly against the yellow bar of the title column, with no gap between them.

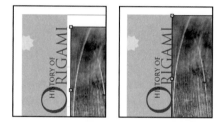

Resizing a graphic frame

The design for this page calls for the purple background image to extend across the page from the title panel to the right edge of the page. Although this image is not yet the right size or shape to do that, you'll start making those adjustments now.

First, you'll stretch the frame to fit the width of your spread.

1 Choose View > Fit Spread in Window so that you can see all of pages 4 and 5 in the document window. If necessary, scroll horizontally so that you can see the right edge of page 5.

2 Using the Selection tool (⬉), click the purple-texture graphic. Drag the lower right handle until the right side of the bounding box snaps into place against the horizontal guide at the 32-pica mark on the vertical ruler and to the edge of page 5.

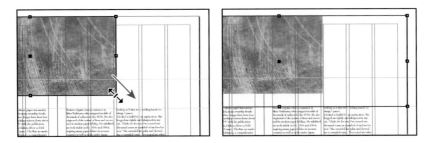

Notice that only the frame bounding box changes, not the purple image itself.

Resizing and moving an image within a frame

You have just finished resizing a graphic frame, but the content image remains unchanged. You'll now resize just the image so that it fills the designated area.

💡 *In addition to the methods we use here, you can also use the context menus to resize pictures to fit within their frame. Do this by right-clicking (Windows) or Ctrl+clicking (Mac OS) and selecting Fitting > Fit Content Proportionally.*

The content and frame for any element are separate things. Unlike with text objects, the frame and content for a graphic each has its own bounding box. Resizing the graphic contents is exactly like resizing the frame, except that you work with the bounding box for the contents. To do that, you need the Direct Selection tool.

1 Press **A** to switch to the Direct Selection tool (⬈), then position the pointer over the purple background image until the pointer appears as a hand, and then click to select the frame contents (the image itself).

2 Select the handle in the lower right corner of the graphic bounding box, and then hold down Shift and drag to enlarge the image. Continue dragging until the image dimensions are even larger than the frame, so that the handle is off the page and onto the pasteboard.

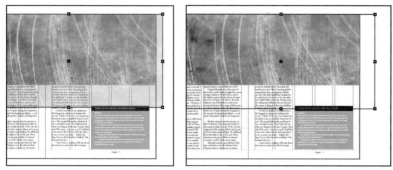

Dragging bounding box of contents, and view after dragging.

3 Move the Direct Selection tool over the purple image so that you see the hand icon. Try dragging the image with the hand icon, and notice how the area of the image that is visible within the frame changes as you drag. If you drag too far to the right, notice that the image no longer covers the left side of the frame area.

Before you start dragging, click and hold down the mouse button until the hand icon turns into a solid arrow (▶) pointer. Then, after you start dragging, you'll see a ghosted image of the hidden areas of the graphic contents, a feature called Dynamic Preview. If you don't wait for the pointer icon to change, you'll still see the bounding box of the graphic as you drag.

4 Make sure that the image entirely fills the frame, and then click a blank area of the page to deselect the purple image. Save your work.

Images expanded beyond 120% of their original size may not contain enough pixel information for high-resolution offset printing. Check with your printer or service provider if you are uncertain as to the resolution and scaling requirements needed for any documents you are having printed.

Changing the shape of the frame

When you resized the frame using the Selection tool, the frame maintained its rectangular shape. Now you will use the Pen tool and the Direct Selection tool to reshape the frame.

1 Press **A** for the Direct Selection tool (⬚). Then move the tip of the pointer over the edge of the purple-image frame, and click when the pointer appears with a small diagonal line (⬚). This selects the path and reveals the anchor points and center point for the frame. Leave the path selected.

2 Press **P** to switch to the Add Anchor Point Pen tool (✒⁺). Carefully position the pointer over the lower edge of the frame path where it intersects with the right margin of page 4 and then click. A new anchor point is added.

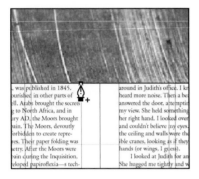

3 Move to page 5, where the lower side of the path intersects with the left margin, and using the Add Anchor Point Pen tool (✒⁺) click again to add another new anchor point.

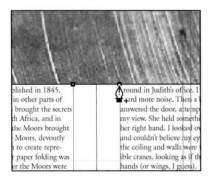

4 Press **A** to switch to the Direct Selection tool. With the second new anchor point still selected, move the pointer over the first new anchor point (on page 4 of the layout) until the pointer arrow appears with a small square (⬚). Then hold down Shift and click to select that anchor point. Now both new anchor points appear solid, showing that they are selected.

5 Drag upwards, holding down Shift as you drag from either one of the new anchor points or the path segment between them. When both anchor points snap into place on the next guide (at 22p on the vertical ruler), release the mouse button and the Shift key.

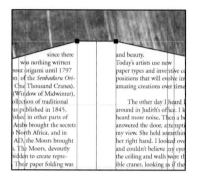

The graphic is now properly shaped and sized for the design.

6 Press **V** to switch to the Selection tool, and select the purple graphic. Then choose Object > Arrange > Send to Back so that the graphic appears to be behind other elements in the Art layer.

💡 *You can simultaneously resize both a graphic image and its frame by using the Selection tool and holding down Ctrl+Shift (Windows) or Command+Shift (Mac OS) as you drag a handle of the frame. In this case, the Shift key maintains the proportions of the bounding boxes, so that the graphic image is not distorted. Using the Shift key is optional if distorting the image doesn't matter to your design.*

Modifying a frame within grouped objects

You can select individual elements of a grouped object using the Direct Selection tool. The black and gray rectangles behind the sidebar story in the lower right corner of page 5 are grouped, so that you can select and modify them as a unit. You'll now change the fill color of just one of the rectangles without ungrouping or changing the other elements of the group.

1 In the Layers palette, make sure the Text layer is locked and that the Art layer is selected.

2 Using the Selection tool (↖), click either the gray or the black background behind the sidebar story. The entire sidebar background is selected, showing the usual eight handles in the bounding box. Notice that a question mark (?) appears in the toolbar Fill box (■), indicating that the grouped items do not all have the same fill color.

3 Press Ctrl+Shift+A (Windows) or Command+Shift+A (Mac OS) to deselect the group.

4 Press **A** to switch to the Direct Selection tool, and click the black fill in the upper part of the sidebar background. Now the four anchor points and center point for the black rectangle appear. Notice that the Fill box in the toolbox is black and that Black is highlighted in the Swatches palette.

5 Make sure that the Fill box (■) is still selected in the toolbox. Then scroll down the Swatches palette and select the Black 80% tint. Now the upper rectangle behind the text block has a dark gray fill but the lower one remains filled with light gray.

6 Save your file.

When you have the smaller rectangle selected, notice what happens if you switch back to the Selection tool: The handles appear, but only for the upper rectangle, not for the entire group as they appeared when you did step 2, above. This can be handy when you have nested objects and want to adjust the frame without ungrouping.

Wrapping text around a graphic

You can wrap text around the frame of an object or around the object itself. In this procedure, you'll see the difference between wrapping text around the bounding box and wrapping text around the graphic.

Your first task is to move the graphic, which couldn't be easier; you just select it and drag. For precise positioning, you can also use the arrow keys to nudge a frame or you can type exact position coordinates on the Transform palette.

1 Using the Selection tool (↖), select the eight-pointed graphics frame with the image of an origami crane that is on page 4. Being careful not to select one of the handles, move the frame down so that the top of the graphic snaps into alignment with the lower guide, at 42 picas on the vertical ruler. Make sure that the center point of the graphic is aligned with the middle of the gutter between the two columns of text. The frame should not have changed size but it should have moved on the page.

Notice that the text appears on top of the image. You'll change this by applying text wrap.

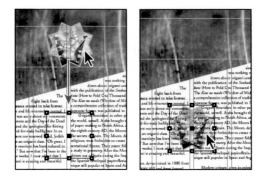

2 Choose Window > Type & Tables > Text Wrap to open the Text Wrap palette, and select the second wrap option so that the text wraps around the bounding box, not around the star-shaped frame.

Text wrapped around bounding box.

3 Next, select the third wrap option so that the text wraps around the contour of the image frame instead of the bounding box. Click a blank area to deselect all.

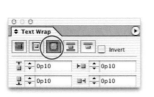

Text wrapped around content.

4 Leave the Text Wrap palette open for now, and choose File > Save.

Creating new frames and adjusting the contents

So far in this lesson, you've changed the size, shape, position, and color of frames and the contents within the frames. In this section, you'll experiment with different ways to create new frames quickly, with a minimum of effort on your part. These include duplicating existing frames, drawing new frames, and replacing the existing contents of a frame. Because frames are independent of their contents, you can replace the contents of any frame with either graphics or text. You'll get experience doing both in these procedures.

Duplicating a frame and its contents

Using the familiar copy-and-paste technique, you can quickly duplicate objects in your design. In this procedure, you'll also use a keyboard shortcut to duplicate and move an object in one action.

1 Using the Selection tool (▶), select the crane graphic, and choose Edit > Copy.

2 Choose Edit > Paste. A duplicate of the crane and its frame appears in the center of the window.

3 Drag the new crane graphic up into the purple background area on page 4 so that the lower edge snaps into position with the guide at 22 picas on the vertical rules.

4 Choose View > Fit Spread in Window.

5 Hold down Alt (Windows) or Option (Mac OS) and drag the crane graphic to page 5. When you release the mouse, you'll see that by using the Alt or Option key, you have moved a new copy of the graphic, as the original remains in place.

If you hold down the mouse button for a few seconds before you start to drag, you'll see the ghosted copy of the duplicate graphic frame and contents as you move it.

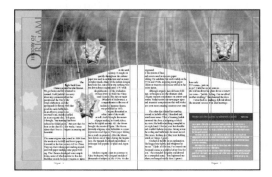

6 Select the Selection tool (✦) and click to select the crane graphic on page 5. Hold down Shift, and click the corner handle, dragging to enlarge it slightly. Then let go of the shift key, click and drag the graphic as needed so that it is approximately centered over the far right column of the page.

Replacing the contents of graphics frames

After you create the two duplicates, it's easy to replace the contents with other graphics or text. Your next task is to resize the new star-shaped frames and replace the crane images with other images. Because the frame and contents are independent, it's easy to swap out one image for another.

1 Using the Selection tool (✦), select the new crane graphic you placed in the upper area of page 4. Hold down Shift to maintain the symmetry of the frame, drag up from the upper right handle to above the top edge of the spread so that part of the image bleeds off the page. Leave the frame selected.

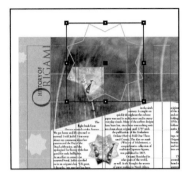

2 Choose File > Place, and browse as needed to find the 03_d.tif file in your ID_03 folder. Select "Replace Selected Item" in the Place dialog box.

3 Double-click the 03_d.tif to place the new image directly into the selected frame, replacing the crane image.

4 With the frame still selected, choose Object > Fitting > Fit Content to Frame. InDesign resizes the graphic so that it fits into the frame.

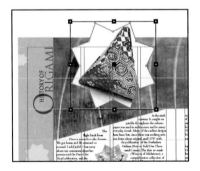

You can also access the fitting commands from the context menus by either right-clicking (Windows) or Option+Clicking (Mac OS).

5 Select the duplicate crane image, on page 5.

6 Choose File > Place, and browse as needed to find the 03_e.jpg file in your ID_03 folder. The image of an origami box replaces the image of the origami crane.

7 With the box graphic still selected, choose Object > Fitting > Fit Content to Frame. Now you've used a single frame shape three times to hold three different images.

Drawing a new graphics frame

Until now, you've used only frames prepared for you for this lesson. Now it's time for you to create a frame on your own, using the drawing tools in the toolbox.

1 In the toolbox, hold down the mouse on the Rectangle tool until you see other options, and select the Polygon tool (⬠).

2 Double-click the Polygon tool to open the Polygon Settings dialog box, and specify the following:

• For Number of Sides, type **4**.

• If necessary, type **20%** for Star Inset and then click OK.

3 Hold down Shift and drag to draw a four-pointed star that it is 12p x 12p, using the H and W values in either the Control or Transform palette as a reference as you drag the star. If you have difficulty getting the values exactly at 12 picas, leave the star selected, type the values in the W and H boxes of the Transform palette, and press Enter or Return.

4 Press **V** to switch to the Selection tool and then drag the new star into position in the purple background on page 5, so that it is slightly off center and entirely within the purple background image. Leave the star selected.

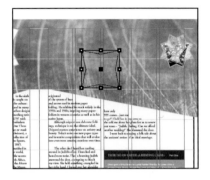

5 Make sure that the Fill box (▣) is selected in the toolbox.

6 Click the Swatches palette tab (or choose Window > Swatches) and select the color named C=0 M=28 Y=100 K=0 to fill the star with a mustard yellow color.

7 In the toolbox, select the Stroke box (▣) and then click the Apply None button (☑) to remove the black stroke color.

Placing and coloring text in a color-filled frame

You can place text in a frame of any closed shape, and the text will flow in to fill the shape from the top. You can even replace a graphic in a frame with text. In this case, however, the frame does not have a graphic as its contents, just a fill. The fill color simply appears as a background for the imported text.

1 Using the Selection tool, select the four-point star and then hold down Alt (Windows) or Option (Mac OS) and drag a short distance to create a duplicate frame.

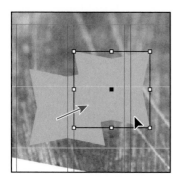

2 In the toolbox, select the Fill box (■⌐), and then in the Swatches palette, select 80% black as the fill color for the new frame.

3 In the Layers palette, click the Text layer lock icon (✗) to unlock the Text layer.

4 With the 80% gray star selected, drag the dot from the Art layer to the Text layer to move the star to that layer. Leave the star selected.

5 Choose File > Place, and then browse to the 03_ID folder and double-click the 03_f.doc file. The text appears in the star, with the same text formatting that it had in the original .doc file. The out port on the bounding box is empty, indicating that all the text for the pull quote fits into the 12-pica star shape.

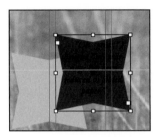

6 Select the frame containing the imported text.

7 Make sure the Text Fill box (T▦) is selected in the Swatches palette then click to select C=0 M=28 Y=100 K=0 so that the text is also mustard-colored.

Orienting objects in space

You've already seen how you can move, reshape, and resize elements on your document layout. In this section, you'll use various features that adjust the orientation of objects on the page and in relationship to each other. To begin, you'll adjust the inset between text and the frame that contains it. Then you'll work with rotation techniques and alignment of selected objects.

Adjusting text inset within a frame

Your next task is to finish up the pull quote items by fitting the text nicely into the star frame. By adjusting the inset between the frame and the text, you make it easier to read.

1 Click to select the Selection tool (▸) in the toolbox, and then select the star with the pull-quote text.

Note: Do not try to use a keyboard shortcut to switch to another tool when the text tool is active, especially if you have text selected or an insertion point placed in a block of text. Doing so would enter text, so the action would not change the tool selection.

2 Choose Object > Text Frame Options to open the Text Frame Options dialog box. If necessary, drag the dialog box aside so that you can still see the star as you set options.

3 In the dialog box, make sure that the Preview option is selected. Then, under Inset Spacing, change the Inset value to shrink the text area until it fits nicely in the frame. (The sample uses 0p4.) Then click OK to close the dialog box.

Rotating an object

There are several options within InDesign for rotating objects. In this topic, you'll use the Transform palette.

1 Using the Selection tool (⬉), select the four-pointed yellow star.

2 In the Transform palette, make sure that the center point is selected on the proxy icon (⊞) so that the object rotates around its center, and then select 45° from the rotation angle pop-up menu.

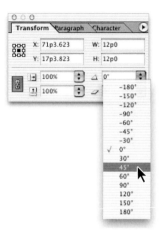

Aligning multiple objects

Now that the two four-pointed stars are set at a 45° angle from each other, you can position one on top of the other so that all eight points radiate from the same center-point position. Precise alignment is easiest when you use the Align palette.

1 Using the Selection tool (↖), select the yellow star and then hold down Shift and click the gray star so that both four-pointed stars are selected.

2 Choose Window > Align to open the Align palette.

3 In the Align palette, select the Align Horizontal Centers button (占). The two stars are now lined up exactly side by side.

4 Again, in the Align palette, click the Align Vertical Centers button (⊟ₒ). The two stars are now centered on the same location in the layout.

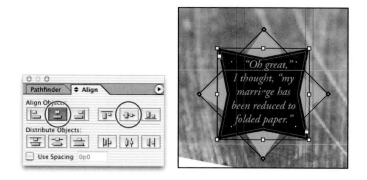

5 Click a blank area to deselect all, and then save your file.

Rotating an image within its frame

You can rotate both the frame and contents in one action by selecting the object with the Selection tool and then dragging one of the handles with the Rotation tool (◌). However, sometimes you just want to set the image at a jaunty angle. That process is just a slight variation on the procedure.

When you rotated the yellow star, you used the Transform palette to set a precise rotation angle. In this procedure, you'll use the rotation tool to rotate the graphic freely.

1 If necessary, press **V** to switch to the Selection tool, and then position the pointer over the origami box image in the star on page 5 and then click.

2 In the Transform palette, make sure that the center proxy icon (▦) is selected.

3 Press **R** to select the Rotation tool (◌).

4 Move the pointer over the corner handle, so that it appears as crosshairs (+).

5 Move the pointer over one of the corner handles and hold down the mouse button and then drag handles counterclockwise to rotate both the image and the frame, stopping when you like the look of the results. The sample uses a rotation of 25°.

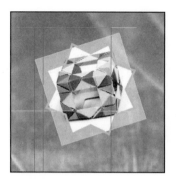

Note: Waiting for the pointer to become a solid arrow lets you preview the contents on-the-fly as you rotate. If you don't wait for the pointer, the bounding box will remain visible as you drag to rotate.

Finishing up

1 Choose Edit > Deselect All.

2 Choose View > Fit Spread in Window.

3 In the toolbox, click the Preview Mode button to hide all guides and frames.

4 Press the Tab key to close all palettes.

5 Save your file one more time, and then choose File > Close to keep InDesign open or File > Exit to end your InDesign session.

Congratulations. You have finished the lesson. Now it's time to admire your work.

On your own

One of the best ways to learn about frames is to experiment on your own. In this section, you will learn how to nest an object inside a shape you create. Follow these steps to learn more about selecting and manipulating frames:

1 Using the Direct Selection tool (⬍), select and copy any image on page 4 or 5.

2 To create a new page, choose Insert Pages from the Pages palette menu and then click OK.

3 Use the Polygon tool to draw a shape on the new page (use any number of sides and any value for the star inset). Select the shape using the Direct Selection tool, and then choose Edit > Paste Into to nest the image inside the frame. (If you choose Edit > Paste, the object will not be pasted inside the selected frame.)

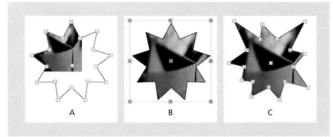

*A. Image pasted into frame. **B.** Image moved and scaled within the frame. **C.** Polygon frame reshaped.*

4 Use the Direct Selection tool to move and scale the image within the frame.

5 Use the Direct Selection tool to change the shape of the polygon frame.

6 Use the Selection tool (⬆) to rotate both the frame and the image. Use the Direct Selection tool to rotate only the image within the frame.

7 When you are done experimenting, close the document without saving.

Review questions

1 When should you use the Selection tool (⬆) to select an object, and when should you use the Direct Selection tool (⬍) to select an object?

2 How do you resize a frame and its contents simultaneously?

3 How do you rotate a graphic within a frame without rotating the frame?

4 Without ungrouping objects, how do you select an object within a group?

Review answers

1 Use the Selection tool (↖) for general layout tasks, such as positioning and sizing objects. Use the Direct Selection tool (↘) for tasks involving drawing and editing paths or frames; for example, to select frame contents or to move an anchor point on a path.

2 To resize a frame and its contents simultaneously, select the Selection tool, hold down Ctrl (Windows) or Command (Mac OS), and then drag a handle. Hold down Shift to maintain the object's proportions.

3 To rotate a graphic within a frame, use the Direct Selection tool to select the graphic within the frame. Select the Rotation tool (⟳), and then drag one of the handles to rotate only the graphic, not the frame.

4 To select an object within a group, select it using the Direct Selection tool.

4 | Importing and Editing Text

With Adobe InDesign you can import text, thread it through frames, and edit text within the frames. Once you import text, you can create and apply styles, find and replace text and formatting, and use different language dictionaries to spell-check any part of your document.

In this introduction to importing and editing text, you'll learn how to do the following:

• Enter text into text frames.

• Flow text manually and automatically.

• Load styles from another document and apply them.

• Thread text.

• Use semi-autoflow to place text frames.

• Find and change text and formatting.

• Find and change a missing font.

• Spell-check a document.

Getting started

In this lesson, you'll work on an 8-page newsletter for Sonata Cycles, a fictitious chain of bicycle stores. Several pages of the newsletter have already been completed. Now that the final article for the newsletter has been written, you're ready to flow the article into the document and add the finishing touches to the newsletter. Before you begin, you'll need to make several preparations:

• If you have not already copied the resource files for this lesson from the ID_04 folder of the *Adobe InDesign CS Classroom in a Book CD*, do so now. See "Copying the Classroom in a Book files" on page 2.

• Restore the default preferences for Adobe InDesign, as described in step 1, below.

When your preparations are complete, you're ready to start work on the lesson.

1 To ensure that the tools and palettes function exactly as described in this lesson, delete or deactivate (by renaming) the InDesign Defaults file and the InDesign SavedData file. See "Restoring default preferences" on page 2.

2 Start Adobe InDesign.

Managing fonts

To begin working, you'll open an existing InDesign document. We have added a font to this document that you do not have on your system, so you will receive an error message relating to the missing font. You will replace this font later in this lesson.

1 Choose File > Open, and open the 04_a.indd file in the ID_04 folder, located inside the Lessons folder within the IDCIB folder on your hard disk.

When you open a file that includes fonts not installed on your system, an alert message indicates which font is missing. The text that uses this missing font is also highlighted in pink. You will fix this missing font problem later in this lesson by replacing the missing font with an available font. This is useful because InDesign makes it clear which fonts might cause problems when printing and provides several opportunities to correct the situation.

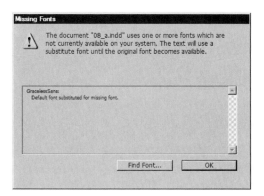

2 Click OK to close the alert message.

Navigate through the pages in the document and you can see that pages 5 through 8 have already been completed. The missing font is located on page 8. In this lesson, you will complete the first four pages of the newsletter and then correct the missing font.

3 Choose File > Save As and name the file **04_News**, and save it in the ID_04 folder.

4 To see what the finished document will look like, open the 04_b.indd file in the same folder. If you prefer, you can leave the document open to act as a guide as you work. When you're ready to resume working on the lesson document, choose its name from the Window menu.

Creating and entering text

You can use InDesign to enter text into your documents or your can import text created in other programs, such as word processing software.

Creating a headline and applying a style

In the area beneath the banner, "Sonata Cycles News," and the space that will contain the start of the article, you'll create a text frame for the article headline, "Team Sonata Captures 24 Hours Race." This headline text frame will span the two columns. You'll then apply a headline style to this headline and format the headline.

1 While viewing page one, double-click the Zoom tool (🔍) to increase the magnification to 100%.

2 To mark the location of the top of your headline frame you will create a guide and then create the frame. Hold down Shift and drag a guide from the horizontal ruler to the 18p6 (18 picas, 6 points) location on page 1. To help you position the guide, watch the Y value in either the Control or Transform palettes as you drag. Holding down Shift constrains the position of the guide in 6-point increments.

3 Using the Type tool (**T**) , position the type cursor next to the left margin over the 18p6 guide. The horizontal crossbar on the type cursor should be at 18p6.

4 Drag to create a text frame in the blank area below the 18p6 guide and above the 21p guide. The text frame should span the two columns, and the top of the frame should snap to the 18p6 guide, while the bottom snaps to the 21p guide.

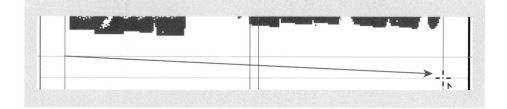

If you need to resize the frame, select the Selection tool, and drag the handles of the frame to snap to the guides. Then select the Type tool and click inside the frame.

After you draw a text frame using the Type tool, an insertion point appears, ready for you to begin typing.

5 In the text frame you just created, type **Team Sonata Captures 24 Hours Race.**

To make this headline consistent with other headlines used in the newsletter, you'll apply the Head 1 style. When you apply a paragraph style, you can place the insertion point anywhere in the paragraph or select any part of the paragraph.

6 With the insertion point anywhere in the headline text you just typed, select Head 1 in the Paragraph Styles palette.

Team Sonata Captures 24 Hours Race

7 Save the file.

Flowing text

The process of taking imported text, such as that from a word processing program, and placing it across several linked text frames is called flowing text. InDesign lets you flow text manually for greater control or automatically to save time.

Tips on flowing text

When your pointer becomes a loaded text icon ( ) after you place text or click an in port or out port, you are ready to flow text onto your pages. When you position the loaded text icon over a text frame, parentheses enclose the icon ( ).

In addition, the icon can appear in one of three forms, which correspond to the method you choose for controlling the flow of text on your pages:

Manual text flow ( ) adds text one frame at a time. It stops flowing text at the bottom of a text frame, or at the last of a series of linked frames. You must reload the text icon to continue flowing text.

Semi-autoflow ( ) works like manual text flow, except that the pointer reloads as a loaded text icon each time the end of a frame is reached, until all text is flowed into your document.

Autoflow ( ) adds pages and frames until all the text is flowed into your document.

–From Adobe InDesign CS online Help.

Flowing text manually

To flow text manually, you first select a word processing file to import. You can then drag to create a frame, or you can click anywhere on the page to create a text frame in a column. In this exercise you will use both methods to flow the text into the columns on the first page of the newsletter.

1 In the Pages palette, double-click the page 1 icon to center the first page in the document window. Click on a blank part of the page to deselect all items.

2 Choose File > Place. In the place dialog box; make sure that Show Import Options is selected, locate and double-click 04_c.doc in the ID_04 folder and click Open.

3 Make certain that Remove Text and Table Formatting is not selected in the import options dialog box. Deselecting this option causes the text to be imported with the same formatting that was applied in the word-processing application. Selecting this option would remove any formatting that was applied to the text. You want to keep the formatting, so you will keep this option deselected.

You will now create a text frame between the light blue guides below the banner on the left side of page 1.

4 Create a text frame in the left column of page 1 by positioning the loaded text icon next to the left margin just below the 21p (21-pica) guide and dragging down to the right side of the first column at the 30p guide.

Dragging to create a text frame.

Notice that the text frame includes an out port in the lower right corner. The red plus sign indicates that there is overset text. There is more text than fits into the existing text frame. You will now flow this text into the second column on page 1.

5 Using the Selection tool (↖), click the out port of the frame you just created.

If you change your mind and decide you don't want to flow overset text, you can click any tool in the toolbox to cancel the loaded text icon. No text will be deleted.

6 Position the loaded text icon in the upper left corner of the second column just below the 21p guide, and click.

The text flows into a new frame from where you clicked to the bottom of the second column. The out port in the new column contains a red plus sign, again indicating that there is still overset text.

Note: While you can create separate, linked frames for each column, it is also possible to work with one large column that is divided into multiple columns using Object > Text Frame Options. Each method has its advantages in certain types of documents.

Flowing text automatically

You will use autoflow to place the rest of the overset text into the document. When you autoflow text, InDesign creates new text frames within column guides on subsequent pages until all the overset text is flowed. If there are not enough pages in your document when you use autoflow, InDesign adds new pages until all the text is placed.

Note: A connected series of text frames is called a story.

1 Using the Selection tool (↖), click the out port in the lower right corner of the frame you just created in the second column on page 1.

While the loaded text icon is active, you can still navigate to different document pages or create new pages. This allows you to continue flowing text onto other pages in your document—even if these pages have not yet been created at the time you click on the out port of a text frame.

2 In the Pages palette, double-click the page 2 icon to center page 2 in the document window. (You may need to scroll down the palette to find the icon for page 2.) Notice that there are no text frames on page 2. Also notice that the text icon is still loaded.

3 Holding down Shift, position the loaded text icon in the upper left corner of the left column on page 2, and click. Release the Shift key.

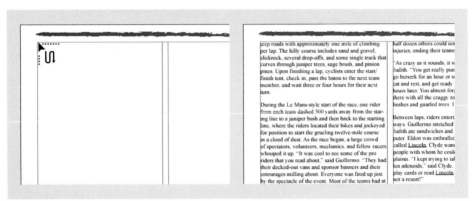

Holding down Shift lets you autoflow text into your document.

Notice that two new text frames were added to each page within the column guides. This is because you held down Shift to autoflow text. All the text in the story is now placed on pages 2 through 4.

Resizing a text frame

When you create a text frame by clicking the loaded text icon, InDesign creates the new text frame as wide as the column where you click. Although these frames are placed within the column margins, you can move, resize, and reshape any of these text frames if necessary.

1 Navigate to page 4 by clicking the page selector in the lower left corner of the document window.

Notice that the text frame in the left column covers the photograph that was placed on this page. When you autoflow text, the text frames are created within the column settings regardless of whether objects appear in those columns. You can fix this overlap by adding a text wrap to the image or by resizing the text frame. In this exercise you will resize the text frame.

2 Using the Selection tool (↖), click the text frame in the left column on page 4 to select the text frame, and then drag the lower middle handle of the text frame above the photograph to approximately the 31p location (you can look at the vertical ruler as you drag or in the transform palette).

Before and after resizing text frame.

3 Choose File > Save.

Flowing text into an existing frame

When you place text, you can flow text into a new frame or into an existing frame. To flow text into an existing frame, you can click an insertion point to flow text at that point, or you can click the loaded text icon in an existing frame, which replaces its contents.

The first page of the newsletter includes a placeholder frame for a sidebar. You'll place the text in this frame that announces upcoming cycling events.

1 Turn to the first page of the newsletter.

2 Choose File > Place. Locate and double-click 04_d.doc in the ID_04 folder.

The pointer becomes a loaded text icon (▤). When you move the loaded text icon over an empty text frame, parentheses enclose the icon (▤).

3 Position the loaded text icon over the placeholder frame near the bottom of page 1, and click.

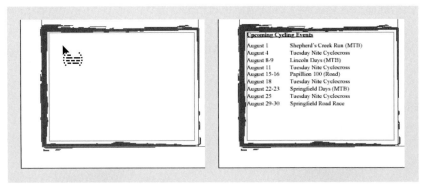

Placing a text file into an existing frame.

You will apply styles to this sidebar text later in this lesson.

4 Choose File > Save.

Note: *If the text formatting in your file looks different than the illustration above, don't worry, because you'll be changing all the formatting for this text block in the next set of steps.*

Working with styles

Styles make it easy to apply repetitive formatting across an entire document. For example, to keep all headlines formatted consistently through your document, you can create a headline style that contains the necessary formatting attributes. Styles can save time when you apply and revise text formatting and can help provide a consistent look to your documents.

Applying a style

To make the appearance of the article consistent with the other articles in the newsletter, you will apply a paragraph style called Body Copy. We created this style for formatting the body text of the main articles in the newsletter.

1   Click the Paragraph Styles palette (or choose Window > Type > Paragraph Styles) to make the palette visible, if it is not already open.

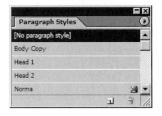

The Paragraph Styles palette for this document now includes four styles: Body Copy, Head 1, Head 2, and Normal. The Normal style has a disk icon next to it, indicating that the style was imported from a different application. In this case, Normal is a Microsoft Word style that was imported when you placed the article. You'll now apply the InDesign style, Body Copy, to the text.

Note: *There are no default paragraph styles when you first create a document with InDesign. You can create new styles or add styles from other InDesign documents. Styles are also added to InDesign documents when you import text with styles from Microsoft Word.*

2   Using the Type tool (**T**), click an insertion point anywhere in the main article you placed. Then choose Edit > Select All to select all the body text in the story. Notice that the sidebar text is not selected; this text belongs to a different story.

3 Once all the text is selected, select Body Copy in the Paragraph Styles palette.

4 Choose Edit > Deselect All. The article is now formatted in a different font, and the first line of each paragraph is now indented.

"Sour grapes," lamented Clyde, when asked if the opponents' protest tarnished their gold-medal effort. "If they can't take a little jostling during a race, maybe they're in the wrong sport. Maybe they should try golf or badminton or tiddlywinks or something." Clyde quickly changed the subject to his recent vacation to Oaxaca, Mexico.

The 24 Hours of Springfield race began at noon on Saturday and finished shortly after noon on Sunday in an area called Behind the Gorge, a remote wilderness region between Springfield and Lincoln. Competing in teams of four, cyclists carry a baton around a twelve-mile course of rolling terrain on moderate to technical

The 24 Hours of Springfield race began at noon on Saturday and finished shortly after noon on Sunday in an area called Behind the Gorge, a remote wilderness region between Springfield and Lincoln. Competing in teams of four, cyclists carry a baton around a twelve-mile course of rolling terrain on moderate to technical jeep roads with approximately one mile of climbing per lap. The hilly course includes sand and gravel, slickrock, several drop-offs, and some single track that curves through juniper trees, sage brush, and pinion pines. Upon finishing a lap, cyclists enter the start/finish tent, check in, pass the baton to the next team member, and wait three or four hours for their next turn.

During the Le Mans-style start of the race, one rider from each team dashed 500 yards away from the staring line to a juniper bush and then back to the starting line, where the riders located their bikes and jockeyed for position to start the grueling twelve-mile course in a cloud of dust. As the race began, a large crowd of spectators, volunteers, mechanics, and fellow racers whooped it

Before and after style is applied.

Loading styles from another document

Styles appear only in the document in which you create them. However, it's easy to share styles between InDesign documents by loading, or importing, styles from other InDesign documents. In this exercise you will take styles from another Sonata Cycles document. This other document includes several styles that will work well for the text in this newsletter. Instead of re-creating these styles, you'll load the styles from the other document and apply them to text in the newsletter.

1 Click the palette menu button (to the right of the Paragraph Styles tab), and choose Load All Styles from the Paragraph Styles palette menu.

2 In the Open a File dialog box, double-click Styles.indd from the ID_04 folder. In the Paragraph Styles palette, notice the new styles called Sidebar Copy and Sidebar Head. You may need to scroll through the list or resize the palette to see these additional styles.

3 In the document window, change the view so that you can see the sidebar ("Upcoming Cycling Events") on page 1.

4 Using the Type tool (**T**), click an insertion point in the sidebar, and then choose Edit > Select All.

5   Select the Sidebar Copy style in the Paragraph Styles palette.

6   Click an insertion point in the sidebar heading, "Upcoming Cycling Events."

7   In the Paragraph Styles palette, select Sidebar Head.

Before and after applying Sidebar Head paragraph style.

Vertically aligning text

To evenly distribute the space on the top and bottom of the text frame, you will center the text vertically using vertical justification.

1   With the insertion point anywhere in the sidebar frame, choose Object > Text Frame Options.

2   Under Vertical Justification, for Align, select Justify, and then click OK.

3   Choose File > Save.

Note: If the text frame extends over the green artwork framing the text, you may not be able to read the bottom line of text. To fix this, you can select the middle handle at the lower edge of the frame and drag it upwards, just as you did in "Resizing a text frame" on page 156. Because the text is set to be justified vertically, the spacing between lines re-adjusts when you release the mouse.

You have finished formatting the first page of the newsletter.

Threading text

When you autoflowed text into the document, InDesign created links between the frames so that text would flow from one frame to another. These links are called threads. You can break the threads between frames, add new frames between the threaded frames, and rearrange how frames are threaded.

1 In the Pages palette, double-click the numbers below the page 2–3 icons. If the entire spread does not automatically appear in the document window, choose View > Fit Spread in Window to view the spread.

2 Select the Selection tool (➤), and then click the text frame in the right column on page 2 to select it.

3 Choose View > Show Text Threads. Blue lines appear that represent the connections (threads) between text frames in the selected story. Each thread goes from the out port of one frame to the in port of the next frame in the sequence.

4 With the text frame in the right column of page 2 still selected, press Backspace or Delete to delete this text frame. Click to select a different frame in the story so that the text threads become visible.

After deleting a threaded frame.

Note: *Text threads only display when a frame within the text flow is selected.*

Notice that the text flows from the left column on page 2 to the left column on page 3. Although the text frame was deleted, no text in the story was deleted—it flowed into the next frame.

5 Press Ctrl+D (Windows) or Command+D (Mac OS) to open the Place dialog box. If necessary, deselect Replace Selected Item and Show Import Option and then locate and double-click 04_e.tif in the ID_04 folder.

6 Click the loaded graphics icon in the upper left corner of the blank column, just below the guide. If necessary, after placing the graphic, drag the picture so that it snaps to the top margin of the column.

You'll fill the space under the picture by creating a new text frame and threading the placed story through the new frame. To thread a new frame in the middle of a story, you can click the out port of the previous frame or the in port of the subsequent frame.

7 Holding down Ctrl (Windows) or Command (Mac OS) drag a guide from the horizontal ruler to the 28p mark. Holding the modifier key applies the guide across the entire spread rather than the entire page.

💡 *For accuracy, hold down Shift as you drag to move the guide in 1p increments, or you can select the guide with the Selection tool and then type **28p** in the Y box of the Transform palette.*

8 Click the left text frame on page 2 to select it, and then click the out port in the lower right corner of the frame. The out port then appears as a blue arrow, indicating that the story is continued in another frame.

9 Position the loaded text icon just below the 28p guide near the bottom of the right column, and click to create a frame that fills the rest of the column.

Threading a new text frame in the middle of a story.

A text frame is created that is the width of the column. You have now completed page 2 of the newsletter.

10 Choose View > Hide Text Threads.

Now you'll use a keyboard shortcut instead of using a menu, for deselecting.

11 Press Shift+Ctrl+A (Windows) or Shift+Command+A (Mac OS) to deselect everything. Then save the file.

Changing the number of columns on a page

You will now create a full-page sidebar on page 3 that provides three different bike routes for the newsletter readers. To simplify creating the three text frames for these routes, you will change the number of columns on page 3.

1 In the Pages palette, double-click the page 3 icon to center the page in the document window. Make sure that only page 3 in the Pages palette is highlighted so that the column change will affect only page 3. If necessary, click another page icon, and then click the page 3 icon.

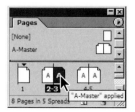

2 Choose Layout > Margins and Columns. Under Columns, type 3 for Number and click OK.

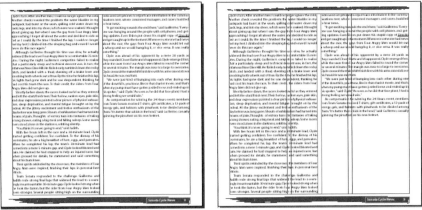

Even though the number of columns changed, the widths of the existing text frames did not change.

Notice that the text frames are independent of the number of columns. Column margins can determine how text frames are created, but the text frame widths do not change when you redefine columns. One exception to this rule is when Layout Adjustment is turned on—you can learn more about Layout Adjustment in "On your own" at the end of this lesson.

3 Using the Selection tool (⬉), select a text frame on page 3 and press Backspace or Delete.

4 Select the other text frame on page 3 and press Backspace or Delete. Both text frames on page 3 should be deleted.

Once again, you have deleted text frames, but you did not delete any text; the text flowed into the text frames on page 4. Now you'll place an Adobe Illustrator file that has been sized to fit within the newsletter page.

5 Press Ctrl+D (Windows) or Command+D (Mac OS) to open the Place dialog box. Deselect Show Import Options, then locate and double-click 04_f.ai in the ID_04 folder.

6 Click the loaded graphics icon in the upper left corner of page 3. If necessary, drag the illustration so that it snaps to the margin guides at the top, left, and right sides of the page.

Using semi-autoflow to place text frames

Now you will use semi-autoflow to place a text file into the three columns below the map illustration. Semi-autoflow lets you create text frames one at a time without having to reload the text icon.

1 Choose File > Place to open the Place dialog box, and then locate and double-click 04_g.doc in the ID_04 folder. Be sure to deselect Replace Selected Items in the Place dialog box.

2 Holding down Alt (Windows) or Option (Mac OS), position the loaded text icon in the left column just below the 28p guide, and click.

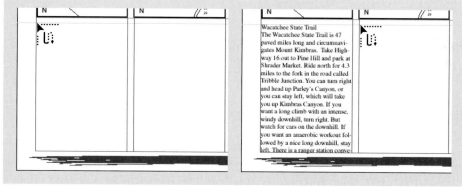

Flowing text semi-automatically.

The text flows into the left column. Because you held down Alt or Option, the pointer is still a loaded text icon, ready for you to flow text into another frame.

3 Holding down Alt or Option, position the loaded text icon in the second column just below the guide, and click. Release the Alt or Option key.

Now you will create the final column. You won't hold down Alt or Option since there will only be three frames in this story.

4 Position the loaded text icon in the third column just below the guide, and click.

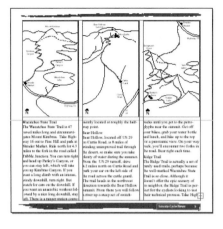

The text is overset in the third column, but after you format the text with styles, the text should then fit within the frames, leaving no overset text remaining.

Applying and editing the sidebar styles

To make the text consistent with the rest of the newsletter, you'll apply the sidebar styles to the text you just added. You will also edit the Sidebar Head style so that each heading starts at the top of the next column. You'll start by using the keyboard to select all the text in the story.

1 Using the Type tool (**T**), click an insertion point in the sidebar. Then press Ctrl+A (Windows) or Command+A (Mac OS) to select all the text in the story.

2 Select the Sidebar Copy style in the Paragraph Styles palette.

3 Click an insertion point inside the "Wacatchee State Trail" heading, and then select the Sidebar Head style in the Paragraph Styles palette.

4 Apply the Sidebar Head style to the other two headings, "Bear Hollow" and "Ridge Trail."

To ensure that the headings will always appear at the top of each frame, you'll edit the sidebar heading style.

5 Before you edit the style, deselect all text.

6 In the Paragraph Styles palette, double-click Sidebar Head to open the Modify Paragraph Style Options dialog box for that style.

7 In the left panel, select Keep Options and then select In Next Column from the Start Paragraph pop-up menu. Then click OK.

The sidebar headings on page 3 are now forced to start at the top of each column. Now that you've finished placing text and graphics in the newsletter, you'll use some of InDesign's word-processing features to add finishing touches to the text throughout the newsletter.

8 Save the file.

The context menu gives you another way to move text to the beginning of the next column. To do this, make sure that the cursor is in the place where you want to create the break, and then right-click (Windows) or Control-click (Mac OS) the text frame to open the context menu. Choose Insert Break Character > Column Break. You can also use context menu commands to move text to the next frame, page, odd page, or even page.

Adding a page continuation note

Because the story on page 2 links to another page, you can let readers know where they can resume reading when they get to the bottom of the page. To do this you will add a "(Continued on page x)" frame. You can add an automatic page number that will automatically reflect the number of the next page in the text flow.

1 Center page 2 in the document window by scrolling or using the Pages palette.

2 Drag a guide from the horizontal ruler down to the 46p location. Zoom in so that you can read the text in the column easily.

3 Select the Selection tool (↖), click the text frame in the right column on page 2, and then drag the lower middle handle up to the 46p guide.

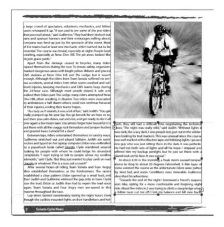

4 Select the Type tool (T), and then drag to create a text frame that fills the space at the bottom of the right-most column on page 2.

5 With a text insertion point active in the new text frame, type (**Continued on page**), including the space and the parentheses. Then use the left arrow key to move the insertion point to the left of the close parenthesis.

6 Right-click (Windows) or Control-click (Mac OS) the text frame, and in the context menu that appears, choose Insert Special Character > Next Page Number. The text now reads "(Continued on page 4)."

Note: The text frame containing the jump line must touch or overlap the frame linked text for the "Next Page Number" character to work properly.

7 If necessary, select the Selection tool, and then drag the top of the new text frame up so that it snaps to the text frame above it.

8 With the Selection tool, click the jump line text frame and then Shift-click to select the text frame immediately above it. Then choose Object > Group. This keeps the story and its jump line together if you move them.

Changing horizontal and vertical text alignment

The jump line text is probably formatted with a different paragraph style than you want to use. Next, you'll reformat that text.

1 Select the Type tool (**T**), and then triple-click "(Continued on page 4)" to select the text.

2 In the Paragraph Styles palette, click Body Copy.

3 In the Character palette, select Italic from the Type Style menu.

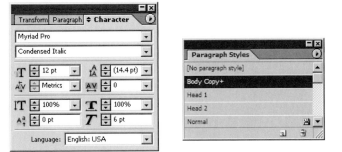

Notice that the Body Copy style has a plus sign (+) next to it in the Paragraph palette. The plus sign next to a style indicates that the current text has formats applied to it in addition to the style.

4 Click the Paragraph palette tab, and then click the Align Right (≡) option.

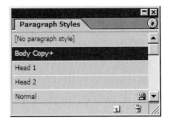

Now you will align the text at the bottom of the frame.

5 Choose Object > Text Frame Options.

6 In the Align pop-up menu under Vertical Justification, select Bottom. Then click OK.

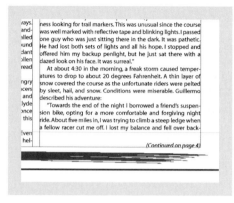

7 Press Shift+Ctrl+A (Windows) or Shift+Command+A (Mac OS) to deselect the text. Then save the file.

Creating and applying a character style

In this lesson, you have applied and loaded paragraph styles. Now you'll learn how to create a character style. A character style allows you to apply consistent formatting to words or groups of words throughout a document. They can be applied to specified text within the body text. You can use the same methods to create character styles and paragraph styles. You can create a style based on formatted text, or you can create a style using the New Character Style dialog box.

Here you'll apply formatting to text and create a new character style based on that text. You'll then apply the formatting to names of bicycles in a story.

1 In the Pages palette, double-click the page 6 icon. Using the Zoom tool (Q), zoom in to a level that allows you to read the type in the right column of page 6.

2 Using the Type tool (T), select "Road Bikes—" (including the em dash) at the beginning of the second paragraph below "New Series of Bicycles" on page 6.

First you will use the Character palette to format the text. Then you will use the Character Styles palette to create a style based on the formatted text.

3 Click the Character palette tab (or choose Window > Type > Character to make the palette visible). Leave the font set in Myriad Pro and select Bold SemiCondensed.

Before and after applying a character style to text within a paragraph.

4 Click the Character Styles tab (or choose Window > Type > Character Styles to make the palette visible). Make sure that the formatted text is still selected.

5 In the Character Styles palette, select the New Character Style command from the palette menu (⊙). For the Style Name type Inline Head then click OK.

6 With the Type tool still selected, select "Mountain Bikes—" at the top of the same column on page 7. Select Inline Head in the Character Styles palette. Then deselect the words and view the new formatting.

The words automatically take on all the formatting attributes you selected for the Inline Head style. Notice that only the selected text was formatted with the style, not the entire paragraph.

7 Apply the Inline Head character style to "Specialty Bikes—" in the second column on page 7.

8 Save the file.

Finding and changing

Like most popular word processors, InDesign lets you find text and replace it. You can also search for and change formatting and special characters.

Finding text and changing formatting

You will search for occurrences of the word "Lincoln" in this document. Make sure that your view-magnification level is set so that you can easily read the text and see the formatting. You do not have to have anything selected for this procedure.

The author of the main article used underline instead of italics to indicate the title of the book, Lincoln. You want to remove the underlining and replace it with italics.

1 Choose Edit > Find/Change. For Find What, type **Lincoln**.

2 Press Tab to move to the Change To box, and make certain that the Change To box is empty. For Search, make sure Document is selected.

These settings tell InDesign to search all text frames throughout the document for the word Lincoln and to keep the same word. Next we will tell InDesign to change the format of the words it locates.

3 Click More Options to display additional formatting options in the dialog box.

4 Under Find Format Settings, click Format to open the Find format dialog box.

5 In the left side of the Find Format Settings dialog box, select Basic Character Formats. Then in the right side, click the Underline check box to place a check mark, indicating that it is selected.

6 Leave the other check boxes as they are: either with grayed-out check marks (Windows) or dashes (Mac OS). These marks indicate attributes that are irrelevant to the search—they will not act as criteria for the search. Click OK to return to the Find/Change dialog box.

Notice the alert icon (⚠) above the Find what box. This icon indicates that InDesign will search for text containing the specified formatting. In this case, InDesign will search for underlined occurrences of "Lincoln."

7 Under Change Format Settings, click Format to open the Change Format Settings dialog box, and set all the following options:

• On the left side of the dialog box, choose Basic Character Formats.

• On the right side, use the pop-up menus to select Adobe Garamond Pro for Font Family and Italic for the font style. (Adobe Garamond is alphabetized on the list under "G," not "A.")

• For Size, select 11 pt.

• For Leading, select 12 pt.

• Click the Underline check box twice to clear it.

• Click OK.

8 Click Change All. A message appears, telling you that InDesign found and changed the three occurrences of underlined "Lincoln."

9 Click OK to close the message, and then click Done to close the Find/Change dialog box. Then save the file.

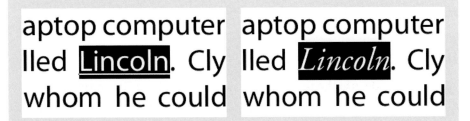

Before and after finding and changing attributes.

Finding and changing special characters

The text in the sidebar on page 1 uses hyphens between date numbers (such as August 8-9) instead of en dashes. You will replace these hyphens (-) with en dashes (–).

1 Turn to page 1, and use the Zoom tool (🔍) to magnify the "Upcoming Cycling Events" text frame.

2 Using the Type tool (T), click inside the "Upcoming Cycling Events" sidebar.

3 Press Ctrl+F (Windows) or Command+F (Mac OS) to open the Find/Change dialog box.

In this case, you want InDesign to replace only the hyphens in the text frame on the first page, so you will limit the search range to only the story, which consists of only the sidebar frame.

4 For Search, choose Story to narrow the search to only the sidebar.

5 For Find what, delete the word "Lincoln" and type - (a hyphen).

6 Press Tab to shift focus to the Change To box. Click the arrow button (▶) to the right of the Change To box and choose En Dash from the pop-up menu. The underlined word "Lincoln" is replaced by ^= (a caret and equal sign), a code for the en dash character.

7 Under Find Format Settings, click Clear. Then click Clear under Change Format Settings. This clears the underline attribute you searched for in your last search so that InDesign will not look for underlines in this step.

8 Click Change All.

The four hyphens (-) are replaced by en dashes (–) in the sidebar.

Note: If you are notified that considerably more than four changes were made, you may have forgotten to choose Story instead of Document for search, or you didn't click an insertion point inside the sidebar frame. Choose Edit > Undo Replace All Text and try again.

9 Click OK to close the message, and then click Done to close the Find/Change dialog box. Save the file.

Finding and changing a missing font

When you opened the document based on the template, the GracelessSans font was missing. You will search for text containing the GracelessSans font and replace it with the Myriad Pro Bold font.

1 In the Pages palette, double-click the page 8 icon (you may need to scroll in the Pages palette). Choose View > Fit Page in Window. The pink highlight indicates that the text is formatted with a missing font.

2 Choose Type > Find Font to open the Find Font dialog box. This dialog box lists all fonts used in the document and the type of font—such as PostScript, True Type or Open Type.

3 Select GracelessSans in the list.

4 For Replace With, select Myriad Pro Bold.

5 Click Change All. Click Done to close the dialog box and see the replaced font in the document.

Note: For your own projects, you may need to add the missing font to your system instead of replacing the missing font. You can fix missing fonts by installing the font on your system, by activating the font using font management software or by adding the font files to the InDesign Fonts folder. For more information, see Adobe InDesign CS online Help.

Spell-checking a story

The text in the "Bad Clams" story on page 5 includes Spanish and Italian phrases. Before you spell-check the story, you will assign the appropriate language to each phrase. InDesign includes the ability to spell check and hyphenate text using multiple languages.

1 In the document window, turn to page 5. Change your view so that you can comfortably read the paragraph below the image in the right column.

2 In the paragraph in the right column beginning "William Johnson," use the Type tool (**T**) to select "¡Yo tengo un cuaderno rojo!"

3 In the Character palette, choose Spanish: Castilian from the Language menu.

Assigning languages lets you spell check a document more accurately and efficiently.

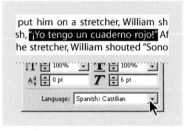

Note: If you do not see the Spanish and other dictionaries on the Language menu, either your dictionaries have been deleted from your hard disk or your installation of InDesign did not include them. To install the dictionaries you need for this task, save your file, quit all programs, and insert your InDesign application CD into your computer CD-ROM drive. Open the CD and double-click the installation icon. Follow the on-screen instructions for a custom installation, specifying only the dictionaries. You do not need to reinstall the InDesign program, only the dictionaries need to be installed. Then reopen your 04_News.indd file and resume your work.

4 In the same paragraph, select "Sono il campione dell mondo" (This is intentionally misspelled). In the Character palette, choose Italian from the Language menu.

The text may shift when you apply the language attribute. This occurs because hyphenation rules are different for English and Italian.

5 Make sure that the insertion point is in the same paragraph, and choose Edit > Check Spelling.

6 For Search, select Story so you don't have to spell-check the entire document.

7 Click Start. When "dell" is highlighted, select "del" under Suggested Corrections, and then click Change. When you finish spell-checking, click Done.

8 Save the file.

Creating text on a path

You can create type that flows along the edge of an open or closed path of any shape. For this lesson, you will draw a circle around the Mr. Tuneup graphic on page 8, and then flow type around the circle.

1 Choose 8 from the Page pop-up menu at the bottom of the document window to turn to page 8.

2 Using the Selection tool (⬉), click the graphic above "It's Mr. Tuneup." Notice the center point of the graphic. You will use this center point to help you draw the circle.

3 Hold down the mouse on the Rectangle tool in the toolbox, and select the Ellipse tool (○). Make sure that None is selected in the toolbox Fill box.

4 Holding down Alt+Shift (Windows) or Option+Shift (Mac OS), place the pointer over the center point of the graphic and drag outward to create a circle slightly larger than the Mr. Tuneup graphic (about 19 picas, as shown in the Transform palette for W and H).

The Shift key constrains the shape to a circle; the Alt or Option key makes the center of the circle the starting point of your drawing so that you draw outward from the center.

5 Using the Type tool (T), select the first two lines below the graphic, "It's Mr. Tuneup! The Maestro Mechanic of Sonata Cycles."

6 Choose Edit > Copy.

7 Click and hold the mouse pointer over the Type tool in the toolbox, and then select the Path Type tool (✎).

8 Position the pointer over the upper left part of the circle until a small plus sign appears next to the pointer (✐), click and drag an arc to the other side of the circle.

If you click an insertion point on a path, the range of type will extend along the entire path. If you drag, type will appear only along the length specified when you dragged.

9 Choose Edit > Paste.

The plus sign (+) in the out port at the end of the text on the path indicates overset text. To display all the text on the path, you will adjust the path type's start and end indicators, which are the blue lines that appear before and after the pasted text.

10 Select the Direct Selection tool (↖) and move it over the blue indicator at the beginning of the text path. When the Direct Selection pointer is properly positioned, it appears as a solid arrowhead with a small vertical line and plus sign (▶ⱨ).

11 Drag the start indicator line (not the in port) down past the left center of the circle. Then drag the end indicator line (not the out port) down until all the text appears.

Finishing up

To complete the newsletter, you will clean up the design on page 8 by removing the circle's stroke and deleting the text box from which you copied the text that is now on the path.

1 Select the Selection tool (✹), and then click the text on the path.

2 Select the Stroke box (▣) in the toolbox, and then click the None button (▨).

3 Using the Selection tool, click the text frame below the graphic from which you copied the text, and press Backspace or Delete.

4 Save the file.

Congratulations. You have finished the lesson.

On your own

Follow these steps to learn more about layout adjustment and styles.

When you changed the number of columns in this lesson, the size of the text frames remained unchanged. However, if you need to change your document setup after you've begun laying out your document, you can turn on the Layout Adjustment option, which can save you time in reformatting your document. Try this:

1 Go to page 4 and choose Layout > Layout Adjustment. Select Enable Layout Adjustment and click OK. Now change the number of columns using the control palette.

Notice that the photograph is resized and the two text frames shrink to fit the first two columns.

2 Resize the text frames and graphics frame to clean up the page. Add threaded text frames as necessary to finish the redesign.

Before column change (left), after column change with Layout Adjustment turned on (middle), and finished redesign (right).

In this lesson, we covered only the basics of creating and applying styles. If you do a lot of your writing in InDesign, you'll want to learn how Next Style works and how to apply styles using shortcut keystrokes.

Note: In Windows, Num Lock must be on for the following shortcut keystrokes to work.

3 With no text selected, double-click the Head 2 style in the Paragraph Styles palette. Click an insertion point in the Shortcut text box. Using numbers from only the keypad, press Ctrl+Alt+2 (Windows) or Command+Option+2 (Mac OS). For Next Style, select Body Copy. Click OK to close the dialog box. Now practice applying the Head 2 style using your keyboard shortcut. Notice that when you press Enter or Return at the end of a Head 2 paragraph, the next paragraph automatically has the Body Copy style.

Note: If text does not appear in the Shortcut text box, make sure that you use the numbers from the numeric keypad. In Windows, make sure that Num Lock is on.

4 Some designers prefer not to indent the first paragraph after a heading. Create a paragraph style called "Body Copy No Indent" that is based on Body Copy and does not have a first-line indent. For the Next Style option in Body Copy No Indent, select Body Copy. Edit the heading styles so that the Next Style option is set to Body Copy No Indent.

Review questions

1 How do you autoflow text? How do you flow text one frame at a time?

2 How can using styles save time?

3 When searching for text using the Find/Change command, you get a "Cannot find match" message. What are some reasons InDesign failed to find a match?

4 While spell-checking your document, InDesign flags words used in other languages. How can you fix this problem?

Review answers

1 When the loaded text icon appears after using the Place command or clicking an out port, hold down Shift and click. To flow text one frame at a time, you can hold down Alt (Windows) or Option (Mac OS) to reload the text icon after you click or drag to create a frame.

2 Styles save time by letting you keep a group of formatting attributes together that you can quickly apply to text. If you need to update the text, you don't have to change each paragraph formatted with the style individually. Instead, you can simply modify the style.

3 If you get a "Cannot find match" message, you may not have typed the text properly, you may have selected Whole Word or Case Sensitive, or you may not have cleared formatting used in a previous search. Another possibility is that you selected Story for Search while the text you're looking for is in a different story. Finally, you may be searching for text that does not exist in your document.

4 Before you spell-check your document, select any phrase from a different language and use the Character palette to specify the language for that text.

5 | Working with Typography

With InDesign you can precisely control the type and formatting of your document. You can easily change font and type styles, modify the alignment, add tabs and indents, and apply colors and strokes to text.

In this lesson, you'll learn how to do the following:

• Prepare and use a baseline grid.

• Change type spacing and appearance.

• Create special characters.

• Create a tabbed table with tab leaders and hanging indents.

• Insert special characters in text using Open Type fonts.

Getting started

In this lesson, you'll create one two-page spread for the annual report of the Sonata Cycles company. Your work in this sample file will involve using one of the Open Type fonts that shipped on the application CD with *Adobe InDesign CS*.

Before you begin, you should restore the default preferences for Adobe InDesign.

1 To ensure that the tools and palettes function exactly as described in this lesson, delete or deactivate (by renaming) the InDesign Defaults file and the InDesign SavedData file. See "Restoring default preferences" on page 2.

2 Start Adobe InDesign.

To begin working, you'll open an existing InDesign document.

3 Choose File > Open, and open the 05_a.indd file in the ID_05 folder, located inside the Lessons folder within the IDCIB folder on your hard disk.

Note: If you have not already copied the resource files for this lesson onto your hard disk from the ID_05 folder from the Adobe InDesign CS Classroom in a Book CD, do so now. See "Copying the Classroom in a Book files" on page 2.

4 Choose File > Save As, rename the file **05_report.indd**, and save it in the ID_05 folder.

5 If you want to see what the finished document will look like, open the 05_b.indd file in the same folder. You can leave this document open to act as a guide as you work. When you're ready to resume working on the lesson document, choose its name from the Window menu.

Adjusting vertical spacing

InDesign provides several options for customizing and adjusting the vertical spacing in your document. You can:

• Set the space between all lines of text using a baseline grid.

• Set the space between each line using the Leading option in the Character palette.

• Set the space between each paragraph separately using the Space Before/Space After options in the Paragraph palette.

• Use the Vertical Justification options in the Text Frame Options dialog box to align text within a frame.

In this section of the lesson, you will use the baseline grid to align text.

Using a baseline grid to align text

Once you've decided on the font size and leading for your document's body text, you may want to set up a baseline grid (also called a leading grid) for the entire document. Baseline grids represent the leading for your document's body text and are used to align the baseline of type in one column of text with the baseline of type in neighboring columns.

Before you set the baseline grid, you'll want to check the margin value for the top of your document and the leading value for the body text. These elements work together with the grid to create a cohesive design.

1 To view the top margin value for the page, choose Layout > Margins and Columns. The top margin is set to 6p0 (6 picas, 0 points). Click Cancel to close the dialog box.

2 To determine the leading value, select the Type tool (T) in the toolbox and click in a body-text paragraph. Then click the Character palette tab (or choose Type > Character) to make the palette visible. Check the leading value (𝐀) in the Character palette. The leading is set to 14 pt (14 points).

3 Choose Edit > Preferences > Grids (Windows, Mac OS) or InDesign > Preferences > Grids (Mac OS) to set your grid options. In the Baseline Grid section, type **6** for Start to match your top margin setting of 6p0. This option sets the location of the first grid line for the document. If you use InDesign's default value of 3p0, the first grid line would appear above the top margin.

4 For Increment Every, type **14pt** to match your leading. When you select another option, InDesign automatically converts the points value to picas (to 1p2).

5 Choose 100% for View Threshold.

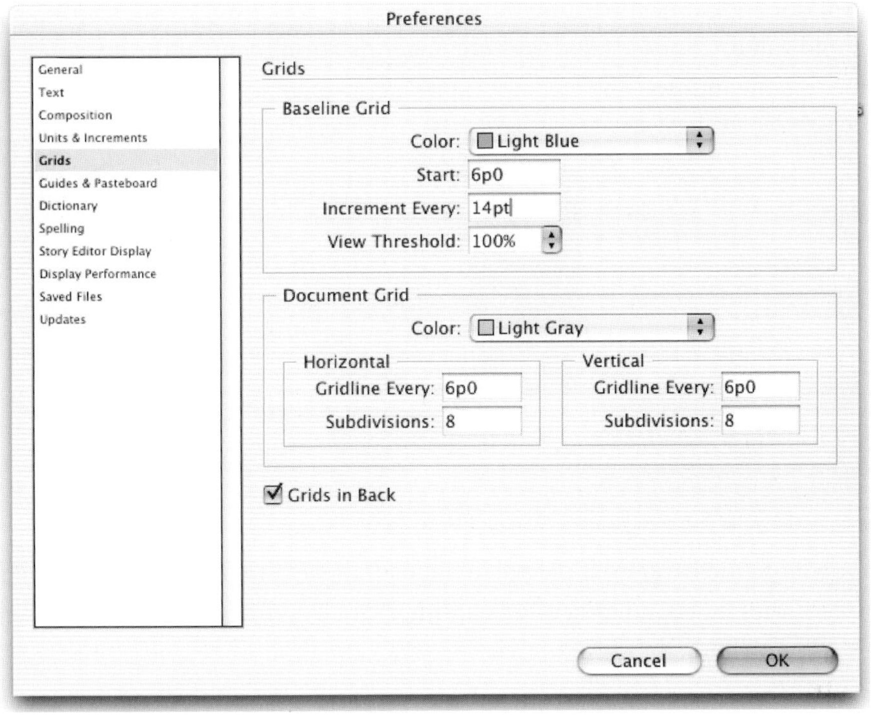

Preferences

General
Text
Composition
Units & Increments
Grids
Guides & Pasteboard
Dictionary
Spelling
Story Editor Display
Display Performance
Saved Files
Updates

Grids

Baseline Grid

Color: ☐ Light Blue

Start: 6p0

Increment Every: 14pt

View Threshold: 100%

Document Grid

Color: ☐ Light Gray

Horizontal

Gridline Every: 6p0

Subdivisions: 8

Vertical

Gridline Every: 6p0

Subdivisions: 8

☑ Grids in Back

Cancel   OK

The View Threshold option sets the minimum value at which you can see the grid on-screen. At 100%, the grid appears in the document window only at magnifications of 100% or higher.

6 Click OK to close the dialog box.

Viewing the baseline grid

Now you'll make the grid you just set up visible on-screen.

1 To view the grid in the document window, choose View > Show Baseline Grid. The grid does not appear because the document view is lower than the grid's View Threshold value. Choose 100% from the magnification menu at the lower left corner of the document window—the grid now appears on-screen.

Now you'll use the Paragraph palette to align all the text to the grid. You can align multiple stories independently of one another, or all at once. You'll align all the stories in this spread simultaneously.

2 Click the Paragraph tab (or choose Type > Paragraph) to make the palette visible.

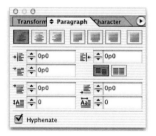

3 With the Type tool still selected, click an insertion point anywhere in the first paragraph on the spread, and then choose Edit > Select All to select all the text in the main story.

When applying paragraph attributes, it is not necessary to select an entire paragraph with the Type tool. Just select a portion of the paragraph or paragraphs you want to format. If you are formatting only one paragraph, you can simply click in the paragraph to make an insertion point.

4 In the Paragraph palette, click the Align to Baseline Grid button (≣). The text shifts so that the baselines of the characters rest on the grid lines.

Before and after aligning the text to the baseline grid.

5 If necessary, scroll to the left side of the spread so you can see the pull quote on the side of the page; then click an insertion point in the pull quote.

6   In the Paragraph palette, click the Align to Baseline Grid button. Because this text is formatted using 18 point leading, not the baseline grid leading value of 14pt or 1p2, aligning to the grid causes the text to expand to every other grid line (using 28 point leading).

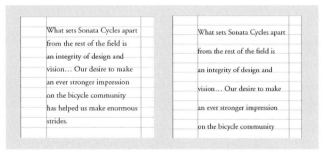

Before and after aligning the pull quote to the baseline grid.

7 Save the file.

Changing the spacing above and below paragraphs

When you apply a space before or after a paragraph that you have previously aligned to the grid, the space automatically adjusts to the next highest multiple of the grid value. For example, if your grid is set to 14 points (1p2) and you specify Space After of any value under 14, InDesign automatically increases the space value to 14; if you specify a value over 14, such as 16, InDesign increases it to the next higher multiple—28. You can use the Space Before or Space After value instead of the Baseline Grid value, by selecting the Do Not Align to Baseline Grid option for the affected paragraph.

No space (left), space adjusted to fit grid at 28 pt (middle), and actual space value at 16 pt (right).

Here you'll increase the space below the second paragraph of the main story. All other paragraphs in the spread have already been formatted with a 1p2 Space After value.

1 Make sure that the Type tool (**T**) is still selected, and click anywhere in the second paragraph on the page on the left (page 2).

2 In the Paragraph palette, type **1p2** for Space After (.≡) and press Enter or Return. The text in the next heading shifts automatically to the next grid line.

Before and after applying a Space After value to the upper paragraph.

Now you'll increase the space before the heading "The Dos Ventanas Cycling Partnership" to give it even more space.

3   Click an insertion point in the heading "The Dos Ventanas Cycling Partnership." In the Paragraph palette, type **0p6** for Space Before (⊤≣) and then press Enter or Return. Because you previously aligned the heading to the baseline grid, the Space Before jumps to 14 points instead of 6 points.

To use the 0p6 value instead of 14, and to add more space between the heading and the following paragraph, you'll unalign the heading from the grid.

4 With an insertion point still in the heading "The Dos Ventanas Cycling Partnership," click the Do Not Align to Baseline Grid button (≣≣) in the Paragraph palette. The heading shifts upward a bit, away from the body text below.

Before and after unaligning the heading from the baseline grid.

This heading and the heading on the page on the right (page 3) are formatted using the Head 1 style. To automatically update the second heading so that it uses the same spacing values as the heading you just edited, you'll redefine the style.

5 Click the Paragraph Styles palette tab (or choose Type > Paragraph Styles) to make the palette visible.

6 Click an insertion point in the heading "The Dos Ventanas Cycling Partnership." Notice that a plus sign (+) appears after the Head 1 style name in the palette. This sign indicates that the formatting for the selected text has been modified from the original formatting for the style.

7 Click the palette menu button (⊙), and choose Redefine Style from the Paragraph Styles palette menu. The Head 1 style now takes on the formatting of the current text.

Notice that the plus sign disappears and that space is added above the heading on page 3.

8 To apply all the same alignment characteristics to another heading, click the Type tool in the "Our New Chain of Stores" heading on page 3, and then select the Head 1 style in the Paragraph Styles palette to apply the redefined style.

9 Save the file.

Changing fonts and type style

Changing the fonts and type styles of text can make a dramatic difference in the appearance of your document. Here you'll change the font family, type style, and size for the text in one of the pull quotes along the border of the spread. You'll make these changes using the Character palette.

About fonts

A font is a complete set of characters—letters, numbers, and symbols—that share a common weight, width, and style, such as 10-pt Adobe Garamond Pro Bold.

Typefaces (often called type families or font families) are collections of fonts that share an overall appearance, and are designed to be used together, such as Adobe Garamond Pro .

A Type Style is a variant version of an individual font in a font family. Typically, the Roman or Plain (the actual name varies from family to family) member of a font family is the base font, which may include type styles such as regular, bold, semibold, italic, and bold italic.

–From Adobe InDesign CS online Help.

---

1 Click the Character palette tab (or choose Type > Character).

2 Using the Type tool (**T**), click inside the pull quote on the left side of page 2, and then choose Edit > Select All to select the entire paragraph.

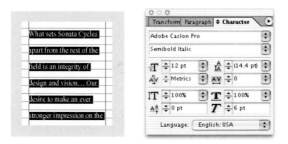

3 In the Character palette, select Adobe Caslon Pro from the Font Family menu and Semibold Italic from the Type Style menu.

4 In Font Size (T͟T), type **15** and press Enter or Return.

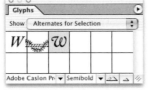

5 Choose Edit > Deselect All to deselect the text. Notice how the text stays aligned to the grid even after changing these attributes.

Because Adobe Caslon Pro is an Open Type font, you can use the Glyphs palette to select alternatives for many characters.

6 Select the first character (the "W") of the pull quote, and then choose Type > Glyphs.

7 In the Glyphs palette, select Alternates for Selection in the pop-up menu, just to see the alternates for "W." Then double-click the more script-like "W" alternate to replace the original character in the pullquote.

Some of the more commonly used glyphs, such as the copyright and trademark symbols are also available from the context menu by right-clicking (Windows) or Control-Clicking (Mac OS) at the text insertion point.

8 You won't be using the baseline grid for the remainder of the lesson, so you can hide it from view. To hide it, choose View > Hide Baseline Grid. Then save the file.

Changing paragraph alignment

You can easily manipulate how a paragraph fits in its text frame by changing the horizontal alignment. You can align text with one or both edges of a text frame or text-frame inset. Justifying text aligns both the left and right edges. In this section, you'll justify the pull quote.

1 Using the Type tool (T), click an insertion point in the pull quote on page 2.

2 Click the Paragraph palette tab (or choose Type > Paragraph), and then click the Justify All Lines button (≡).

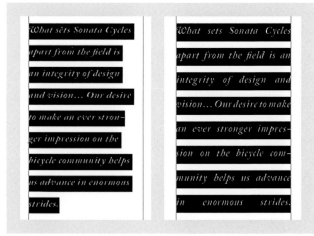

Before and after justifying text.

Adding a decorative font and special character

Now you'll add a decorative font character and a flush space (special character) to the end of the pull quote. Used together, a decorative font and flush space can make a dramatic difference in the look of a justified paragraph.

1 Using the Type tool (T), click an insertion point in the pull quote, just after the final period.

2 If the Glyphs palette is not still open, choose Type > Glyphs.

3 In the Glyphs palette, for Show, select Ornaments.

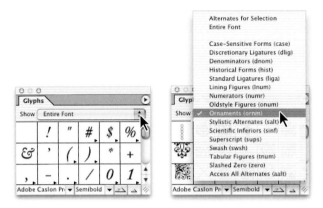

4 From the scrollable list, select the third character in the third row and double-click to insert the character. The character appears at the insertion point in the document. You're finished with the Glyphs palette for this lesson so you can close it now, and then save your work.

Note: This font may display many more glyphs than you are accustomed to seeing because it is an OpenType font. OpenType fonts are able to carry many more characters and glyph alternates than earlier PostScript typefaces. But Adobe's OpenType fonts are built on the same foundation as PostScript. For more information about OpenType fonts, visit www.adobe.com/type.

Notice how the word spacing in the last line of the pull quote has an overly large space in the center. You can address this by adding a flush space to the end of the paragraph. A flush space adds a variable amount of space to the last line of a fully justified paragraph. You'll insert the flush space between the period and the decorative end-of-story character you just added.

You could add a flush space using the Type menu, but this time you'll use the context menu to do the job.

5 Using the Type tool (**T**), click an insertion point between the final period and the Wood Type decorative character.

6 Right-click (Windows) or Control-click (Mac OS) and choose Insert White Space > Flush Space.

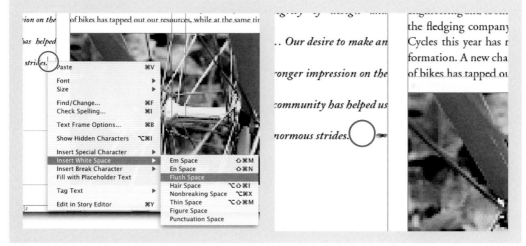

Before and after applying a flush space.

Applying special font features

You can add creative touches to your document using the special InDesign font features. For example, you can make the first character or word in a paragraph a drop cap, or apply a gradient or color fill to text. Other features include superscript and subscript characters, along with ligatures and oldstyle numerals for font families with these features.

Applying a gradient to text

InDesign makes it easy to apply gradients to the fill and stroke of text characters. You can apply gradients to an entire text frame or to different character ranges within a frame. Here you'll apply a gradient to the pull quote on page 2. You'll use a gradient swatch that was previously created and added to the Swatches palette.

1 Click the Swatches palette tab (or choose Window > Swatches) to make the palette visible.

2 Make sure that the Type tool (**T**) is still selected, click in the text of the pull quote on page 2, and then select all of the text in the paragraph.

3 Select the Fill box () in the toolbox, and then select the Text Gradient swatch in the Swatches palette (you may need to scroll). To see the gradient, choose Edit > Deselect All.

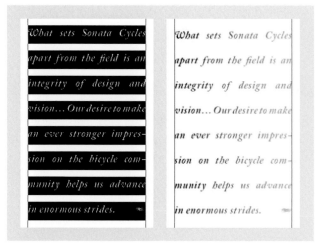

Applying a gradient swatch to selected text creates a left-to-right gradient fill.

Notice how the gradient flows from the left to right. If you want to change the direction of the gradient, you can use the gradient tool. You'll do that now to make the gradient flow from top to bottom, like the pull quote on page 3.

4 Using the Type tool, reselect all the text in the pull quote.

5 Select the Gradient tool (not the Gradient button) in the toolbox (▫), and drag a line from the top to the bottom of the highlighted text. To ensure that you draw a straight line, hold down the Shift key as you drag.

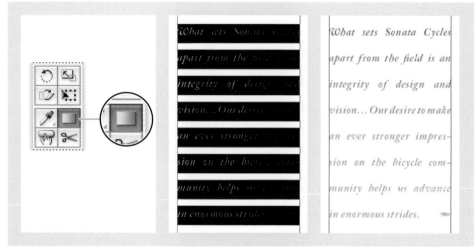

The gradient tool (left) lets you set the direction of the gradient fill.

To view the gradient fill, you'll use a keyboard shortcut to deselect all the text.

6 Press Shift+Ctrl+A (Windows) or Shift+Command+A (Mac OS) to deselect the text.

7 Select File > Save.

Creating a drop cap

Here you'll create a three-letter drop cap in the first paragraph of the document.

1 Using the Type tool (**T**), click an insertion point anywhere in the first paragraph on page 2.

2 In the Paragraph palette, type **3** for Drop Cap Number of Lines (⸾ᴬ≣) to make the letters drop down three lines. Then type **3** for Drop Cap One or More Characters (Ⓐ≣) to enlarge the first three letters. Press Enter or Return.

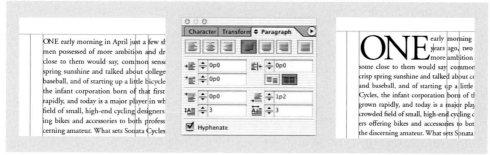

Before and after applying the drop cap.

Applying a fill and stroke to text

Next, you'll add a fill and stroke to the drop cap letters you just created.

1 With the Type tool (**T**) still selected, select the drop cap characters on page 2.

2 If necessary, select the Fill box in the Swatches palette (🇹).

3 In the Swatches palette, select Sonata Red. InDesign fills the letters with red, though you can't see it yet because the text is still selected.

Note: If you don't see Sonata Red in the palette, click the Show All Swatches button (🗗).

4 Select the Stroke box in the toolbox (🇹).

5 In the Swatches palette, select Black. A stroke appears around each of the letters.

The default size of the stroke is 1 point, which is a little thick for the letters. You'll change the stroke to one half point.

6 Choose Window > Stroke to open the Stroke palette.

7 In the Stroke palette, choose 0.5 pt for Weight. Then, press Shift+Ctrl+A (Windows) or Shift+Command+A (Mac OS) to deselect the text to view the fill and stroke effect.

Original drop cap (left), drop cap with color fill (middle), and drop cap with fill and stroke (right).

8 Close the Stroke palette, and then save the file.

Adjusting letter and word spacing

You can change the spacing between words and letters using InDesign's kerning and tracking features. You can also control the overall spacing of text in a paragraph by using the single-line or multi-line composers.

About tracking and kerning

Kerning is the process of adding or subtracting space between specific pairs of characters. Tracking is the process of loosening or tightening a block of text.

You can automatically kern type using metrics kerning or optical kerning. Metrics kerning uses kern pairs, which are included with most fonts. Kern pairs contain information about the spacing of specific pairs of characters. A sample of these are: LA, P., To, Tr, Ta, Tu, Te, Ty, Wa, WA, We, Wo, Ya, Yo, and yo. InDesign uses metrics kerning by default so kern pairs are automatically honored when you import or type text.

Some fonts include robust kern-pair specifications. However, when a font includes only minimal built-in kerning or none at all, or if you use two different typefaces or sizes in one or more words on a line, you may want to use the optical kerning option. Optical kerning adjusts the spacing between adjacent characters based on their shapes.

–From Adobe InDesign CS online Help.

Adjusting the kerning and tracking

With InDesign you can control the space between letters by using the kerning and tracking features. Kerning is the process of adding or subtracting space between specific letter pairs. Tracking is the process of creating an equal amount of spacing across a range of letters. You can use both kerning and tracking on the same text.

Here you'll manually kern some letters in the heading "The Dos Ventanas Cycling Partnership" to close up noticeable gaps. Then you'll track the heading to bring it all onto one line.

1 To distinguish the amount of space between letters more easily and to see the results of the kerning more clearly, select the Zoom tool (🔍) in the toolbox and drag a marquee around the heading "The Dos Ventanas Cycling Partnership."

2 If necessary, increase the zoom level in the magnification menu in the lower left corner of the document window.

3 Select the Type tool (T) and click an insertion point between the "V" and the "e" in the word "Ventanas."

4 Press Alt+Left Arrow (Windows) or Option+Left Arrow (Mac OS) to move the letter "e" to the left. Press this key combination repeatedly until the two adjacent letters look visually pleasing to you. We pressed it four times.

Note: The kerning value changes in the Character palette as you press the key combination. You can also use the Character palette to make these changes if you prefer.

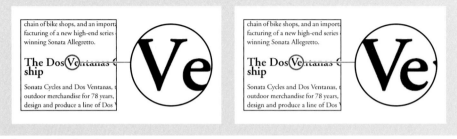

Before and after kerning.

5 If you've moved the letter too far, press Alt+Right Arrow (Windows) or Option+Right Arrow (Mac OS) to move the letter to the right.

6 Click an insertion point between the "P" and the "a" in the word "Partnership."

7 Press Alt/Option+Left Arrow to move the letter "a" to the left. Press this key combination repeatedly until the two adjacent letters look visually pleasing to you. We pressed it four times.

Before and after kerning.

Now you'll set a tracking value for the entire heading "The Dos Ventanas Cycling Partnership" to condense the overall spacing and bring it all onto one line. To set tracking you must first select the entire range of characters you want to track.

8 Choose 200% from the magnification menu at the lower left corner of the document window to view more of the page on-screen.

9 Triple-click "The Dos Ventanas Cycling Partnership" to select the entire heading.

10 Click the Character palette tab (or choose Type > Character). Then select -5 for Tracking ($\overset{A\,V}{\leftrightarrow}$) and press Enter or Return.

chain of bike shops, and an important market transition into manu-facturing of a new high-end series of bicycles, including the award-winning Sonata Allegretto.

The Dos Ventanas Cycling Partner-ship

Sonata Cycles and Dos Ventanas, the first and last name in reliable outdoor merchandise for 78 years, have announced a partnership to design and produce a line of Dos Ventanas Edition bicycles, acces-sories, and sportswear that will appeal to active-lifestyle consumers. The bicycles, related accessories, and the clothing will be sold only

chain of bike shops, and an important market transition into manu-facturing of a new high-end series of bicycles, including the award-winning Sonata Allegretto.

The Dos Ventanas Cycling Partnership

Sonata Cycles and Dos Ventanas, the first and last name in reliable outdoor merchandise for 78 years, have announced a partnership to design and produce a line of Dos Ventanas Edition bicycles, acces-sories, and sportswear that will appeal to active-lifestyle consumers. The bicycles, related accessories, and the clothing will be sold only through authorized retailers and will be available in time for the

Before and after tracking.

Now you'll use a keyboard shortcut to deselect the text.

11 Press Shift+Ctrl+A (Windows) or Shift+Command+A (Mac OS).

12 Press Ctrl+1 (Windows) or Command+1 (Mac OS) to return to a 100% view.

13 Save the file.

Applying the paragraph and single-line composers

The density of a paragraph (sometimes called its color) is determined by the composition method used. When composing text, InDesign considers the word spacing, letter spacing, glyph scaling, and hyphenation options you've selected, and then evaluates and chooses the best line breaks. InDesign provides two options for composing text: the paragraph composer, which looks at all the lines in the paragraph, or the single-line composer, which looks separately at each individual line.

When you use the paragraph composer, InDesign composes a line by considering the impact on the other lines in the paragraph; in the end, the best overall arrangement of the paragraph is established. As you change type in a given line, previous and subsequent lines in the same paragraph may break differently, making the overall paragraph appear more evenly spaced. When you use the single-line composer, which is the standard for other layout and word-processing programs, only the lines following the edited text are recomposed.

The text in this lesson was composed using the default, the Adobe Paragraph Composer. To see the difference between the two, you'll recompose the pull quote text using the single-line composer.

1 With the Type tool (**T**) still selected, click an insertion point in the pull quote on page 2.

2 Click the Paragraph tab (or choose Type > Paragraph). Choose Adobe Single-line Composer from the Paragraph palette menu.

The single-line composer looks at each line individually and, consequently, can make some lines in a paragraph appear more dense or sparse than others.

Because the paragraph composer looks at multiple lines at once, it makes the density of the lines in a paragraph more consistent.

3 On the Paragraph palette menu, choose Adobe Paragraph Composer. Notice that the lines of text now have a consistent density and all the text fits neatly in the text frame.

Pull quote formatted using the Adobe Single-line Composer (left), and the Adobe Paragraph Composer (right).

Working with tabs

You can use tabs to position text in specific horizontal locations in a frame. Using the Tabs palette, you can organize text and create tab leaders, indents, and hanging indents. Here you'll format the information at the top of page 3 using the Tabs palette. The tab markers have already been entered in the text, so all you will be doing is setting the final location of the text.

1 If necessary, scroll to the top of page 3 until the table appears on-screen.

2 To view the tab markers in the table, choose Type > Show Hidden Characters, and make sure that Normal View Mode (▣) is selected in the toolbox. If you decide not to keep them showing as you work, choose Type > Hide Hidden Characters.

3 Using the Type tool (**T**), click in the word "Category" at the top of the table.

4 Choose Type > Tabs to open the Tabs palette. When an insertion point is in a text frame, the Tabs palette snaps to the border of the frame so that the measurements in the palette's ruler exactly match the text.

5 To center the page on your screen, double-click the page 3 icon in the Pages palette. Because the Tabs palette moves independently of the table, the two are no longer aligned.

6 Click the magnet icon (🔩) in the Tabs palette to realign the palette with the text.

Clicking the magnet icon in the Tabs palette aligns the ruler with the selected text.

Note: *If the Tabs palette did not snap to the text frame, part of the text block may be hidden from view, or there may not be enough room for the Tabs palette between the text frame and the top of the document window. Scroll as necessary, and then click the magnet icon (🔩) again.*

7 Using the Type tool, select all the text in the table's text frame, from the word "Category" to the number "$110,000."

8 In the Tabs palette, click the Center-Justified Tab button (↓) so that when you set the new tab positions, they will align from the center.

9 In the Tabs palette, position the pointer in the top third of the ruler, just above the numbers, and then click to set tab markers at the following locations: 24, 29, 34, 40, and 45. You can view the location of the pointer on the ruler in the X: text box (above the left side of the ruler). To precisely set the value, drag in the ruler while watching the X value before releasing the mouse button or type the value directly into the X value of the Tabs palette.

The value in the X: text box indicates the location of the selected tab.

Note: *If you don't get the tab locations correct the first time, you can select the tab in the ruler and type the location in the X value. You can also click on a tab in the Tabs palette and drag up to remove a tab.*

10 Press Shift+Ctrl+A (Windows) or Shift+Command+A (Mac OS) to deselect the text and view the new tab settings.

THE BIKES IN SONATA CYCLES' 2000 MODEL YEAR ARE DISTRIBUTED ACROSS THESE MAJOR CATEGORIES:

CATEGORY	UNITS	SOLD	% OF SALES	1999	2000
Mountain Bikes					
Full Suspension & Front Suspension	400	350	47	$175,000	$185,000
Road Bikes					
Full Suspension & Non-Suspended	250	225	35	$120,0000	$122,000
Recreational					
Hybrid, Tandem, & Touring	187	135	18	$81,000	$110,000

Now you'll set a tab leader for some of the tabs.

11 Select all the text in the table from "Mountain" to "$110,000."

12 In the Tabs palette, click the first tab arrow along the ruler to select it so that the leader you create will affect any selected tabs at that tab marker.

13 In the Leader text box, type ._ (period, space) and press Enter or Return. You can use any character as a tab leader. We used a space between periods to create a more open dot sequence.

14 Deselect the table text and view the leaders.

Creating a hanging indent

Now you'll use the Tabs palette to create hanging indents. The text frame for this table has an inset value of 6 points at the top and 9 points on the sides and bottom. (To see the inset values, choose Object > Text Frame Options.) An inset sets the text apart from the frame; now you'll set it apart even more by indenting the three categories in the table.

You can set an indent in the Tabs palette or the Paragraph palette. You'll keep the Paragraph palette visible so you can see how the values change there, too.

1 Make sure that the Paragraph palette is visible. If necessary, select Type > Paragraph.

2 In the table, use the Type tool (**T**) to select all the text from "Mountain" to "$110,000."

3 Make sure that the Tabs palette is still aligned directly above the table. If it has moved, click the magnet icon (⌂).

4 In the Tabs palette, drag the indent markers (▶) on the left side of the ruler to the right until the X value is 2p0. Dragging the bottom marker moves both at once. Notice how all the text shifts to the right and the indent option in the Paragraph palette changes to 2p0. Keep the text selected.

Now you'll bring just the category headings back to their original location in the table to create a hanging indent.

5 In the Tabs palette, drag the top half of the indent marker to the left until the X value is -2p0. Deselect the text and view the hanging indent.

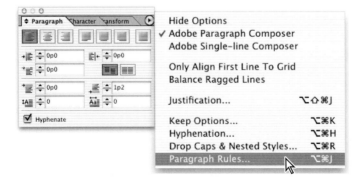

6 Close the Tabs palette and save the file.

Note: You can also create tables of information using the Table menu and Table palette. For more information, see Lesson 8, "Creating Tables."

Adding a rule below a paragraph

You can also add a rule, or line, above or below a paragraph. Here you'll add a rule under the table headings.

1 Using the Type tool (**T**), click an insertion point in the word Category in the table.

2 From the Paragraph palette menu, choose Paragraph Rules.

3 In the Paragraph Rules dialog box, choose Rule Below from the menu at the top of the dialog box, and then select Rule On to activate the rule.

4 To view the rule as you select your options, select Preview and move the dialog box so that it is not obstructing your view of the heading.

5 For Weight, choose 1 pt; for Color, choose Sonata Red; for Width, choose Column; and for Offset, type **0p9**. Then click OK.

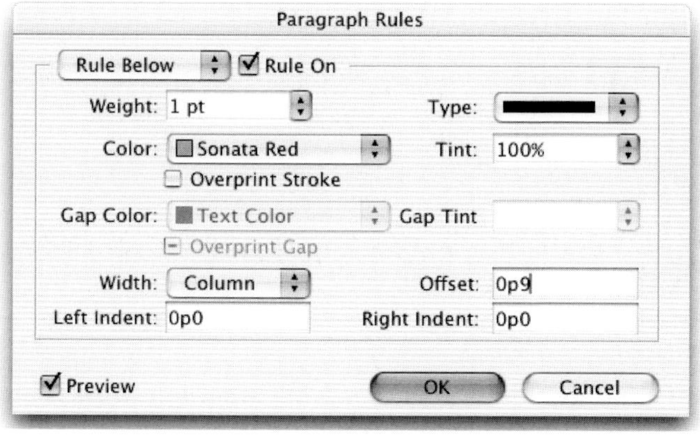
Paragraph Rules
Rule Below
Rule On
Weight: 1 pt
Type:
Color: Sonata Red
Tint: 100%
Overprint Stroke
Gap Color: Text Color
Gap Tint
Overprint Gap
Width: Column
Offset: 0p9
Left Indent: 0p0
Right Indent: 0p0
Preview
OK
Cancel

6 Save the file.

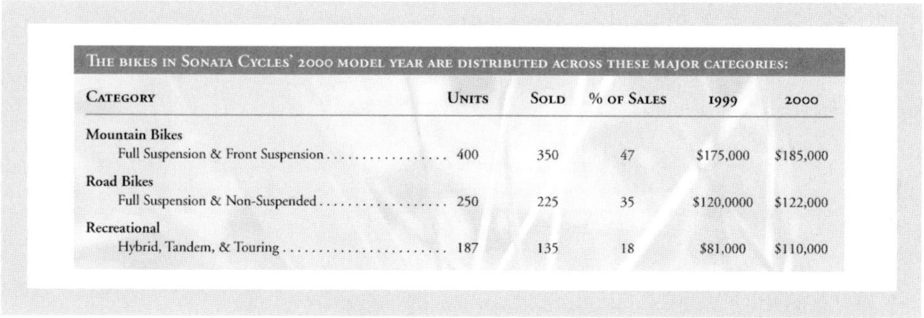

THE BIKES IN SONATA CYCLES' 2000 MODEL YEAR ARE DISTRIBUTED ACROSS THESE MAJOR CATEGORIES:

CATEGORY	UNITS	SOLD	% OF SALES	1999	2000
Mountain Bikes					
Full Suspension & Front Suspension	400	350	47	$175,000	$185,000
Road Bikes					
Full Suspension & Non-Suspended	250	225	35	$120,0000	$122,000
Recreational					
Hybrid, Tandem, & Touring	187	135	18	$81,000	$110,000

On your own

Now that you have learned the basics of formatting text in an InDesign document, you're ready to apply these skills on your own. Try the following tasks to improve your typography skills.

1 Click your cursor within various paragraphs and experiment with enabling and disabling hyphenation from the Paragraph palette. Select a hyphenated word and choose No Break from the Character palette menu to individually stop a word from hyphenating.

2 Click your cursor within the body copy and choose Edit > Edit in Story Editor. Make some edits to the text and then select Edit > Edit in Layout. Notice how the edits made in the story editor are reflected back in the layout. Explore the formatting and editing commands that are available while working in the Story Editor.

Original drop cap (left), raised cap (right).

3 Create a nested style that combines both character and paragraph styles. This lets you start the first portion of a paragraph using one style while the remaining portion is another style. Start by creating a character style that will be used on the initial portion of a paragraph, then create a new paragraph style and select Drop Caps and Nested Styles. Define the number of characters to which the style should apply.

Use the Eyedropper tool ( ) to apply an image's color to text.

4 Use the context menu to add a copyright symbol (©) to the end of the company name "Sonata Cycles" in the first paragraph on page 2.

5 Apply Optical Margin Alignment to each paragraph in the main story (everything except the pull quotes and table). You can access the Optical Margin Alignment feature from the Story command in the Type menu. Make sure to set the font size correctly.

Review questions

1   How do you view a baseline grid?

2   When and where do you use a flush space?

3   How do you apply a gradient to only a few words or characters in a paragraph?

4   What is the difference between the multi-line composer and the single-line composer?

Review answers

1   To view a baseline grid, choose View > Show Baseline Grid. The current document view must be at or above the View Threshold set in the Baseline Grid preferences. By default, that value is 75%.

2   You use a flush space on justified text. For example, if used with a special character or decorative font at the end of a paragraph, it absorbs any extra space in the last line.

3   To apply a gradient to a specific range of characters, you first select the text with the Type tool. Next, you apply the gradient to the text. If the entire range of colors does not appear, select the gradient tool and drag from one end of the selected text to the other in the direction you want the gradient to flow.

4   The multi-line composer evaluates multiple lines at once when determining the best possible line breaks. The single-line composer looks at only one line at a time when determining line breaks.

6 | Working with Color

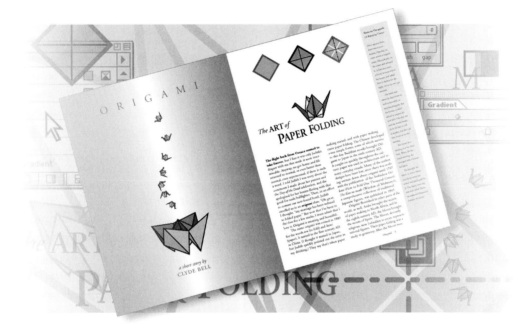

You use the Swatches palette to apply, modify, and save colors, tints, and gradients in your document. You can create and apply process and spot colors including CMYK, RGB and LAB colors. You can also apply tints, and blended gradients to frames, borders and text.

In this introduction to working with colors, you'll learn how to do the following:

- Add colors to the Swatches palette.

- Apply colors to objects.

- Create dashed strokes.

- Create and apply a gradient swatch.

- Adjust the direction of the gradient blend.

- Create a tint.

- Create a spot color.

Getting started

In this lesson, you'll work on a 2-page spread for a magazine article about origami. If you've gone through several of the previous lessons, the design of this document will look somewhat familiar. The document includes two layers (Art and Text), two master pages (B is based on A), and a separate main story and sidebar. Before you begin, you'll need to restore the default preferences for Adobe InDesign. Then you'll open the finished document for this lesson to see what you'll be creating.

1 To ensure that the tools and palettes function exactly as described in this lesson, delete or deactivate (by renaming) the InDesign Defaults file and the InDesign SavedData file. See "Restoring default preferences" on page 2.

2 Start Adobe InDesign.

3 Choose File > Open, and open the 06_a.indd file in the ID_06 folder, located inside the Lessons folder within the IDCIB folder on your hard disk

Note: *If you have not already copied the resource files for this lesson onto your hard disk from the ID_06 folder from the Adobe InDesign CS Classroom in a Book CD, do so now. See "Copying the Classroom in a Book files" on page 2.*

4 Choose File > Save As, rename the file **06_Color.indd**, and save it in the ID_06 folder.

5 If you want to see what the finished document will look like, open the 06_b.indd file in the same folder. You can leave this document open to act as a guide as you work. When you're ready to resume working on the lesson document, choose its name from the Window menu.

Note: As you work through the lesson, feel free to move palettes around or change the magnification to a level that works best for you. For more information, see "Changing the magnification of your document" on page 53 and "Using the Navigator palette" on page 60.

Defining printing requirements

It's a good idea to know printing requirements before you start working on a document. For example, meet with your prepress service provider and discuss your document's design and use of color. Because your prepress service provider understands the capabilities of their equipment, they may suggest ways for you to save time and money, increase quality, and avoid potentially costly printing or color problems. The magazine article used in this lesson was designed to be printed by a commercial printer using the CMYK color model.

Adding colors to the Swatches palette

You can add color to objects using a combination of palettes and tools. The InDesign color workflow revolves around the Swatches palette. Using the Swatches palette to name colors makes it easy to apply, edit, and update colors for objects in a document. Although you can also use the Color palette to apply colors to objects, there is no quick way to update these colors, called unnamed colors. Instead, you'd have to update the color of each object individually.

You'll now create most of the colors you'll use in this document. Since this document is intended for a commercial press, you'll be creating CMYK process colors.

1 Make sure that no objects are selected, and then click the Swatches palette tab. (If the Swatches palette is not visible, choose Window > Swatches.)

The Swatches palette stores the colors that have been preloaded into InDesign, as well as the colors, tints, and gradients you create and store for reuse.

2 Choose New Color Swatch from the Swatches palette menu.

3 Deselect Name With Color Value, and for Swatch Name, type **Purple**. Make sure that Color Type and Color Mode are set to Process and CMYK, respectively.

The Name With Color Value option names a color using the CMYK color values that you enter, and automatically updates the name if you change the value. This option is available only for process colors and is useful when you want to use the Swatches palette to monitor the exact composition of process-color swatches. For this swatch you deselected the Name With Color Value option, so that you can use a name (Purple) that's easier to read for this lesson.

4 For the color percentages, type the following values: **C = 67, M = 74,**

Y = 19, and **B = 12**, and then click OK.

5 Repeat the previous three steps to name and create the following colors:

	C	M	Y	K
Red	0	69	60	12
Green	51	19	91	12
Gold	0	31	81	4

If you forget to type the name for a color or if you type an incorrect value, double-click the swatch, change the name or value, and then click OK.

New colors added to the Swatches palette are stored only with the document in which they are created. You'll apply these colors to text, graphics, and frames in your document.

Applying colors to objects

There are three general steps to applying a swatch color: (1) selecting the text or object, (2) selecting either stroke or fill in the toolbox, depending on what you want to change, and (3) selecting the color in the Swatches palette. You can also drag swatches from the Swatches palette to objects.

1 Select the Selection tool (↖), and click the path or one of the lines in any one of the diamond shapes at the top of the right page to select it.

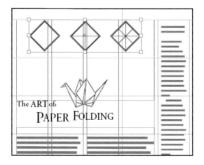

Notice that these three objects are grouped, so all are now selected. You will ungroup these objects and lock them in place. Locking objects prevents you from accidentally moving them.

2 With the group of objects still selected, choose Object > Ungroup and then choose Object > Lock Position.

3 Deselect the objects. To deselect an object, you can choose Edit > Deselect All, you can click a blank area in your document window, or you can press Shift+Ctrl+A (Windows) or Shift+Command+A (Mac OS).

4 Select the Zoom tool (🔍) in the toolbox and drag across the three diamonds to draw a marquee around the shapes. The view magnification changes so that the area defined by the marquee now fills the document window. Make sure that you can see all three diamond shapes.

💡 *To fine-tune the zoom magnification, you can press Ctrl+= (Windows) or Command+= (Mac OS). To zoom out, you can press Ctrl+- (Windows) or Command+- (Mac OS).*

5 Select the Selection tool (▸), and then click the border of the middle diamond to select it. Select the Stroke box (⬚) in the toolbox, and then click Purple in the Swatches palette.

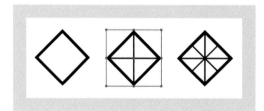

The stroke of the diamond shape is now purple. However, the color is not applied to the lines inside the shape because they are separate objects.

6 Deselect the object.

7 Click the border of the left diamond to select it. Select Red in the Swatches palette to apply a red stroke.

8 With the left diamond still selected, select the Fill box (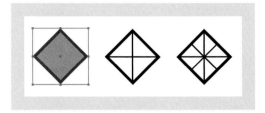) in the toolbox, and then select Gold in the Swatches palette (you may need to scroll down the list of swatches).

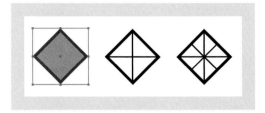

The right diamond requires the same Red stroke and Gold fill. You'll use the eyedropper to copy the stroke and fill attributes from the left diamond in one quick step.

9 Select the Eyedropper tool (), and click the left diamond. Notice that the eyedropper is now filled (), indicating that it picked up the attributes from the clicked object.

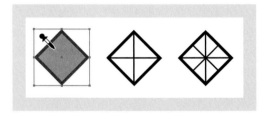

10 With the filled Eyedropper tool, click the white background of the rightmost diamond. The right diamond takes on the left diamond's fill and stroke attributes.

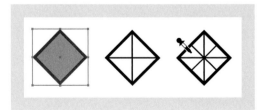

Now you'll change the color of the two diagonal lines in the right diamond.

11 Select the Selection tool (), and then deselect the objects.

12 Holding down Shift, select the two diagonal lines inside the right diamond. Release Shift. Select the Stroke box (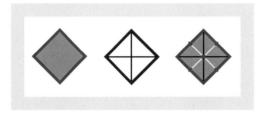) in the toolbox, and then select [Paper] in the Swatches palette.

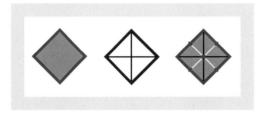

[Paper] is a special color that simulates the paper color on which you're printing. Objects behind a paper-colored object won't print where the paper-colored object overlaps them. Instead, the color of the paper on which you print shows through.

Creating dashed strokes

You'll now change the lines in the center and right diamonds to a custom dashed line. Because you will only be using the custom dashed line on one object, you will create it using the Stroke palette. If you need to save a stroke for repetitive use throughout a document, you can easily create a stroke style. For more information about saving Stroke styles, including dashes, dots and stripes, see Adobe InDesign CS online Help.

1 Deselect the objects. Holding down Shift, use the Selection tool (➤) to select the four vertical and horizontal lines in the middle and right diamonds. Release Shift.

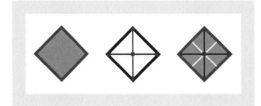

2 If the Stroke palette is not already visible, choose Window > Stroke to open it, and then choose Show Options from the Stroke palette menu to expand the palette so that you see several previously hidden options.

3 For Type, select Dashed.

Six dash and gap boxes appear at the bottom of the Stroke palette. To create a dashed line, you specify the length of the dash, and then the gap, or spacing, between the dashes.

4 Type the following values in the Dash and Gap boxes: **6, 4, 2, 4** (press Tab after you type each value to move to the next box). Leave the last two dash and gap boxes empty.

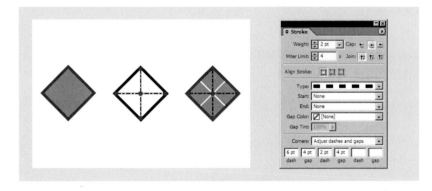

5 Deselect the lines and close the Stroke palette. Then choose File > Save.

Working with gradients

A gradient is a graduated blend between two or more colors, or between tints of the same color. You can create either a linear or a radial gradient.

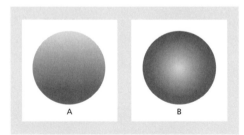

A. *Linear gradient.* **B.** *Radial gradient.*

Creating and applying a gradient swatch

Every InDesign gradient has at least two color stops. By editing the color mix of each stop and by adding additional color stops in the Gradient palette, you can create your own custom gradients.

1 Make sure no objects are selected, and choose New Gradient Swatch from the Swatches palette menu.

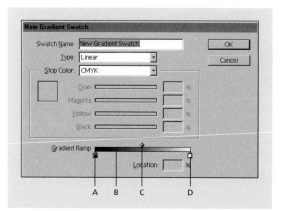

A. Left stop. B. Gradient bar. C. Ramp slider. D. Right stop.

Gradients are defined by a series of color stops in the gradient bar. A stop is the point at which a gradient changes from one color to the next and is identified by a square below the gradient bar.

2 For Swatch Name, type **Green/Gold Gradient**.

3 Click the left stop marker (⌂). For Stop Color, select Swatches, and then scroll down the list of color swatches and select Green.

Notice that the left side of the gradient ramp is green.

4 Click the right stop marker. For Stop Color, select Swatches, and then scroll down the list and select Gold.

The gradient ramp shows a color blend between green and gold.

5 Click OK.

Now you'll apply the gradient to the fill of the middle diamond.

6 Click the border of the middle diamond to select it.

7 Select the Fill box (■ꞁ) in the toolbox, and then click Green/Gold Gradient in the Swatches palette.

Adjusting the direction of the gradient blend

Once you have filled an object with a gradient, you can modify the gradient by using the gradient tool (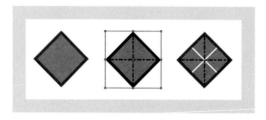) to "repaint" the fill along an imaginary line you drag. This tool lets you change the direction of a gradient and change the beginning point and endpoint of a gradient. You'll now change the direction of the gradient.

1 Make sure the middle diamond is still selected, and then select the gradient tool ( ) in the toolbox.

Now you'll experiment with the gradient tool to see how you can change the direction and intensity of the gradient.

2 To create a more gradual gradient effect, place the pointer an inch or so outside the selected diamond and drag across and past it.

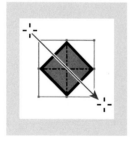

When you release the mouse button, you'll notice that the blend between green and gold is more gradual than it was before you dragged the gradient tool.

3 To create a sharper gradient, drag a small line in the center of the diamond. Continue to experiment with the gradient tool so that you understand how it works.

4 When you have finished experimenting, drag from the top corner of the diamond to the bottom corner. That's how you'll leave the gradient of the middle diamond.

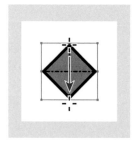

5 Choose File > Save.

Creating a tint

In addition to adding colors, you can also add tints to the Swatches palette. A tint is a screened (lighter) version of a color. You'll now create a 30% tint of the green swatch you saved earlier in this lesson.

Tints are helpful because InDesign maintains the relationship between a tint and its parent color. For example, if you changed the Green color swatch to a different color, the tint swatch you create in this procedure would become a lighter version of the new color.

1 Deselect all objects.

2 Click Green in the Swatches palette. Choose New Tint Swatch from the Swatches palette menu. For Tint percentage, type **30** and then click OK.

The new tint swatch appears at the bottom of the list of swatches. The top of the Swatches palette displays information about the selected swatch, with a Fill/Stroke box showing that the green tint is currently the selected fill color and a Tint option showing that the color is 30% of the original Green color.

3 Choose View > Fit Page in Window to center the right page of the spread in the document window. Using the Selection tool (↖), click the sidebar text frame on the right side of the page.

4 Make sure the Fill box (◼) is selected, and then click the Green tint that you just created in the Swatches palette.

Before and after adding fill tint.

About spot and process color types

A spot color is a special premixed ink that is used instead of, or in addition to, CMYK inks, and requires its own printing plate on a printing press. Use spot color when few colors are specified and color accuracy is critical. Spot color inks can accurately reproduce colors that are outside the gamut of process colors. However, the exact appearance of the printed spot color is determined by combination of the ink as mixed by the commercial printer and the paper it's printed on, so it isn't affected by color values you specify or by color management. When you specify spot color values, you're describing the simulated appearance of the color for your monitor and composite printer only (subject to the gamut limitations of those devices).

A process color is printed using a combination of four standard process inks: cyan, magenta, yellow, and black (CMYK). Use process colors when a job requires so many colors that using individual spot inks would be expensive or impractical, such as when printing color photographs. Keep the following guidelines in mind when specifying a process color:

*   *For best results in a printed document, specify process colors using CMYK values printed in process color reference charts, such as those available from a commercial printer.*

*   *The final color values of a process color are its values in CMYK, so if you specify a process color using RGB or LAB, those color values will be converted to CMYK when you print color separations. These conversions will work differently if you turn on color management; they'll be affected by the profiles you've specified.*

*   *Don't specify a process color based on how it looks on your monitor, unless you are sure you have set up a color management system properly, and you understand its limitations for previewing color.*

*   *Avoid using process colors in documents intended for online viewing only, because CMYK has a smaller color gamut than a typical monitor.*

Sometimes it's practical to print process and spot inks on the same job. For example, you might use one spot ink to print the exact color of a company logo on the same pages of an annual report where photographs are reproduced using process color. You can also use a spot color printing plate to apply a varnish over areas of a process color job. In both cases, your print job would use a total of five inks—four process inks and one spot ink or varnish. You can mix process and spot colors together to create mixed ink colors.

–From Adobe InDesign CS online Help.

Creating a spot color

This publication will be printed by a commercial printer using the standard CMYK color model, which requires four separate plates for printing—one each for cyan, magenta, yellow, and black. However, the CMYK color model has a limited range of colors, which is where spot colors come in handy. Because of this, spot colors are used to create additional colors beyond the range of CMYK or to create consistent, individual colors such as those used for company logos.

In this publication, the title design calls for a metallic ink not found in the CMYK color model. You'll now add a metallic spot color from a color library.

1 Deselect all objects.

2 In the Swatches palette menu, select New Color Swatch.

3 In the New Color Swatch dialog box, select Spot on the Color Type pop-up menu.

4 In Color Mode, select Pantone Solid Matte.

5 In the PANTONE M text box, type **876** to automatically scroll the list of Pantone swatches to the color you want for this project, which is PANTONE 876 M.

*To select an item in a palette using the keyboard, hold down Ctrl+Alt (Windows) or Command+Option and click an item in the palette. Then quickly type the color number. In this case, you would quickly type **876** to select PANTONE 876 M.*

6 Click OK. The metallic spot color is added to your Swatches palette. Notice the icon (⊚) next to the color name in the Swatches palette. This icon indicates that it is a spot color.

Note: The color you see on your monitor does not reflect the actual printed color. To determine the color you want to use, look at a chart provided by the color system, such as a PANTONE Color Formula Guide, or an ink chart obtained from your printer. Each spot color you create generates an additional spot-color plate for the press. In general, commercial printers typically produce either 2 color using black and one spot color, or 4 color CMYK work with the possibility of adding one or more spot color. Using spot colors beyond these can increase your printing costs. It is a good idea to consult with your printer before using spot colors in your document.

Applying color to text

As with frames, you can apply a stroke or fill to text itself. You'll apply colors to the text inside the frames on page 2 of the document.

1 In the Pages palette, double-click the page 2 icon to center page 2 in the document window.

2 Using the Selection tool (⬦), click the word "Origami" to select the title.

3 In the toolbox, make sure the Fill box (■) is selected and then click the small "T" icon (the formatting affects text button) in the row below the Fill box.

4 In the Swatches palette, click PANTONE 876 M, and then click a blank area to deselect. The text now appears in the spot color.

Your monitor probably shows the text in a dull brown shade, but the actual printed color of the text will be the metallic spot color. Next, you'll insert another text frame and apply colors to the text.

5 Select the Type tool (T) and triple-click "a short story by" at the bottom of the page to select that paragraph.

6 Make sure the Fill box (T) is selected in the toolbox, and then click Purple in the Swatches palette.

7 Triple-click "Clyde Bell" to select the name, and then click Red in the Swatches palette.

8 Choose Edit > Deselect All so that you can see the colored text. Then choose File > Save.

Applying colors to additional objects

Now you'll apply the same colors used by the small cranes to the large crane image at the bottom of the page. First you'll look at a magnified view of one of the small cranes to see which colors are used.

1 In the toolbox, select the magnification tool (Q), and then drag across one of the small cranes to zoom in.

2 Select the Direct Selection tool (↳), and then click any of the objects in the crane image. Notice that the corresponding swatch in the Swatches palette becomes highlighted when you select the object to which the swatch is applied.

Now you'll apply these colors to the larger image at the bottom of the page.

3 Choose View > Fit Page in Window. Select the Selection tool (▶), and click the large image at the bottom of page 2 to select the object. Choose Object > Ungroup.

Notice that the image consists of many smaller shapes grouped together. Now you'll apply orange to two of these shapes.

4 Deselect all objects, and then select the Fill box (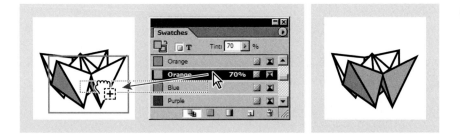) in the toolbar. Holding down Shift, click the two objects indicated below, and apply the Orange fill color (not the Orange tint).

5 Deselect all objects. Drag the Orange 70% fill swatch from the Swatches palette to the object indicated below. Be sure to drop it inside the object and not on the object's stroke.

Dragging and dropping can be a more convenient way to apply color when an object is a large, easy target because you don't have to select the object first. However, in the next step the area is small, so you'll go back to applying a color by selection.

6 Deselect all objects, select the object indicated below, and apply the Blue fill.

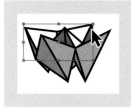

If you applied the color to the wrong object, choose Edit > Undo Swatch and try again.

Creating another tint

You'll now create a tint based on the Blue color. When you edit the Blue color, the tint that is based on the color will also change.

1 Deselect all objects.

2 Click Blue in the Swatches palette. Choose New Tint Swatch from the Swatches palette menu. Type **70** in the Tint box, and then click OK.

3 Select the object shown below and apply the Blue 70% fill.

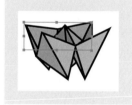

Notice how the large image shares the same colors with the small cranes. Next you'll change the Blue color. Blue 70% is based on the Blue swatch, so the tint will also change.

4 Deselect all objects.

5 Double-click Blue (not the Blue tint) to change the color. For Swatch Name, type Violet Blue. For the color percentages, type the following values: **C = 59, M = 80, Y = 40, B = 0**. Click OK.

Notice that the color change affects all objects to which Blue and Blue 70% were applied. As you can see, adding colors to the Swatches palette makes it easy to update colors in multiple objects.

6 Choose File > Save.

Using advanced gradient techniques

Earlier you created and applied a gradient and adjusted its direction using the gradient tool. InDesign also lets you create gradients of multiple colors and control the point at which the colors blend. In addition, you can apply a gradient to individual objects or to a collection of objects.

Creating a gradient swatch with multiple colors

Earlier in this lesson, you created a gradient with two colors—green and gold. Now you'll create a gradient with three stops so that a green color on the outside will fade to white in the middle. Make sure that no objects are selected before you begin.

1 On the Swatches palette menu, choose New Gradient Swatch, and then type **Green/ White Gradient** for Swatch Name.

The colors from the previous blend appear in the dialog box.

2 Click the left stop marker (▲), select Swatches for Stop Color, and make sure that Green (not the tinted Green) is selected in the list box. Click the right stop marker (▲), select Swatches for Stop Color, and make sure that Green (not the tinted Green) is selected in the list box.

The gradient ramp is now entirely green. Now you'll add a stop marker to the middle so that the color fades toward the center.

3 Click just below the center of the gradient bar to add a new stop. For Location, type **50** to make sure the stop is centered.

4 For Stop Color, select CMYK and then drag each of the four color sliders to 0 (zero) to create white.

5 Click OK, and then choose File > Save.

Applying the gradient to an object

To finish page 2, you'll create a full-page box and then apply the gradient to its fill. First, let's change the view size so that you can see all of page 2.

1 Choose 50% from the magnification pop-up list at the bottom of the document window.

Before you create the graphics frame, make sure that the Art layer is selected. It's a good idea to get into the habit of making sure that your objects are placed on the appropriate layer, so you can hide or lock a set of objects easily.

2 Choose Edit > Deselect All. Click the Layers palette tab to bring the Layers palette to the front, and then select Art. (Do not select either box to the left of Art, or you'll hide or lock the objects on the Art layer.)

3 Select the Fill box (■) in the toolbox, and then select Green/White Gradient in the Swatches palette, if it's not already selected. Select the Stroke box (◻) in the toolbox, and then click the None button (☒) at the bottom of the toolbox.

A. Apply last-used color.
B. Apply last-used gradient.
C. Remove color or gradient.

Now that the Fill box is set to the gradient and the Stroke box is set to none, the next object you draw will contain the gradient fill with no stroke.

4 Select the Rectangle tool (▢), and then draw a frame that covers all of page 2, including the margins.

5 With the frame still selected, choose Object > Arrange > Send to Back (not Send Backward).

You are now finished with page 2.

Applying a gradient to multiple objects

Previously in this lesson, you used the Gradient tool (⬛) to change the direction of a gradient and to change the gradient's beginning point and end point. You'll now use the gradient tool to apply a gradient across multiple objects in the crane on page 3.

1 Double-click the Zoom tool (🔍) to change the view to 100%. Click the Pages palette tab to display the Pages palette, and then double-click the page 3 icon.

2 Click the Layers palette tab to display the Layers palette. Click the empty box just to the left of the Text layer name to prevent you from selecting the text frame accidentally. A crossed-out pencil icon (✘) appears in the box.

3 Select the Selection tool (▶), and then click the crane image above "The Art of Paper Folding."

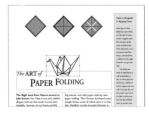

4 With the object selected, choose Object > Ungroup, and then deselect all the objects.

5 To zoom in, press **Z** to switch to the Zoom tool, and drag across the crane object above "The Art of Paper Folding." Then press **V** to switch back to the Selection tool.

6 Select the object shown below, make sure the Fill box () in the toolbox is selected, and apply the Red swatch.

7 Select the object shown below and apply the Green swatch (not the Green tint) as a fill.

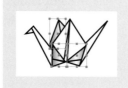

Now you'll apply the Green/White gradient to three different objects.

8 Deselect all objects. Holding down Shift, select the three objects shown below, and then apply the Green/White Gradient.

Notice that the gradient affects each object on an individual basis. Now you'll use the gradient tool to apply the gradient across the three selected objects as one.

9 With the three objects still selected, select the Gradient tool (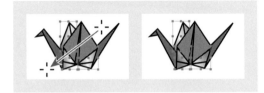) in the toolbox. Drag an imaginary line as shown.

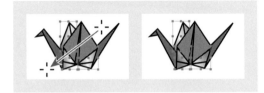

Now the gradient runs across all three selected objects.

Viewing the completed spread

You have finished the spread. Now you'll look at the spread without frame edges or the pasteboard.

1 Choose Edit > Deselect All.

2 To view your spread, choose View > Fit Spread in Window.

3 In the toolbox, select the Preview Mode button.

4 Save the file.

Congratulations. You have completed the lesson.

On your own

Follow these steps to learn more about importing colors and working with gradients.

1 To create a new document, choose File > New > Document, and then click OK in the New Document dialog box.

2 To import the colors from a different InDesign document, use the following procedure:

• Use the Swatches palette menu and choose New Color Swatch.

• In the Color Mode pop-up menu, select Other Library and browse to find the ID_06 folder.

• Double-click 06_Color.indd (or 06_b.indd). Notice that the colors you created earlier in this lesson appear in this dialog box list for the new document.

• Select the Green/Gold Gradient and click OK to close the dialog box and add the color to the Swatches palette.

• Repeat this entire process a few more times to add other colors to the Swatches palette.

3 Using the lesson files or your own InDesign document, double-click the color swatch Paper and change its composition. Notice how the color of the document changes to reflect the color of the paper on which the document will be reproduced.

4 Create a new mixed ink color swatch that combines at least one spot color with either a CMYK color or another spot color. Choose New Mixed Ink Swatch from the swatches palette to create the mixed ink swatch. You may want to add some additional spot colors to your document before experimenting with this feature.

5 Create a new gradient swatch that is radial instead of linear. Apply the new gradient to the fill of a different shape you draw. Use the Gradient tool to change the gradient.

6 When you are done experimenting with colors, close the document without saving it.

Review questions

1 What is the advantage of applying colors using the Swatches palette instead of the Color palette?

2 What are the pros and cons of using spot colors versus process colors?

3 After you create a gradient and apply it to an object, how do you adjust the direction of the gradient blend?

Review answers

1 If you use the Swatches palette to apply a color to several objects, and then decide you want to use a different color, you don't need to update each object individually. Instead, change the color in the Swatches palette and the color of all the objects will be updated automatically.

2 By using a spot color, you can ensure color accuracy. However, each spot color requires its own plate at the press, so using spot colors is more expensive. Use process colors when a job requires so many colors that using individual spot inks would be expensive or impractical, such as when printing color photographs.

3 To adjust the direction of the gradient blend, use the Gradient tool to repaint the fill along an imaginary line in the direction you want.

7 Importing and Linking Graphics

You can easily enhance your document with photographs and artwork imported from Adobe Photoshop, Adobe Illustrator, or other graphics programs. If these imported graphics change, InDesign can tell you that a newer version of a graphic is available. You can update or replace imported graphics at any time.

In this lesson, you'll learn how to do the following:

• Distinguish between vector and bitmap graphics.

• Place Adobe Photoshop and Adobe Illustrator graphics into an Adobe InDesign layout.

• Import clipping paths with graphics, and create clipping paths using InDesign and Photoshop.

• Place Adobe PDF files.

• Manage placed files using the Links palette.

• Use and create libraries for objects.

Getting started

In this lesson, you'll assemble a booklet for a compact disc by importing and managing graphics from Adobe Photoshop and Adobe Illustrator. After printing and trimming, the insert will be folded so that it fits into a CD box.

This lesson includes a procedure that you can perform using Adobe Photoshop, if you have a copy of that program installed on your computer.

Before you begin, restore the default preferences for Adobe InDesign, using the procedure in "Restoring default preferences" on page 2.

1 Start Adobe InDesign.

2 Choose File > Open, and open the 07_a.indd file in the ID_07 folder, located inside the Lessons folder within the IDCIB folder on your hard disk.

Note: If you have not already copied the resource files for this lesson onto your hard disk from the ID_07 folder from the Adobe InDesign CS Classroom in a Book CD, do so now. See "Copying the Classroom in a Book files" on page 2.

3 A message appears, saying that the publication contains missing or modified links. Click Don't Fix; you will fix this later in the lesson.

4 If necessary, move the Links palette out of the way so it doesn't obscure your view of the document. The Links palette opens automatically whenever you open an InDesign document that contains missing or modified links.

5 To see what the finished document will look like, open the 07_b.indd file in the same folder. If you prefer, you can leave the document open as you work to act as a guide. When you're ready to resume working on the lesson document, select 07_a.indd from the Window menu.

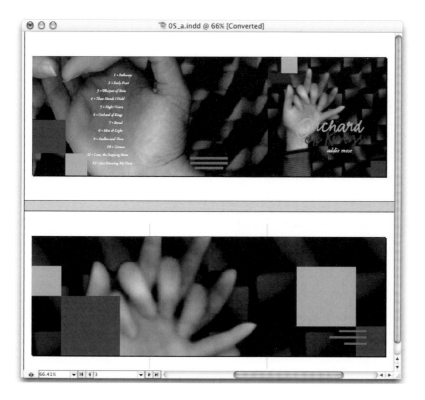

6 Choose File > Save As, rename the file **07_cdbook.indd**, and save it in the ID_07 folder.

Note: As you work through the lesson, feel free to move palettes around or change the magnification to a level that works best for you. For more information, see "Changing the magnification of your document" on page 53 and "Using the Navigator palette" on page 60.

Adding graphics from other programs

InDesign supports many common graphics file formats. While this means that you can use graphics that were created using a wide range of graphics programs, InDesign works most smoothly with other Adobe professional graphics programs, such as Photoshop and Illustrator.

By default, imported graphics are linked, which means that InDesign displays a graphics file on your layout without actually copying the entire graphics file into the InDesign document.

There are two major advantages to linking resource files. First, it saves disk space, especially if you reuse the same graphic in many InDesign documents. Second, you can edit a linked document in the program you used to create it and then simply update the link in the InDesign Links palette. Updating a linked file maintains the current location and settings for the resource so you don't have to redo that work.

All linked graphics and text files are listed in the Links palette, which provides buttons and commands for managing links. When you create final output using PostScript® or PDF, InDesign uses the links to produce the highest level of quality available from the original, externally stored versions of placed graphics.

Comparing vector and bitmap graphics

The drawing tools of Adobe InDesign and Adobe Illustrator create vector graphics, also called draw graphics, which are made up of shapes based on mathematical expressions. Vector graphics consist of smooth lines that retain their clarity when scaled. They are appropriate for illustrations, type, and graphics such as logos that are typically scaled to different sizes.

Bitmap images are based on a grid of pixels and are created by image-editing applications, such as Adobe Photoshop. In working with bitmap images, you edit individual pixels rather than objects or shapes. Because bitmap graphics can represent subtle gradations of shade and color, they are appropriate for continuous-tone images, such as photographs or artwork created in painting programs. A disadvantage of bitmap graphics is that they lose definition and appear "jagged" when enlarged. Additionally, bitmap images are typically larger in file size than a similar vector file.

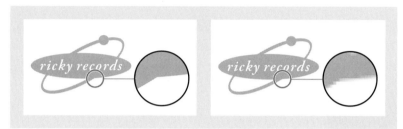

Logo drawn as vector art (left), and rasterized as bitmap art (right).

In general, use vector drawing tools to create art or type with clean lines that look good at any size, such as a logo used on a business card and also on a poster. You can create vector artwork using the InDesign drawing tools, or you might prefer to take advantage of the wider range of vector drawing tools available in Illustrator. You can use Photoshop to create bitmap images that have the soft lines of painted or photographic art and for applying special effects to line art.

Managing links to imported files

When you opened the document, you saw an alert message about problems with linked files. You'll resolve those issues using the Links palette, which provides complete information about the status of any linked text or graphics file in your document.

Identifying imported images

To identify some of the images that have already been imported into the document, you'll use three different techniques involving the links palette. Later in this lesson, you'll also use the Links palette to edit and update imported graphics.

1 If necessary, zoom or scroll the document window so that you can see both spreads in the document. Alternatively, choose View > Entire Pasteboard.

2 If the Links palette is not visible, choose Window > Links.

3 Using the Selection tool (➤), select the Orchard of Kings logotype on page 4, the far right page of the first spread. Notice that the graphic's filename, 07_i.ai, becomes selected in the Links palette when you select it on the layout.

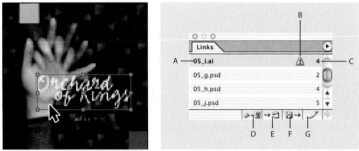

A. Linked file name. *B. File Modified icon.*
C. Page on which linked item appears. *D. Relink button.* *E. Go To Link button.*
F. Update Link button. *G. Edit Original button.*

4 Using the Selection tool, select the large hand graphic that spans the second spread (pages 5–7). The filename for this graphic, 07_j.psd, is now selected in the Links palette.

Now you'll use the Links palette to locate a graphic on the layout.

5 In the Links palette, select 07_h.psd, and then click the Go To Link button (···🗎). The graphic becomes selected and centered on the screen. This is a quick way to find a graphic when you know its file name.

If the Links palette is still in the center of the document window, you can move it now so that it doesn't block your view of the page as you work through the rest of the lesson.

These techniques for identifying and locating linked graphics are useful throughout this lesson and whenever you work with a large number of imported files.

Viewing information about linked files

You can use the Links palette to manage placed graphics or text files in many other ways, such as updating or replacing text or graphics. All the techniques you learn in this lesson about managing linked files apply equally to graphics files and text files that you place into your document.

1 If the Links palette is not visible, choose Window > Links to display it. If you cannot see the names of all the linked files without scrolling, drag the lower right corner of the palette to enlarge it so that all the links are visible.

2 Double-click the link 07_g.psd. The Link Information dialog box appears, describing the linked file.

3 Click Next to view information about the following file on the Links palette list, 07_h.psd. You can quickly examine all the links this way. Some of the other links may display an alert icon (⚠) under Content Status; this icon indicates a linking problem, which you'll address in the next topic. After you've examined the link information, click Done.

By default, files are sorted in the Links palette so that files that are listed first are those that may need to be updated or relinked. You can use commands in the Links palette menu to sort the file list in different ways.

4 In the Links palette, choose Sort by Page from the Links palette menu. The palette now lists the links in numerical order by the page on which the linked item appears.

Updating revised graphics

Even after you place text or graphic files in your InDesign document, you can still use other programs to modify those files. The Links palette indicates which files have been modified outside of InDesign and gives you the choice of updating your document with the latest versions of those files.

In the Links palette, the file 07_i.ai has an alert icon (⚠), indicating that the original has recently been modified. This is the file, as well as some others, that caused the alert message when you opened this document. You'll update its link so that the InDesign document uses the current version.

Viewing link status in the Links palette

A linked graphic can appear in the Links palette in any of the following ways:

• *An up-to-date graphic displays only the file name and its page in the document.*

• *A modified file displays a yellow triangle with an exclamation point (⚠). This icon means that the version of the file on disk is more recent than the version in your document. For example, this icon will appear if you import a Photoshop graphic into InDesign, and then another artist edits and saves the original graphic using Photoshop.*

• *A missing file displays a red hexagon with a question mark (❓). The file isn't at the location from which it was originally imported, though the file may still exist somewhere. This can happen if someone moves an original file to a different folder or server after it's been imported into an InDesign document. You can't know whether a missing graphic is up to date until its original is located. If you print or export a document when this icon is displayed, the graphic may not print or export at full resolution.*

–From "About the Links palette" in Adobe InDesign CS online Help

1 In the Links palette, select the file 07_i.ai, and click the Go To Link button (⸱⸱⸱→🗐). You don't have to do this step to update a link, but it's a quick way to double-check which imported file you are about to update.

2 Click the Update Link button (🗐⸱⸱⸱→). The appearance of the image in the document changes to represent its newer version. However, the new image is larger than the previous version, so the existing frame now crops the updated graphic. Select the other files displaying the modified icon (⚠) and click the update button. You can hold down the shift key to select multiple consecutive files to be updated in a single step or Ctrl+click (Windows) Command+click (Mac OS), to select non-consecutive items in the Links palette.

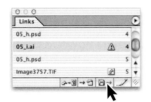

💡 *All the buttons at the bottom of the Links palette are also available as commands on the Links palette menu.*

3 Using the Selection tool (↖), click the "Orchard of Kings" image to select it, and then choose Object > Fitting > Fit Frame to Content. This command resizes only the frame, not the image.

You'll replace the large, wide image of the hands that spans the second spread (pages 5–7) with a modified image. You'll use the Relink button to reassign the link to another graphic.

4 Go to pages 5–7 (the second spread) and choose View > Fit Spread in Window.

5 Select the 07_j.psd image, which is the photograph of two hands that extends across pages 5–7. You can tell when you've selected the right image because the filename becomes selected in the Links palette.

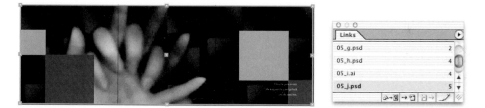

6 Click the Relink button (⟿-▣) in the Links palette.

7 Browse to find the 07_h.psd file in the ID_07 folder, and then click Open. The new version of the image (which has a greenish cast, especially noticeable in the background) replaces the original image (with its predominantly red colored background), and the Links palette is updated accordingly.

8 Click a blank area of the pasteboard to deselect all objects in the file.

9 Choose File>Save to save your work.

Placing a Photoshop file and adjusting view quality

Now that you've resolved all the file's links, you're ready to start adding more graphics. You'll place a Photoshop file in the InDesign document. InDesign imports Photoshop files directly; there is no need to save them in other file formats and no need to flatten the file before importing.

As you place the image, InDesign automatically creates a low-resolution (proxy) version of it, corresponding to the current settings in the Preferences dialog box. This and any other images in this document are currently low-resolution proxies, which is why the image appears to have jagged edges. You can control the degree of detail InDesign uses to display placed graphics. Reducing the on-screen quality of placed graphics displays pages faster, and doesn't affect the quality of final output.

1 Using the pop-up menu in the status bar of the document window, go to page 7 of your document. If necessary, zoom or scroll the document window so that you can see the entire page.

2 In the Layers palette, click the Photos layer to target it.

3 Make sure that no objects are selected. Then choose File > Place, and double-click the file 07_c.psd in the ID_07 folder.

4 Position the loaded graphics icon to the left and slightly below the top edge of the green square, and click.

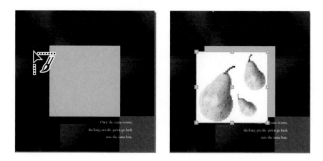

Don't be concerned about the white rectangular background behind the image. You'll remove it in the next section of this lesson. Now you'll zoom-in, using a high magnification so that you can learn about options for display quality.

5 Click the Navigator palette tab (or choose Window > Navigator to make the palette visible). Use the palette to zoom to 400%, keeping the image you placed in the center of the view.

6 Right-click (Windows) or Control-click (Mac OS) the pear image, and then choose Display Performance > High Quality Display from the context menu that appears. The pears image appears at full resolution. Notice that the resolution display of the other images in the document is not affected by this process. Use this process to confirm the clarity, appearance or position of a placed graphic in your InDesign layout.

On-screen display using Typical Display (left) and High Quality Display (right).

7 Choose File > Save.

Working with clipping paths

You can remove unwanted backgrounds from images using InDesign. You'll get some experience doing this in the following procedure. In addition to removing the background using Adobe InDesign, you can also create paths or Alpha Channels in Photoshop, which can then be used to silhouette an image in an InDesign layout.

The image you just placed has a solid rectangular background that is blocking your view of the area behind it. You can hide unwanted parts of an image using a clipping path—a drawn vector outline that acts as a mask. InDesign can create clipping paths from many kinds of images:

• If you drew a path in Photoshop and saved it with the image, InDesign can create a clipping path from it.

• If you painted an Alpha Channel in Photoshop and saved it with the image, InDesign can create a clipping path from it. An Alpha Channel carries transparent and opaque areas, and is commonly created with images used for photo or video compositing.

• If the image has a light or white background, InDesign can automatically detect its edges and create a clipping path.

The pear image you placed doesn't have a clipping path or an Alpha Channel, but it does have a solid white background that InDesign can remove.

Removing a white background using InDesign

You can use the Detect Edges option of the Clipping Path command to remove a solid white background from an image. The Detect Edges option hides areas of an image by changing the shape of the frame containing the image, adding anchor points as necessary. For more information about frames and anchor points, see the "About frames, paths, and selections" sidebar in Lesson 3.

1 Using the Selection tool (￪), select the pear image 07_c.psd by clicking the image. Switch to the Direct Selection tool (￪), and click the image when the pointer appears as a hand (￧), to activate the frame.

Note: Activating the image frame with the Direct Selection tool makes the anchor points visible, so that you can see exactly how InDesign changes the frame into a clipping path as you work. The process will still work if you select the image or its bounding box instead of its frame, but you won't get as much visual feedback.

2 Choose Object > Clipping Path. If necessary, drag the Clipping Path dialog box so that you can see the pear image.

3 In the Type pop-up menu, choose Detect Edges. Select the Preview check box so that you see that the white background is almost entirely eliminated from the image.

4 For Threshold, drag the slider and watch the image on page 7 until the Threshold setting hides as much of the white background as possible without hiding parts of the subject (darker areas). We used a Threshold value of 15.

Note: If you can't find a setting that removes all the background without affecting the subject, specify a value that leaves the entire subject visible along with small bits of the white background. You'll eliminate the remaining white background by fine-tuning the clipping path in the following steps.

The Threshold option works by hiding light areas of the image, starting with white. As you drag to the right to choose a higher value, increasingly darker tones are included within the range of tones that become hidden. Don't try to find a setting that matches the pears perfectly. You'll learn how to improve the clipping path a little bit later.

5 For Tolerance, drag the slider slightly to the left until the Tolerance value is between about 1 and 1.8.

Clipping Path	
Type: Detect Edges	OK
	Cancel
Threshold: 15	☑ Preview
Tolerance: 1	
Inset Frame: 0p0	
☐ Invert	
☐ Include Inside Edges	
☐ Restrict to Frame	
☑ Use High Resolution Image	

The Tolerance option determines how many points define the frame that's automatically generated. As you drag to the right, InDesign uses fewer points so that the clipping path fits the image more loosely (higher tolerance). Using fewer points on the path may speed up document printing, but may also be less accurate.

6 For Inset Frame, specify a value that closes up any remaining background areas, and click OK. We specified a value of 0p1 (zero picas, one point). This option shrinks the current shape of the clipping path uniformly, and is not affected by the lightness values in the image. Then click OK to close the Clipping Path dialog box.

Before and after applying an inset of 1 point.

7 (Optional) You can refine the clipping path. Make sure that the path is activated, or click one of the pear images with the Direct Selection tool ( ) to activate it. You can then drag individual anchor points and use the drawing tools to edit the clipping path around the pears. For information about drawing, see Lesson 9, "Drawing Vector Graphics."

Now you'll switch the quality setting for the pear image back to low-resolution, to speed up performance.

8 Right-click (Windows) or Control-click (Mac OS) the pear image, and then choose Display Performance > Typical Display from the context menu to set the image for low-resolution display.

9 Save the file.

You can also use the Detect Edges feature to remove a solid black background. Just select the Invert option and specify a high threshold value.

Working with Alpha Channels

When an image has a background that isn't solid white or black, the Detect Edges feature may not be able to remove the background effectively. With such images, hiding the background's lightness values may also hide parts of the subject that use the same lightness values. Instead, you can use the advanced background-removal tools in Photoshop to mark transparent areas using paths or Alpha Channels, and let InDesign make a clipping path from those areas.

Note: *If you place a Photoshop file (.psd) that consists of an image placed on a transparent background, InDesign honors the transparency with no dependence on clipping paths or Alpha Channels. This can be especially helpful when you place an image with a soft or feathered edge.*

Importing a Photoshop file and Alpha Channels

You imported the previous image using the Place command. This time, use an alternate method: You'll simply drag a Photoshop image directly onto an InDesign spread. InDesign can use Photoshop paths and Alpha Channels directly—you don't need to save the Photoshop file in a different file format.

1 In the Layers palette, make sure that the Photos layer is selected so that the image will appear on that layer.

2 Go to page 2 of your document. Then resize and arrange your Explorer window (Windows), Finder window (Mac OS), and your InDesign windows as needed so that you can simultaneously see the list of files on the desktop and the InDesign document window. Make sure that the lower left quarter of page 2 in your document is visible.

3 In Explorer (Windows) or the Finder (Mac OS), open the ID_07 folder, which contains the file 07_d.psd file.

4 Drag the file 07_d.psd to page 2 in the InDesign document. Then use the Selection tool (➤) to reposition the graphic so that it is in the lower left corner of the page.

Note: When you place the file, be careful to drop it outside the solid-color squares. If you drop it in an object drawn using InDesign, it will be placed inside the object. If this happens, choose Edit > Undo, and try again.

5 If necessary, you can now maximize the InDesign window to its previous size, because you've finished importing the file.

Examining Photoshop paths and Alpha Channels

In the Photoshop image that you just dragged into InDesign, the hand and the background share many of the same lightness values. Therefore, the background can't easily be isolated using the Detect Edges option in the Clipping Path command.

Instead, you'll set up InDesign to use a path or alpha channel from Photoshop. First you'll use the Links palette to open the image directly in Photoshop to see what paths or Alpha Channels it already includes.

The procedure in this topic requires a full version of Photoshop 4.0 or later and is easier if you have enough RAM available to leave both InDesign and Photoshop open as you work. If your configuration doesn't include these two standards, you can still read these steps to help you understand what Photoshop Alpha Channels look like and do, and resume your work in the next section of this lesson.

1 If necessary, use the Selection tool to select the 07_d.psd image in InDesign.

2 If the Links palette is not already open, choose File > Links. The image filename appears selected in the Links palette.

3 In the Links palette, click the Edit Original button (✎). This opens the image in a program that can view or edit it. This image was saved from Photoshop, so if Photoshop is installed on your computer, InDesign starts Photoshop with the selected file.

Note: Sometimes the Edit Original button opens an image in a program other than Photoshop or the program that created it. When you install software, some installer utilities change your operating system's settings for associating files with programs. The Edit Original command uses these settings for associating files with programs. To change these settings, see the documentation for your operating system.

4 If an Embedded Profile Mismatch dialog box appears as the image opens in Photoshop, do one of the following:

• If you are not using color management, select Use the Embedded Profile (Instead of the Working Space).

• If you've properly configured all Photoshop and InDesign color-management settings for your workflow using accurate ICC profiles, select Convert Document's Colors to the Working Space to reproduce the image properly in Photoshop.

5 In Photoshop, choose Window > Channels to display the Channels palette, or click the Channels palette tab.

The Channels palette contains three Alpha Channels in addition to the standard RGB channels. These channels were drawn using the masking and painting tools in Photoshop.

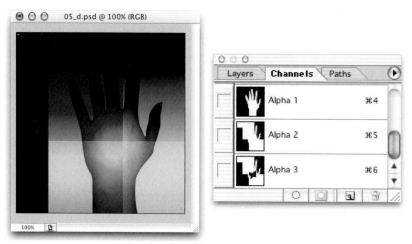

Photoshop file saved with three Alpha Channels.

6 In the Channels palette in Photoshop, click Alpha 1 to see how it looks, then click Alpha 2 and Alpha 3 to compare them.

7 In Photoshop, choose Window > Paths to open the Paths palette, or click the Paths palette tab.

The Paths palette contains two named paths, Shapes and Circle. These were drawn using the Pen tool and other Path tools in Photoshop, although they could also be drawn in Illustrator and pasted into Photoshop.

8 In the Photoshop Paths palette, click Shapes to view that path. Then click Circle.

You're finished using Photoshop, so you can now quit that program.

Using Photoshop Alpha Channels in InDesign

Now you'll return to InDesign and see how you can create different clipping paths from the Photoshop paths and Alpha Channels.

1 Switch to InDesign. Make sure that the 07_d.psd Photoshop file is still selected on the page; if necessary, select it using the Selection tool ( ).

2 (Optional) Right-click (Windows) or Control-click (Mac OS) the hand image, and choose Display Performance > High Quality from the context menu that appears. This step isn't necessary, but it lets you precisely preview the following steps.

3 With the hand image still selected, choose Object > Clipping Path to open the Clipping Path dialog box. If necessary, move the Clipping Path dialog box so that you can see the image as you work.

4 Make sure that Preview is selected in the Clipping Path dialog box, and then choose Alpha Channel from the Type menu. The Alpha menu becomes available, listing the three Alpha Channels you saw in Photoshop by the names used in that program.

5 In the Alpha menu, choose Alpha 1. InDesign creates a clipping path from the alpha channel. Then choose Alpha 2 from the same menu, and compare the results.

The first clipping path you see represents the default settings for defining the edges of an alpha channel. You can fine-tune the clipping path that InDesign creates from an alpha channel by adjusting the Threshold and Tolerance options, as you did for the Detect Edges feature earlier in this lesson. For Alpha Channels, start with a low Threshold value such as 1.

6 Choose Alpha 3 from the Alpha menu, and then select the Include Inside Edges option. Notice the changes in the image.

Selecting the Include Inside Edges option makes InDesign recognize a butterfly-shaped hole painted into alpha channel 3, and adds it to the clipping path.

You can see how the butterfly-shaped hole looks in Photoshop by viewing alpha channel 3 in the original Photoshop file, as you did in the previous procedure, "Examining Photoshop paths and Alpha Channels.

7 Choose Photoshop Path from the Type menu, and then choose Shapes from the Path menu. InDesign reshapes the image's frame to match the Photoshop path.

8 Choose Circle from the Path menu. Since this is the effect wanted for this design, click OK.

Since you're done working with this graphic, you can reset its display resolution to the document default.

9 Right-click (Windows) or Control-click (Mac OS) the hand image to open the context menu, and choose Display Performance > Typical Display. Then save the file.

Importing an Illustrator file

InDesign takes full advantage of the smooth lines provided by EPS vector graphics such as those from Adobe Illustrator. When you use InDesign's high-quality screen display, EPS vector graphics and type appear with smooth edges at any size or magnification. Most EPS vector graphics don't require a clipping path because most programs save them with transparent backgrounds. In this section, you'll drag an Illustrator graphic from a folder to the InDesign document.

1 Make sure that the ID_07 folder and the InDesign document window are both visible simultaneously. In InDesign, zoom or scroll if necessary so that pages 5 and 6 are both visible. You may find it useful to view the entire spread by selecting View > Fit Spread in Window.

2 In the Layers palette, target the Graphics layer.

3 Drag the Illustrator file 07_e.ai to the InDesign document. Position it as shown below.

4 If you want, resize the InDesign window once you've finished importing the file.

Now you'll see how the InDesign high-resolution display affects vector graphics.

5 Display the Navigator palette. With the Illustrator graphic selected, type **1000** in the magnification box and press Enter or Return.

6 If necessary, drag the view box in the Navigator palette so that you can see more detail in the Illustrator graphic.

7 Right-click (Windows) or Control-click (Mac OS) the ivy graphic to open the context menu, and choose Display Performance > Typical Display. Notice the jagged quality of the images. Then use the context menu again and choose Display Performance > High Quality Display.

On-screen image resolution with Typical and High Quality.

Display settings for display performance

With the High Quality Display setting, you can see the Illustrator graphic at the greatest possible level of detail and with sharp, crisp edges. Because the display is this accurate, you may be able to use sight alone to precisely position and align Illustrator and EPS graphics, particularly when you work at an increased magnification. However, you may also notice a slight decline in computer performance when using high–quality display. You'll switch back to a low-resolution quality in order to speed–up image display for the rest of the lesson.

8 Right-click (Windows) or Control-click (Mac OS) the ivy graphic, and then choose Display Performance > Typical Display from the context menu that appears.

9 Save the file.

Placing an Adobe PDF file

You can include Adobe Portable Document Format (PDF) files in your InDesign layout. PDF is a popular format for exchanging documents and graphics such as advertisements, because it preserves professional-quality color, vector graphics, bitmap images, and text across a wide range of programs and computing platforms. You can use PDF to publish the same document on paper and on the Internet while maintaining quality appropriate for both media. In this section, you'll import a PDF file that contains a company logo created and saved directly from Adobe Illustrator.

1 Go to page 3 in the document, and make sure that all of the page is visible. In the Layers palette, make sure that the Graphics layer is targeted.

Now you'll use a keyboard shortcut to open the Place dialog box.

2 Press Ctrl+D (Windows) or Command+D (Mac OS). In the Place dialog box, deselect Replace Selected Item and then select Show Import Options. In the ID_07 folder, locate and double-click the file 07_f.pdf.

The import options for PDF files let you customize how a PDF file is placed into your document. For example, when you place a multiple-page PDF file, you can choose which page to place. This file contains only one page, however. You can also set the cropping of the file, which you will do in the next step.

3 Under Option, in the Crop To menu, select Bounding Box. This sets the size of the placed PDF file to the smallest rectangle that encloses all of the objects in the file. For example, in this case the logo is much smaller than the page size, so it makes sense for the frame of the imported file to be the size of the logo, not of the page.

4 Leave the other settings as they are, click OK. Then click the loaded graphics icon above the address on page 3 of your document.

5 Save the file.

Using a library to manage objects

Object libraries let you store and organize graphics, text, and pages that you frequently use. You can also add ruler guides, grids, drawn shapes, and grouped images to a library. Each library appears as a separate palette that you can group with other palettes any way you like. You can create as many libraries as you need—for example, different libraries for each of your projects or clients. In this section, you'll import a graphic currently stored in a library, and then you'll create your own library.

1 Type **5** into the page navigation box at the bottom of the InDesign document window to go to that page, and then press Enter or Return.

2 Choose File > Open, select the file 07_k.indl in the ID_07 folder, and then click Open. Drag the lower right corner of the palette to reveal more of the items it contains.

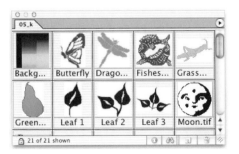

3 In the 07_k.indl library palette, click the Show Library Subset button (🔍). In the last box for the Parameters option, type **Tree**, and click OK.

4 Make sure that the Links palette is visible. In the Layers palette, make sure that the Graphics layer is targeted.

5 Out of the two objects visible in the 07_k.indl library palette, drag Tree.tif to page 5. The file is added to the page, and notice how the file name appears in the Links palette.

Note: Because you copied the Tree.tif from its original location to your hard drive, InDesign may alert you to the fact that the file is in a new location by displaying a modified link icon in the links palette. You can remove warning by choosing the Update Link command from the Links palette menu.

6 Using the Selection tool (▸), position the Tree.tif image as shown below.

7 With the Tree.tif image selected, choose Object > Arrange > Send Backward.

Creating a library

Now you'll create your own library.

1 Choose File > New > Library. Type CD Projects as the library filename, navigate to the ID_07 folder, and click Save. The library appears in its own floating palette, labeled with the filename you specified.

2 Go to page 3 and, using the Selection tool, drag the "ricky records" logo to the library you just created. The logo is now saved in the library for use in other InDesign documents.

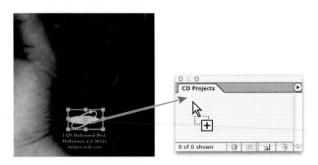

3 In the CD Projects library, double-click the "ricky records" logo. For Item Name, type Logo, and then click OK.

4 Using the Selection tool, drag the address text block to the library you created. It appears in the CD Projects library palette.

5 In the CD Projects library, double-click the address text block. For Item Name, type **Address**, and then click OK. Now your library contains both text and graphics. As soon as you make changes to the library, InDesign saves the changes.

Note: Graphics stored using an InDesign library still require the original, high resolution file for printing. The entire graphic file is not copied into the library, and it maintains a link to the original source file.

6 Close the Library.

7 Save the file.

Congratulations! You've created a CD booklet by importing, updating, and managing graphics from many different graphics file formats.

On your own

Now that you've had some practice working with imported graphics, here are some exercises to try on your own.

1 Place different file formats with Show Import Options turned on in the Place dialog box, and see what options appear for each format. For a full description of all the options available for each format, see Chapter 8, "Importing, Exporting, and Managing Graphics" in Adobe InDesign CS online Help.

2 Place a multiple-page PDF file with Show Import Options turned on, and import different pages from it.

3 Create libraries of text and graphics for your work.

Review questions

1 How can you determine the filename of an imported graphic in your document?

2 What are the three options in the Clipping Path command, and what must an imported graphic contain for each option to work?

3 What is the difference between updating a file's link and replacing the file?

4 When an updated version of a graphic becomes available, how do you make sure that it's up to date in your InDesign document?

Review answers

1 Select the graphic and then choose File > Links to see if the graphic's filename is highlighted in the Links palette. The graphic will appear in the Links palette if it takes up more than 48KB on disk and was placed or dragged in from the desktop.

2 The Clipping Path command in InDesign can create a clipping path from an imported graphic by using:

• The Detect Edges option, when a graphic contains a solid white or solid black background.

• The Photoshop Path option, when a Photoshop file contains one or more paths.

• The Alpha Channel option, when a graphic contains one or more Alpha Channels.

3 Updating a file's link simply uses the Links palette to update the on-screen representation of a graphic so that it represents the most recent version of the original. Replacing a selected graphic uses the Place command to insert another graphic in place of the selected graphic. If you want to change any of a placed graphic's import options, you must replace the graphic.

4 Check the Links palette and make sure that no alert icon is displayed for the file. If an alert icon appears, you can simply select the link and click the Update Link button as long as the file has not been moved. If the file has been moved you can locate it again using the Relink button.

8 | Creating Tables

Tables are an efficient and effective way to communicate large amounts of information. With InDesign you can easily create visually rich tables. You can either create your own tables or import tables from other applications.

In this lesson you'll learn how to do the following:

• Import formatted tables from other applications, such as Microsoft Word and Microsoft Excel.

• Format tables with alternating row colors.

• Format cell and border strokes.

• Apply colors to individual rows.

• Delete and resize columns.

• Set precise column dimensions.

• Place single or multiple graphics within a cell.

• Format text in tables by columns and by rows.

Getting started

In this lesson you'll work on a fictional magazine spread that takes tables of information and brings them into the world of effective visual design. You'll develop tables using the Table palette that gives you complete control over table features.

To ensure that the tools and palettes function exactly as described in this lesson, delete or deactivate (by renaming) the InDesign Defaults file and the InDesign SavedData file. See "Restoring default preferences" on page 2.

1 Start Adobe InDesign.

2 Choose File > Open, and open the 08_a.indd file in the ID_08 folder inside the Lessons folder located in the IDCIB folder on your hard disk.

Note: If you have not already copied the resource files for this lesson onto your hard disk from the ID_08 folder from the Adobe InDesign CS Classroom in a Book CD, do so now. See "Copying the Classroom in a Book files" on page 2.

3 Choose File > Save As, name the file **08_Gardens**, and save it in the ID_08 folder in the IDCIB folder on your hard disk.

4 To see what the finished document will look like, open the 08_b.indd file in the same folder. You can leave this document open to act as a guide as you work. When you're ready to resume working on the lesson document, choose Window > 08_Gardens.indd.

In the Pages palette of your 08_Gardens.indd document, notice that page 1 and page 2 are on different spreads. You want those pages to face each other in a single spread, numbering them pages 2 and 3.

5 In the Pages palette click to select page one. Choose Layout > Numbering & Section Options, and then select the Start Page Numbering At option and type **2**. Click OK to close the dialog box.

6 If necessary, choose Window > Pages. On the Pages palette menu, choose Keep Spread Together. If you were to add or remove pages, doing this would keep this pair of pages together.

7 Open the Layers palette, and make the following adjustments:

• (Optional) Click the eye icon (👁) for the Background layer to hide that layer. This will make it easier to see guides and frame edges.

• Select the Tables layer to target it.

• Click to lock the Text and Trees layers (🔏) so that you don't accidentally change them while you work on the first table.

Importing and formatting a table

If you've worked with tables before, you already know that tables are grids of individual cells set in rows (horizontal) and columns (vertical). The border of the table is a stroke that lies on the outside perimeter of the entire table. Cell strokes are lines within the table that set the individual cells apart from each other. Many tables include special rows or columns that describe the category of information they contain. Typically, these are in the top row or the first column.

InDesign CS can import tables from other applications, including Microsoft Word and Microsoft Excel. In this section, you'll import a table that was created in Word. This table contains all the information about the garden tour that you want in your InDesign layout, organized into rows and columns.

1 In the Pages palette, double-click page 3 to center it in the document window.

2 On the View menu, make sure that the Snap to Guides command is selected, as indicated by a checkmark. If the Show Guides command is available in the View menu, select it now.

3 Choose File > Place, and then navigate to the ID_08 folder and double-click the 08_c.doc file.

4 Move the pointer, which now appears as a loaded text icon (), to the intersection of the left margin of page 3 and the guide at the 1.5-inch mark of the vertical ruler. Click once to place the Microsoft Word table into your InDesign document.

Because it is a table, text wraps within the cells. You can edit text and make selections according to rows, columns, or the entire table.

The frame for the table fills the page from margin to margin, although the table itself does not cover that much space. Leave the frame in its current size because your table will grow larger as you set cell dimensions, add graphics, and format text.

Formatting borders and alternating row colors

InDesign CS includes many easy-to-use formatting options for tables. You can use these to make your tables both attractive and easy for readers to understand, so that they find the information they need quickly and comfortably.

1 Using the Zoom tool (Q), click the upper left area of page 3 to increase the magnification to 100% or more. Then select the Type tool (**T**).

2 Move the pointer to the upper left corner of the imported table, so that the pointer appears as a heavy diagonal arrow, and click once to select the entire table.

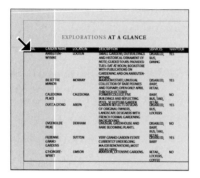

Increase the magnification if you experience difficulty getting the diagonal arrow to appear. An alternate way to select an entire table is to click the Type tool anywhere in the table and then choose Table > Select > Table. If the Type tool is not selected, this command is not available.

3 Choose Table > Table Options > Table Setup. (Or, choose the same command on the Table palette menu.) The Table Options dialog box opens at the Table Setup tab.

4 Under Table Border, set the following options: the Weight as 1, the Type as Solid, and the Color as [Black].

5 Then click the Fills tab and set the following options:

• For Alternating Pattern, select Every Other Row.

• Under First, select Color as **C = 75, M = 5, Y = 100, K = 0**, and then type **25%** for Tint.

• Under Next, select Color as [Paper].

• In Skip First, type **1** so that the alternating colors start on row 2 (the row below the headings).

6 Click OK to close the dialog box, and then choose Edit > Deselect All so that you can see the results.

The even-numbered rows now have a pale green fill color behind the black text.

Adding cell strokes

Another way you can help your readers to interpret table information is to add strokes around each cell.

1 Select the Type tool (T) and move the pointer to the upper left corner of the table until it turns into a diagonal arrow, then click to select the entire table.

2 Choose Table > Cell Options > Strokes and Fills (or choose the same command from the Table palette menu).

3 In the Cell Stroke area of the dialog box, select the following options:

• For Weight, select 0.5 pt.

• For Type, select Solid.

• For Color, select [Black], and then click OK.

4 Choose Edit > Deselect All to see the results of your formatting.

Formatting the heading cells

Another element that makes reading a table easier is to set the categories apart from the table data. By making the categories visually distinctive, your readers are more likely to comprehend the table information more easily. In this procedure, you'll create insets, so that the text doesn't run into the strokes on each cell, and then you'll give the heading row a unique color fill.

1 Using the Type tool (**T**), move the pointer over the left edge of the first row until it appears as a heavy horizontal arrow (→). Then click to select the entire first row.

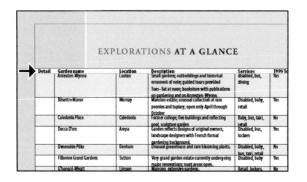

2 Choose Table > Cell Options > Text.

3 On the Text tab, set the following options:

• Under Cell Insets, type **0.086"** (or 0.086 in) for Bottom. If the Top, Left, and Right values are not already 0.0556", type that number in each of those options.

• Under Vertical Justification, for Align, select Bottom.

• For First Baseline, make sure that the Offset is set as Ascent. Leave the dialog box open.

4 On the Strokes and Fills tab, leave the Cell Stroke value as it is (0.5 pt, Solid, [Black], 100%). For the Color option under Cell Fill, select **C = 15, M = 100, Y = 100, K = 0.** Leave the Tint at 100%, and leave the dialog box open.

5 On the Rows and Columns tab, for Row Height, select Exactly on the pop-up menu, and then type **0.5"**.

6 Click OK to close the dialog box, and then deselect to see the results of your work.

The heading row of the table now appears formatted with white type against a deep red background.

Deleting a column

After you create or import a table, you can add or delete entire rows or columns to or from your table structure. Sometimes, you'll want to delete just the contents of a cell, row, or column. Other times, you'll want to delete the cell, row, or column itself, including its contents. The techniques for these two procedures differ slightly so that you make the exact edits that you intend.

The information in the column on the far right of this table is out of date and no longer relevant, so you'll delete the entire column now.

1 Using the Type tool (**T**), move the pointer to the top edge of column 6 (the last column, on the right) until the pointer turns into a heavy downward-pointing arrow (↓). Then click to select the entire column.

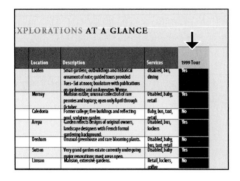

2 Choose Table > Delete > Column. Now the entire column disappears.

Note: *To delete only the content of a column, you can select the column and use the delete key on your keyboard.*

💡 *You'll find additional commands on the Table menu and Table palette menu for inserting additional columns and rows, for deleting rows and entire tables, and for selecting rows, columns, cells, and entire tables.*

Using graphics within tables

You can use InDesign tables to create effective tables that combine text, photographs, and illustrations. The techniques involved are as easy as working with text.

In this section, you'll adjust your table formatting so that the cells are the correct sizes for the graphics you'll place in them. Then you'll put graphics into those cells.

Setting fixed column and row dimensions

You can define the sizes of cells, columns, or rows to fit precise measurements. In this topic, you will adjust the size of the first column so that the one-inch photographic images fit nicely within the cells.

1 Using the Type tool (T), select the first column, either by dragging from top to bottom or by clicking the top edge of the column when the heavy downward-pointing arrow (↓) appears. Or, you can click in any cell of the column and select Table > Select > Column.

2 Choose Window > Type & Table > Table to show the Table palette, if it is not already visible. In the Column Width option (⊞), type **1.15 in** (or **1.15"**), and press Enter. Then click anywhere in the table to deselect the column.

3 Using the Type tool (T), drag down from the second cell in the first column. Select all the cells except the heading cell at the top of the column.

4 In the Table palette, select Exactly in the Row Height option and type **1.15 in**. Press Enter.

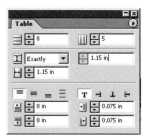

Placing graphics in table cells

To save you some time, most of the images you'll place within the table are already placed on the pasteboard of this document. In this procedure, you'll just cut and paste these images one by one into the cells of the first table column. To begin, you'll import one image that is not yet part of the InDesign file.

1 Using the Type tool, click to place the insertion point in the first cell in the second row (just below the "Detail" cell).

2 Choose File > Place, and locate the 08_d.tif file in your ID_08 folder. Double-click to open the file. The photographic image appears in the first cell.

3 Adjust the document-window magnification and scroll horizontally as needed so that you can see both the first column and the vertical row of photographs on the pasteboard, just to the right of page 3.

4 Using the Selection tool (↖), select the top photograph on the pasteboard to the right of the spread. Then choose Edit > Cut.

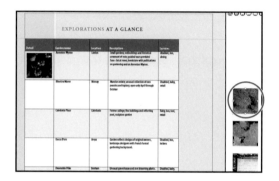

5 Switch to the Type tool (**T**) and click to place a cursor in the third row of the first column, just below the photograph you placed in the previous step.

6 Choose Edit > Paste.

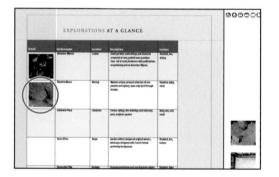

7 Continue cutting and pasting to place each of the remaining five photographs into the empty cells in column 1, proceeding from top to bottom.

You can temporarily switch between the Selection tool and the Type tool by holding the Ctrl key (Windows) or Command key (Mac OS).

Note: *You cannot simply drag items into table cells. Dragging would merely position the item above or below the table in the layout stacking order, not place the item within a cell. Tables require you to use the Type tool as you place or paste content into cells.*

Placing multiple graphics in a cell

Essentially, the images you place or paste into table cells are inline graphics in text. Because of this, you can add as many images to a single cell as you need. You are limited only by the actual size of a cell.

1   Using the Selection tool (![arrow]( )), select the wheelchair graphic on the pasteboard.

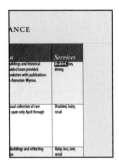

2   Choose Edit > Copy.

3   Switch to the Type tool, and look in column 5 for the first instance of the word Disabled. Click and drag to select the entire word and the comma. It is probably easiest to also select the space between that word and the next one.

4 Choose Edit > Paste. If you selected the space after the comma, press the spacebar to add a space after the graphic.

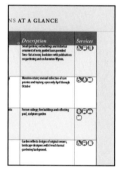

5 Find the remaining instances of the word Disabled in the remaining cells of that column, select them, and paste to replace the text with the wheelchair graphic.

6 Repeat this entire process for each of the remaining words and icons: Baby, Bus, Taxi, Lockers, Retail, Coffee, and Dining.

Note: If you are unsure which icon is which, select the icon with the Selection tool and then look at the Links palette to see which file is selected. The icon files have descriptive names.

Because you haven't yet adjusted the column widths, your icons may overlap each other vertically at this phase of your work. You'll fix that in the next section.

Formatting text within a table

All that remains in your table project is to make some final adjustments so that the spacing of the text, graphics and table are in harmony with the rest of the spread.

Applying character styles to text in a table

If you are already comfortable formatting text in text frames, then formatting text in tables will be an easy and natural extension of your InDesign skills.

1 Using the Type tool (T), click anywhere in the words Garden name in the first row of your table. Then choose Table > Select > Row.

2 Choose Type > Character Styles to make the Character Styles palette visible, and then select the Table Head character style in that palette to apply that style to the first-row text.

If some of the text no longer fits into the cells, it will be fixed in the next step. Overset text inside of cells is represented by a red dot inside the cell.

3 In the second column, double-click the name Anreuten-Wynne to select it and then drag down to select all the garden names in that column, being careful not to include the text in the header at the very top of the column.

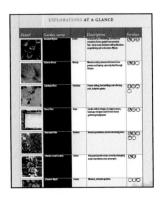

4 In the Character Styles palette, select Table Names to apply that style to the selected text.

5 Select all the cells in columns 3 and 4 except those in the first row, using the same technique as in step 3. Then use the Character Styles palette to apply the style Table Details to this text.

6 Select all the cells except for the headings of each column, using the same technique from steps 3 and 5.

7 In Table palette, under Top Cell Inset (▤), type **0.08"** and press Enter.

Dragging to adjust column size

When an ordinary text frame contains a story that doesn't completely fit into the assigned space, the out port for the frame displays a red plus sign (+), indicating that there is overset text. You would solve that either by enlarging the text frame or continuing the story in another text frame.

In tables, text or graphics that don't fit into their cells are also called overset, indicated by a small colored circle in the lower right corner of the cell. Unlike ordinary frames, you can't just carry over the excess data into another cell of the table. Instead, you must either resize the cell to hold the information or resize the content (by scaling the graphic or deleting some of the text).

For this table, you'll resize the columns so that everything fits nicely into the table.

1 Choose View > Fit Page in Window.

2 Move the Type tool over the vertical line separating columns 2 and 3 until the pointer icon becomes a double arrow (↔), and then drag the column margin to resize it until the words Garden and name fit on the same line.

3 Moving from left to right, resize each of the columns so that the contents fit inside. Also set the right edge of the table to snap against the vertical margin guide on the right side of the page. Make sure that the last column on the right is wide enough so that all the services icons fit on a single line, as shown in the illustration.

4 Choose View > Fit Spread in Window, and then save your work.

Working with tables within existing text frames

The imported table you've been working on is the only text in its frame. Next, you'll make a minor adjustment that affects the other table in the two-page spread. That table, on page 2, is part of a frame that includes other text.

1 In the Layers palette, click the empty box between the eye icon (👁) and the Table layer name to lock that layer. Then unlock the Text layer by clicking in the column immediately to the left of the layer name in the Layers palette then click the layer name to select the layer.

2 In the Pages palette, double-click the page 2 icon to center the page in the document window.

3 Using the Type tool (T), click to place an insertion point immediately in front of the words "As always" (about two-thirds of the way down the long paragraph). Notice the position of the table near the bottom of the page.

4 Press Enter to separate the text into two paragraphs. Choose Edit > Deselect All. Notice how the table moves down the page, adjusting to the new spacing.

Note: *Because tables are placed inside of text boxes, their position can be changed by the formatting of the text surrounding them*

Finishing up

You're almost finished with your work on this lesson.

1 Choose View > Fit Spread in Window.

2 In the Layers palette, make sure that all layers are visible, with the eye icon (☻) displayed for each one.

3 In the toolbox, click the Preview Mode button.

4 Press Tab to hide all the palettes and review the results of your work.

Congratulations! You have now completed this lesson.

For more information about working with tables, see online Help, and the Adobe Web site.

On your own

Now that you're skilled in the basics of working with tables using InDesign, you can experiment with other techniques to expand your table-building abilities.

1   To create a new table, scroll beyond the spread to the pasteboard, and drag the Type tool (T) to create a new text frame. Then choose Table > Insert Table and enter the number of rows and columns you want in your table.

2   To enter information in your table, make sure that the blinking insertion point is in the first frame and then type. To move forward to the next cell in the row, press Tab. To move to the next cell down in the column, press the down arrow key.

3   To add a column by dragging, move the Type tool over the right edge of one of the columns in your table, so that the pointer becomes a double-headed arrow. Hold down Alt (Windows) or Option (Mac OS) and drag a short distance to the right, perhaps half an inch or so. When you release the mouse button, a new column appears, having the same width as the distance you dragged.

4   To combine several cells into one cell, select all the cells in the new column you created in the previous "On your own" exercise (number 3). Then choose Table > Merge Cells. To convert the table to text, choose Table > Convert Table to Text. You can have tabs separate what were previously columns and have paragraph breaks separate the columns. You can also modify these options. Similarly, you can convert tabbed text into a table by selecting the text and choosing Table > Convert Text to Table.

5   To create rotated text, click the Type tool inside the merged cell you created "On your own" exercise number 4. Choose Window > Table to bring the Table palette forward, and select the Rotate Text 270° option (⊢). Then type the text you want in this cell.

Review questions

1 What are the advantages of using tables rather than just typing text and using tabs to separate the columns?

2 When might you get an overset cell?

3 What tool is used most frequently when you work with tables?

Review answers

1 Tables give you much more flexibility and are far easier to format. In a table, text can wrap within a cell, so you don't have to add extra lines to accommodate cells with many words. Also, you can assign styles to individual rows, columns, and cells, including character styles and even paragraph styles, because each cell is considered a separate paragraph.

2 Overset cells occur when the dimensions of the cell are limited and the contents don't fit inside it. For this to occur, you must actively define the width and height of the cell (or its row and column). Otherwise, when you place text in the cell, the text will wrap within the cell, which then expands vertically to accommodate the text. When you place a graphic in a cell that does not have defined size limits, the cell also expands vertically but not horizontally, so that the row column keeps its original width.

3 The Type tool must be selected to do any work with the table. You can use other tools to work with the graphics within table cells, but to work with the table itself, such as selecting rows or columns, inserting text or graphic content, adjusting table dimensions, and so forth, you use the Type tool.

9 Drawing Vector Graphics

You can use the Pen tool to draw straight lines and smooth, flowing curves with great precision. The Pen tool will be familiar to you if you've used the Pen tools in Adobe Illustrator and Photoshop. Shapes you draw with the Pen tool can enhance your page designs in combination with text and imported graphics.

In this lesson, you'll learn how to do the following:

• Draw and edit straight and curved path segments and open and closed paths with the Pen tool.

• Create a hole in a filled shape by combining paths into a compound path.

• Apply a shape (such as an arrowhead) to the end of a path.

• Slice paths into smaller pieces.

• Paste an image inside a drawn path.

• Scale, reflect, and duplicate objects.

• Add a graphic so that it becomes part of a text story and flows with it.

Getting started

In this lesson, you'll create the front and back of a direct-mail piece. You'll use the InDesign drawing tools to draw some of the vector objects, or paths, in the design. Before you begin, you'll need to restore the default preferences for Adobe InDesign.

1 To ensure that the tools and palettes function exactly as described in this lesson, delete or deactivate (by renaming) the InDesign Defaults file and the InDesign SavedData file. See "Restoring default preferences" on page 2.

2 Start Adobe InDesign.

To begin working, you'll open an existing InDesign document.

3 Choose File > Open, and open the 09_a.indd file in the ID_09 folder, located inside the Lessons folder on your hard disk.

Note: *If you have not already copied the resource files for this lesson onto your hard disk from the ID_09 folder from the Adobe InDesign CS Classroom in a Book CD, do so now. See "Copying the Classroom in a Book files" on page 2.*

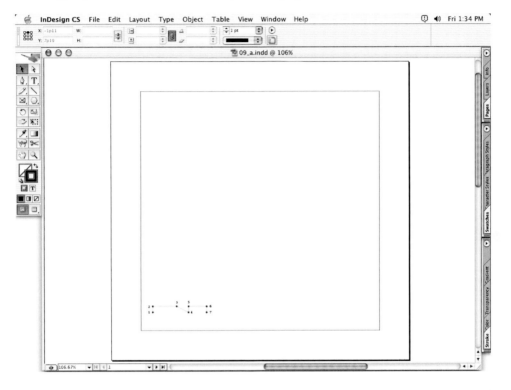

4 Choose File > Save As, rename the file **09_Mailer.indd**, and then click Save.

You'll notice that the page is blank except for a shape near the bottom left corner of the page. This document contains everything you need to create the completed version of the document, but to keep things simple, it uses layers to hide everything except the tracing template for the shape you're currently drawing. Right now, you see the tracing template for the first shape you'll draw.

As you progress through the lesson, you'll use the Layers palette to show and hide other parts of the document. When you're finished, you'll display all layers except the layers containing the tracing templates. For more information, see "Working with Layers" in Adobe InDesign CS online Help.

5 To see what the finished document will look like, open the 09_b.indd file in the same folder. You can leave this document open to act as a guide as you work. When you're ready to resume working on the lesson document, choose its name from the Window menu.

Note: You'll use the Layers and Swatches palettes frequently in this lesson. It may be helpful to enlarge those palettes so that you can easily see all of their items. You can move palettes around and change the magnification of the layout to a level that works best for you. See "Changing the magnification of your document" on page 53 and "Using the Navigator palette" on page 60 of this book.

Setting up the document grid

Many of the paths you draw in this lesson will be straight lines, precise corners, and symmetrical curves. It's easier to draw these kinds of paths if you set up the document grid in a convenient way. You'll now define and display the grid and grid options.

1 Choose Edit > Preferences > Grids (Windows, Mac OS) or InDesign CS > Preferences > Grids (Mac OS).

2 In the Document Grid area under Horizontal, type **10p0** (10 picas, 0 points) for Gridline Every and type **10** for Subdivisions. Type these values (**10p0** and **10**) again for the similar options under Vertical. Then click OK.

3 Choose View > Show Document Grid.

4 Choose View > Snap To Document Grid to select it.

Sometimes the grids are hard to see because they're covered by objects on the layout. You can move grids to the front of the display by choosing Edit > Preferences > Grids (Windows) or InDesign > Preferences > Grids (Mac OS), and deselecting the Grids in Back option.

Drawing straight segments

You can use the Pen tool to draw straight lines by clicking two anchor points, which define a segment. To create straight lines that are vertical, horizontal, or 45-degree diagonals, you can hold down Shift as you click the Pen tool. This is called constraining the line.

This lesson makes extensive use of templates to facilitate the drawing process for you as you learn to use InDesign. These templates are non-writing layers that display the final shapes. You simply trace those shapes so that your results will look exactly like the finished sample file.

Drawing an open path of straight segments

You'll begin by drawing a simple open path, tracing over a template at the bottom left corner of page 1. This template for the shirt-collar top is on the Template 1 layer. You will draw the collar on the Collar layer.

1 Click the Layers palette tab (or choose Window > Layers) to make the palette visible, and scroll down the palette to the Collar and Template 1 layers near the bottom of the list.

The eye icon (👁) indicates that the layers are visible, and the crossed-out pencil icon (✗) for the Template 1 layer indicates that the layer is locked. All the template layers are locked so that you don't draw on them by accident.

2 In the Layers palette, select the Collar layer. The pen icon (🖋) appears to the far right of the Collar layer name, indicating that anything you add to the page will be written on this layer.

3 In the toolbox, select the Zoom tool (🔍) and then click the shirt-collar template one or more times to zoom until you can easily read the numbers on the template.

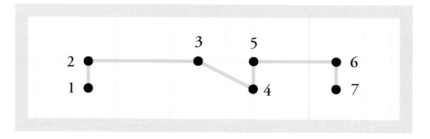

4 Press Shift+Ctrl+A (Windows) or Shift+Command+A (Mac OS) to make sure that no objects are selected.

5 Choose Window > Stroke to display the Stroke palette, and make sure that the Weight is 1 point. Then move or close the Stroke palette, as needed, so that it doesn't obstruct your view of the template.

Note: When you adjust any option while no objects are selected, you adjust the default setting for that option. For this lesson, you want the default stroke weight to be 1 point, so that the paths you draw don't obscure the lines on the template layer.

6 In the toolbox, select the Pen tool (🖋), and move the pointer over point 1 on the template, for the lower edge of the shirt collar.

The pointer has a small hollow arrowhead (🖋ₓ) next to it to remind you that you selected the Snap to Grids option. When you click, the pointer will snap to the closest guide or grid intersection and place the first anchor point at that location.

7 Click point 1.

8 Move the Pen tool over point 2 on the template and click again.

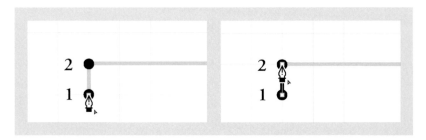

💡 *When the Snap To Document Grid command is not on, you can still position points at 45-degree angles by holding down Shift as you click.*

9 Click each of the remaining numbered points (3, 4, 5, 6, and 7) in order. Because you're clicking at positions that fall on the grid, the shape is a perfect match with the template.

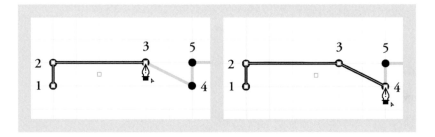

10 To end the path, do one of the following:

• Choose Edit > Deselect All.

• Click the Pen tool in the toolbox.

• Hold down Ctrl (Windows) or Command (Mac OS) to temporarily activate the most recently used Selection tool, and then click in an empty area to deselect the path. If you use this method, make sure that you're not selecting any white objects.

As you draw paths with the Pen tool, you'll see many visual cues along the way. These cues provide you with useful information. By this step, you're already able to observe the following:

• A third point appears between the first and second anchor points of any segment you draw. This is the center point of the segment, which automatically appears on any path that has at least two points. A center point makes it easier to select and align objects. As you progress through this lesson, watch how the center point automatically keeps itself at the center of a path as you change a path's shape.

• When you click the second point, a caret (^) appears next to the pointer as long as the tip of the Pen tool icon is on the new endpoint. The caret indicates an opportunity to create a curve out of that anchor point. You'll create curves later in this lesson.

• The path and anchor points you've drawn appear in lavender. This is because the Collar layer uses lavender as its layer color, indicated by the colored square immediately to the left of the Collar layer name in the Layers palette. The layer color identifies the layers that contain the currently selected objects.

Note: Don't confuse the layer color with the stroke color, which does not print. The layer color represents the stacking order of objects.

Applying color to a path

The path you just drew appears in the default stroke color, so now you'll apply the correct colors for the design. The colors for this illustration are already stored in the Swatches palette for you.

Before you apply color to the collar shape, you'll hide the Template 1 layer so that you can see the path more clearly.

1 In the Layers palette, click the eye icon (👁) for the Template 1 layer to hide that layer.

2 Using the Selection tool (▸), select the path.

3 Click the Swatches palette tab (or choose Window > Swatches) to make the palette visible.

4 In the toolbox, select the Stroke box (🔲) to bring it forward.

5 In the Swatches palette, select TRUMATCH 25-c1 (you may need to enlarge the palette or scroll through it).

6 In the toolbox, select the Fill box (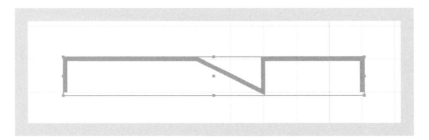) to bring it forward and make sure that [None] is selected in the Swatches palette.

7 Choose Edit > Deselect All, and then choose File > Save to save the file.

Copying and altering an existing path

You'll start the process of drawing a closed shape that will appear below the open shape you just drew. First, you'll show the Template 2 layer, which contains the shape of the bottom part of the shirt collar that you'll create next.

1 In the Layers palette, click the square to the far left of the Template 2 layer to display the eye icon (👁) and select the Collar layer to target that layer. If necessary, adjust the view in the document window so that you can see the entire collar shape.

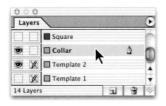

Notice that the top edge of the template you just displayed is the same as the collar top you've already drawn. You can save time by duplicating the collar top and editing the copy.

2 Using the Direct Selection tool (↳), click the top collar path (the one you've already drawn), and then click the center point to select all points in the path.

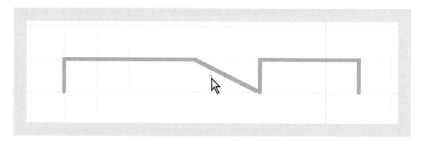

3 Hold down Shift+Alt (Windows) or Shift+Option (Mac OS) as you drag the top collar path down until it lines up with the top edge of the template for the collar bottom. When you release the mouse, you'll see that you've actually created and dragged a copy of the path, not the original.

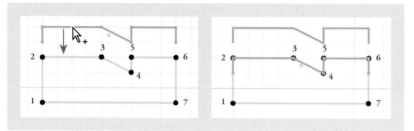

Dragging a copy of upper path (left), and the new copy in position (right).

Note: If you find yourself dragging one point instead of the entire shape, choose Edit > Undo and try again, making sure all points on the path are selected (solid) before you begin dragging.

By using the Direct Selection tool for this move, you aligned the path itself to the grid, not the stroke. If you had used the Selection tool, the object would have aligned the outer edge of its stroke width to the grid, not the path.

Changing how stroke weight affects bounding box and path dimensions

When you change the stroke weight of a path, the outer dimensions of the path's bounding box are preserved by default. This maintains the position of the stroke's outer edge while its inner edge grows or shrinks with the stroke weight. The position and dimensions of the path (which lies at the center of the stroke) are changed accordingly. If you want to constrain the path's position and dimensions, select the Weight Changes Bounding Box. This will have less effect on how much of a path's fill or contents are visible, but will cause the total area of the fill and stroke to change whenever you change a stroke weight.

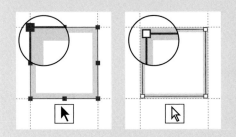
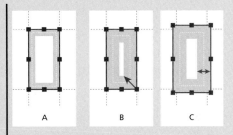

The Selection tool activates the bounding box at the outer edge of the stroke weight (left). The Direct Selection tool displays the path at the center of the stroke (right).

A. Original path. **B.** *Stroke weight increased.* **C.** *Stroke weight increased after selecting the Weight Changes Bounding Box option.*

–From Adobe InDesign CS online Help.

4 Choose Edit > Deselect All.

5 Using the Direct Selection tool, drag a selection marquee around the bottom left point to select it. With the point still selected, hold down Shift as you use the Direct Selection tool to drag a selection marquee around the bottom right point. Now both points should be selected, so they appear as tiny solid squares rather than hollow ones.

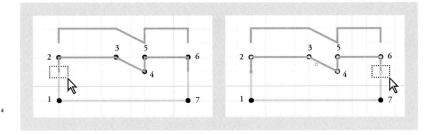

6 Position the pointer on the lower right endpoint of the collar path. Then drag it down to the point numbered 7 on the template to extend both the selected segments.

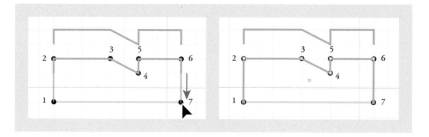

Closing and applying colors to a drawn object

In order to apply a solid fill to the collar, you must first close the collar shape. Your work continues with the Collar label targeted (selected in the Layers palette) and the Template 2 layer visible.

1 Press the **P** key to select the Pen tool, and move the pointer tip directly over the endpoint labeled 1, so that a slash ( ) appears next to the pointer. The slash indicates that clicking will continue the path from the endpoint rather than starting a new path.

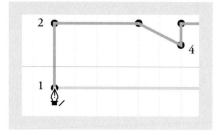

 By learning the keyboard shortcuts for drawing (such as the Pen tool shortcut you just used), you save many trips to the toolbox. That helps you work faster and more smoothly. Many users find it efficient to keep the mouse in one hand, and keep the other hand over the keyboard to press tool shortcut and modifier keys.

2 Click and release on endpoint 1. You may notice that the slash next to the pointer momentarily changes to a caret ( ).

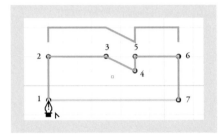

3 Move the pointer over point 7, and notice that a loop now appears next to the pointer ( ), indicating that a click will close the path. Click point 7 to close the collar shape.

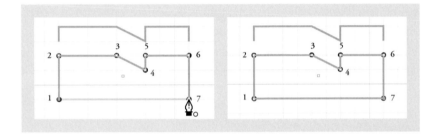

4 In the Layers palette, click the eye icon ( ) for the Template 2 layer to hide that layer. Leave the path selected.

5 In the toolbox, select the Fill box ( ), and then in the Swatches palette select TRUMATCH 25-c1 50% (the second instance of the color).

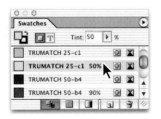

6 Press the **X** key to bring the Stroke box forward in the toolbox.

7 Click the Apply None button ( ) (below the Fill/Stroke boxes) to remove the stroke color.

8 Press Shift+Ctrl+A (Windows) or Shift+Command+A (Mac OS) to deselect all, or choose Edit > Deselect All.

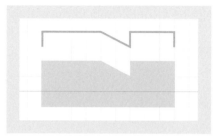

9 Choose View > Fit Page in Window, and then save the file.

Drawing with the Pencil tool

In this procedure, you'll draw a flower shape that is free-form rather than a precise representation. Since the shape is informal, you'll use the Pencil tool to sketch the shape intuitively. As you work, you'll take advantage of the new Fidelity and Smoothness controls for the pencil and Smooth tools to make it easier to create the smooth shape you want for the flower.

Preparing to draw with the Pencil tool

Before you begin drawing, you'll set up your document so that you are drawing on the appropriate layer and with the correct stroke.

1 In the Layers palette, click the eye icon (👁) for the Collar layer to hide it, and then click the eye icon boxes for Template 3 and the Flower layers to make them visible, selecting the Flower layer so that it is targeted.

2 In the magnification pop-up menu in the lower left corner of the document window, select 600% (or higher) and scroll so that you can see the flower template easily.

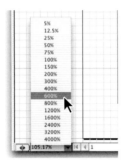

Or, you can use the Zoom tool (Q) to drag a marquee around the flower shape on the template to define the view magnification.

3 In the toolbox, double-click the Pencil tool to open the Pencil tool Preferences dialog box, and then set the following options:

• For Fidelity, drag the slider or type to set the value at **15 pixels**.

• For Smoothness, drag the slider or type to set the value at **50%**.

• Make sure that the Edit Selected Paths option is selected, with the value of Within 12 Pixels so that you can add to an existing path by clicking the Pencil tool (✏) within that distance from the endpoint. Then click OK to close the dialog box.

Drawing the flower shape with the Pencil tool

Now you're all set to draw the flower.

1 Move the Pencil tool (✎) over the grayed shape of the flower and start to trace the path. A dotted red line indicates where the line you are drawing will appear. After you draw a segment of one flower petal, release the mouse so that you can see the results.

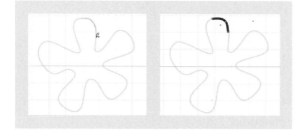

Notice that the path that appears is much smoother than the dotted red line that appeared as you drew. This is because you set a high Smoothness value for the Pencil tool.

2 Place the tip of the Pencil tool pointer near the endpoint of the line you drew so that the small X to the right of the pointer icon disappears, and then continue drawing the petal in short segments.

It is important that the path is continuous, that is, that the segments join as a single path. As long as the Pencil tool pointer appears without the small X in it as you begin drawing each successive segment, you can be confident that the path you draw will be unbroken.

It is not important that your flower shape match the template exactly for two reasons: First, it's an informal shape, and second, you can refine the path after you finish drawing it, as explained in the next procedure. However, if you are dissatisfied with a segment you draw, you can choose Edit > Undo to remove just that segment and try again.

Note: *InDesign CS has multiple levels of undo, so you can choose Edit > Undo to step back through many recent actions. The exact number of undo steps possible may be limited by the amount of RAM on your computer, but can be as high as several hundred undos.*

3 When you come back to the starting point, hold down Alt (Windows) or Option (Mac OS) so that the Pencil tool displays a small loop ( ); then the final segment you draw will close the flower shape.

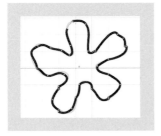

If the shape is less precise than you like, you can correct that by using the Smooth tool ( ).

Merging two pencil-drawn paths

If you accidentally create a segment that is its own path rather than a continuation of your path drawing, you don't have to undo that segment and start over. Instead, you can attach the two independent segments. Use the following procedure whenever you need to unite the two paths. If you have more than two separate segments to merge, attach them one at a time.

1 *In the toolbar, select the Selection tool (✸).*

2 *Select the first of the paths and then hold down Shift and select the second path.*

3 *In the toolbar, select the Pencil tool (✐) and move it over the endpoint of one path that you want to connect to the second path.*

4 *Start to drag toward the endpoint of the second path and hold down Ctrl (Windows) or Command (Mac OS) as you draw to the second endpoint. The Pencil tool pointer appears with a small loop indicating that what you draw will merge the two paths.*

5 *When you finish drawing, release the mouse and then release the Ctrl (Windows) or Command (Mac OS) key; then choose Edit > Deselect All.*

If necessary, repeat steps 2 through 5 to connect the end of the newly merged path with other separate segments, attaching the segments to the path one at a time.

Smoothing out the path drawing

The Smooth tool can eliminate slight wobbles and irregularities in paths that you draw with the Pencil tool. Like the Pencil tool, the Smooth tool includes controls that you can adjust for Fidelity and Smoothness.

If you are already satisfied with the shape of your flower drawing, you do not need to do this procedure.

1 Using the Direct Selection tool ( ), select the path.

2 In the toolbox, hold down the Pencil tool until the button expands, showing you other tools, and select the Smooth tool ( ).

Smooth Tool Preferences

Tolerances

Fidelity: 10 pixels

Smoothness: 50 %

OK

Cancel

Defaults

Options

☑ Keep Selected

3 Double-click the Smooth tool to open the Smooth tool Preferences dialog box, and set Fidelity at 15 and Smoothness at 50%. Then click OK.

4 Drag the Smooth tool over any areas of your flower path that you want to smooth.

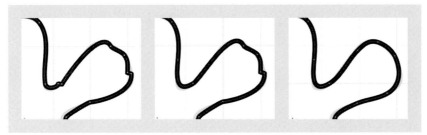

Using the Smooth tool (left), after smoothing a segment (center), finished smoothing (right).

5 Repeat step 4 as necessary until you are satisfied with the shape of the path. If you smooth too much, choose Edit > Undo to undo the smoothing actions.

Finishing the flower drawing

Now you'll finish up your flower shape.

1 In the toolbox, select the Fill box (⬛), and then in the Swatches palette select TRUMATCH 25-cl.

2 Press X to select the Stroke box (⬜) in the toolbox, and then click the Apply None button in the toolbox to remove the stroke on the flower.

3 Choose Edit > Deselect All, press Ctrl+0 (Windows) or Command+0 (Mac OS) to fit the page in the window, and save your file.

Note: *If the keyboard shortcut for Fit Page in Window doesn't work for you, make sure that you pressed the number zero key above the letter keys, not the letter O or the zero on the numeric keypad.*

You'll do the rest of the drawing in this lesson with the Pen tool rather than the Pencil tool; the Pen tool is ideal for creating precise shapes and curves.

Later on, when you are comfortable with the Pen tool, you can challenge yourself to create a precise replica of the template shape for the flower by using the Pen tool. That procedure is described in the "On your own" section at the end of this lesson.

Drawing curved segments with the Pen tool

In this part of the lesson, you'll learn how to draw smooth curved lines using the Pen tool. As with the straight-line segments you drew earlier to create the collar, drawing curves with the Pen tool involves positioning points that anchor the path. However, instead of simply clicking the Pen tool, you'll drag to extend the two direction lines that precisely influence curve direction. When you release the mouse, a curve's starting point is created with its direction lines. Then you drag the Pen tool to end the curve and to set the starting point and direction of the next curve.

1 Choose View > Snap to Document Grid to deselect it.

2 In the toolbox, select Preview Mode to hide all guides, grids, and frame edges.

Selecting a point on a curve

When you select a point that's part of a curved segment, the segment displays additional controls that you can use to adjust a curve precisely. Before you begin drawing curves, it's helpful to recognize these controls.

1 In the Layers palette, click the square to the far left of the Hair layer to display the eye icon (👁). This contains the wavy lines you'll use in this section.

2 Using the Zoom tool, zoom in on the set of wavy lines.

Pressing the **Z** key selects the Zoom tool in the toolbox.

3 Press the **A** key to switch to the Direct Selection tool (⟨k⟩), and then click any of the wavy lines. In the Layers palette, the Hair layer becomes selected, and the path and its anchor points appear in the Hair layer's color of magenta.

4 With the Direct Selection tool still selected, select the second anchor point from the left on any of the wavy lines. When selected, the anchor point becomes solid and displays two direction lines.

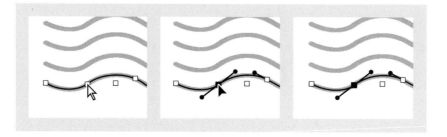

The direction lines cause the anchor point to connect the two adjacent path segments as a continuous curve shaped by the direction lines. The angular collar path you drew in the previous section only has corners because its anchor points don't have any direction lines.

As their names imply, the anchor points anchor the curved segments, and the direction lines control the direction of the curves. You can drag the direction lines or their endpoints, called direction points, to adjust the shape of the curve.

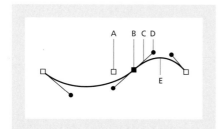

*A. Center point. **B.** Anchor point. **C.** Direction line.*
***D.** Direction point. **E.** Path segment.*

Anchor points, direction points, and direction lines are aids to help you draw. Anchor points are square and, when selected, appear solid. When unselected, anchor points appear hollow. Direction points are always round and solid. Direction lines and points do not appear in print or in any other output; they exist only to help you draw precisely.

5 When you finish examining the anchor points, click a blank area of the page to deselect.

Drawing combinations of curved and straight segments

When you drew curves for the previous shape, two direction lines pivoted together around each anchor point. Those anchor points are called smooth points because they connect segments as a continuous curve. You can use the Pen tool with a modifier key to drag each of the two direction lines at different angles, converting a smooth point into a corner point with two direction lines that move independently. The only difference between the corner points you first created in this lesson and the corner points you'll create in this section is that these corner points will have direction lines.

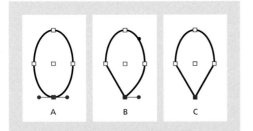

*A. Smooth point. **B.** Corner point with direction line.*
C. Corner point without direction lines.

Preparing to draw the head shape

The final head shape includes a mix of curves and straight segments joined by corner points. Before you begin using the Pen tool, you need to see and activate all the needed items.

1 In the Layers palette, click the eye icons (👁) to the far left of both the Flower layer and the Template 3 layer to hide them. Then click the square to the far left of the Template 4 layer to make it visible.

2 In the document window, scroll or zoom if necessary so that you can easily see all of the numbers and direction lines on the tracing template for the head.

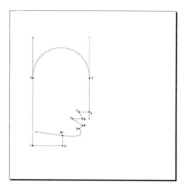

3 In the Layers palette, click the square to the far left of the Head/eye layer to make it visible. In the document window, a partially complete path appears, beginning at point 1 and ending at point 6.

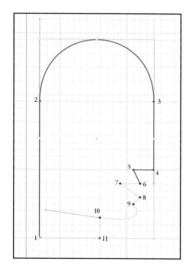

4 In the Layers palette, select the Head / eye layer to target it.

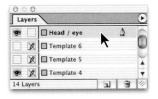

Now you'll use keyboard shortcuts to make the grid visible and make objects snap to it.

5 Make sure that Normal view mode is selected in the toolbox, or select it now.

Note: If you still do not see the document grid lines, press Ctrl+' (Windows) or Command+' (Mac OS) to show them.

6 Press Shift+Ctrl+' (Windows) or Shift+Command+' (Mac OS) to make objects snap to the document grid. You can look on the View menu to confirm that the Snap to Document Grid command has a checkmark, indicating that it is selected.

Drawing the head shape

Now that everything is ready for the head shape, you can start drawing. In this procedure, you'll combine straight lines and curved ones, but you'll also leave some straight segments that you'll refine with curves later in this lesson.

1 Press **P** to select the Pen tool (✒). Position the pointer on point 6 on the template so that the pointer appears with a slash; then click point 6. The slash indicates that the anchor points you add will connect to the existing path rather than to a separate path.

2 Click points 7, 8, and 9, in that order.

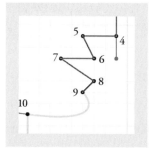

💡 *To reposition an anchor point while drawing, hold down the spacebar as you drag.*

You'll draw the chin by drawing a curved segment in between two straight segments.

3 Position the pointer on point 10. Drag left from point 10 to the red and let go of the mouse.

4 Click point 11. Notice that the new path segment is curved, not a straight line as shown in the template, so you'll need to correct that in the next steps.

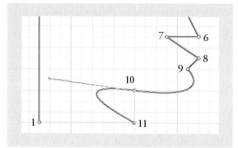

5 Choose Edit > Undo. The line disappears.

6 Position the pointer over point 10 (the pointer appears with a small caret next to it) and click point 10.

The left direction line for point 10 is removed, so that the red line of the template is visible where the green directional line used to be. This makes it possible to make the next segment perfectly straight. Notice that the green directional line on the right of point 10 remains in place and that the chin curve still matches the curve of the template.

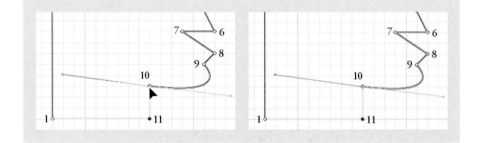

7 Click point 11, and then position the pointer over point 1. Click the point when you see the pointer icon appear with a small circle, indicating that clicking point 1 will close the path, completing the head drawing.

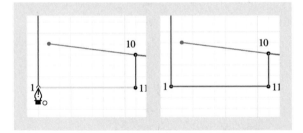

8 In the Layers palette, click the eye icon (👁) for the Template 4 layer to hide it, and then choose File > Save.

You'll adjust the fill and stroke of this path later, after you've edited the mouth and drawn the eye.

Changing the shape of existing segments

Now you'll create a more expressive mouth by changing some of the straight segments to curves. It's easy to change the shape of existing segments at any time.

1 Click the square to the far left of the Template 5 layer to display the eye icon (👁). The Template 5 layer contains a template for the finished mouth.

2 In the document window, zoom in so that you can see the nose, mouth, and chin.

3 With the path for the head still selected in the document window, press A to select the Direct Selection tool (⟍). You must use the Direct Selection tool because the Selection tool displays the path's bounding box, not its anchor points.

4 Press **P** to select the Pen tool (✒), and position it on point 6 (but don't click). You'll know it's positioned on the point when you see a minus sign next to the pointer (✒).

5 With the Pen tool still positioned, hold down Alt (Windows) or Option (Mac OS). Notice that the pointer changes to the icon for the Convert Direction Point tool (⌁) — this switches to the actual tool, not the pen with a caret. Continue holding down Alt or Option as you drag down from point 6 to the red dot. Direction lines appear, converting the corner point to a smooth point.

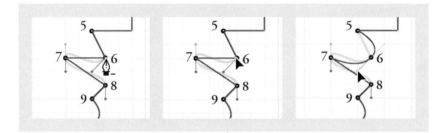

Don't be concerned that the segments between points 5, 6, and 7 don't match the template. You'll fine-tune the segments in the following steps. First you'll retract the upper direction line to restore the straight segment between points 5 and 6.

💡 *If you Alt/Option-click a smooth point, you convert it to a corner point, removing its direction lines.*

6 Position the Pen tool on the upper direction point for point 6. Then hold down Alt (Windows) or Option (Mac OS) as you drag the upper direction point down into point 6.

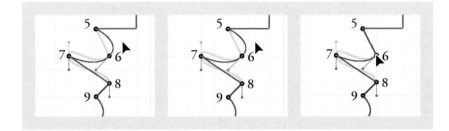

7 Position the Pen tool on point 7, and then hold down Alt/Option as you drag from point 7 down to the red dot. You've converted point 7 from a corner point to a smooth point. Extending the direction lines also shapes the left half of the segment between points 6 and 7 so that it now matches the template.

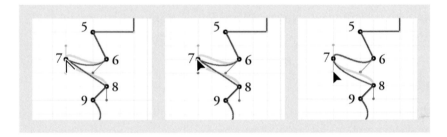

8 Position the Pen tool on point 8, and then hold down Alt/Option as you drag from point 8 down to the red dot so that the segment between points 8 and 9 becomes curved.

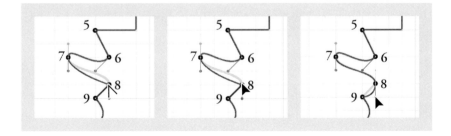

9 Position the Pen tool on point 8's lower direction point. Then hold down Alt or Option as you drag the lower direction point up into point 8.

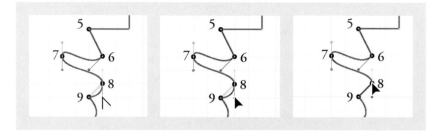

10 Press Ctrl+0 (Windows) or Command+0 (Mac OS) to fit the page in the window.

11 In the Layers palette, click the eye icon for the Template 5 layer to hide it.

12 Deselect everything, and then save the file.

Different artists use various drawing styles. Some prefer to lay down all corners and curves correctly the first time, and others prefer to rough out a shape by clicking corner points, and then returning later to create and refine the curves as you did in this section. With practice, you'll discover which way you prefer to draw.

Drawing the eye

To draw the eye for the head, you'll practice more techniques for interactively controlling corner angles and curve shapes as you draw. First, you'll use keyboard shortcuts to quickly turn off and hide the document grid, which you don't need for this section.

Ordinarily, the directional lines that control the curves around an anchor point mirror each other, so that they have equal lengths and are 180 degrees from each other. In this procedure, you'll use keyboard shortcuts to drag one directional line independently of its partner for the anchor point.

1 Press Ctrl+' (Windows) or Command+' (Mac OS) to hide the document grid.

2 Press Shift+Ctrl+' (Windows) or Shift+Command+' (Mac OS) to turn off the Snap to Document Grid option.

3 Click the square to the far left of the Template 6 layer to display the eye icon (👁).

This layer contains the template for the eye. In the document window, zoom in on the eye template.

4 Make sure that the Head / eye layer is targeted in the Layers palette.

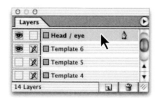

5 Using the Pen tool (✎), position the pointer on point 1 on the template, and then click.

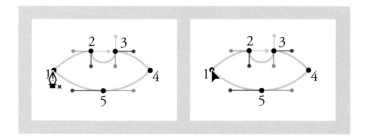

6 Position the pointer on point 2, and click first and then hold down Shift as you drag right to the gray dot.

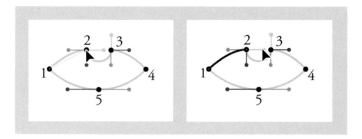

7 Position the pointer over the right direction point (on the gray dot) for point 2. Hold down Alt (Windows) or Option (Mac OS) and drag the direction point down to the red dot. Notice that the left direction line for point 2 does not change.

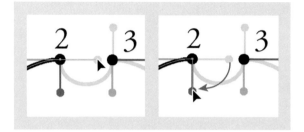

8 Click and then hold down Shift as you drag from point 3 up to the gray dot.

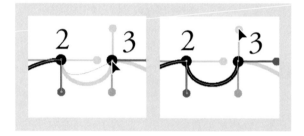

9 Hold down Alt/Option as you drag point 3's upper direction line down and right to the red dot. This will shape the left half of the next segment.

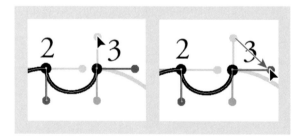

10 Click the Pen tool at point 4.

11 Click and then hold down Shift as you drag from point 5 to the red dot.

Holding down Shift constrains the directional lines so that they are exactly horizontal.

Note: *If you have trouble with this step, choose Edit > Undo and make sure that you start dragging before you press Shift.*

12 Click point 1 to close the path, and then press Shift+Ctrl+A (Windows) or Shift+Command+A (Mac OS) to make sure that the path is deselected.

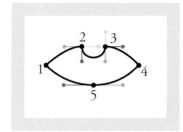

13 In the Layers palette, click the eye icon for the Template 6 layer to hide it, and then save the file.

Notice that as you clicked new segments, the Pen tool preserved any existing smooth and corner points, and that pressing Alt/Option changed the default behavior of the Pen tool.

Creating a compound path

Now you'll combine the eye with the head as a compound path. When you make a compound path, overlapping areas become holes. In this illustration, the eye will become a hole in the head through which you will be able to see the background behind the head.

A compound path isn't the same as a group, where different objects in the group retain their own attributes. All parts of a compound path have to be paths, and they will all share the same set of attributes such as color and stroke weight.

1 In the document window, scroll or zoom if necessary so that you can easily see the entire head.

In order to make it easier to see the effect of creating a compound path, you'll temporarily fill the image.

2 Using the Selection tool (➤), click the head path to select it.

3 In the toolbox, make sure that the Fill box (▪) is selected. In the Swatches palette, select any color except White or None.

4 With the head still selected, hold down Shift as you click the eye to select both paths.

5 Choose Object > Compound Paths > Make.

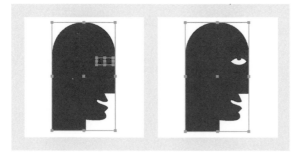

The head and the eye are now two subpaths of the same compound path. The compound path uses the eye shape as a hole.

6 Make sure that the Fill box is selected in the toolbox, and click the Apply None button to remove the temporary colored fill. Then deselect everything and save the file.

Note: When you use the Selection tool to select a compound path, it selects the entire compound path. To select a subpath, select the Direct Selection tool and Alt-click (Windows) or Option-click (Mac OS) as a subpath.

Creating a perfect semicircle

The finished document contains a semicircle outside another circle, both located inside the head shape. Although you could draw the semicircle using the Pen tool, it's easier to slice an arc out of a circle.

Duplicating as you scale

The semicircle you'll create must be larger than, and concentric with, an existing circle. In a single action, you can scale the existing circle from the center and make a copy of the result.

1 In the Layers palette, click the eye icon for the Head / eye layer to hide it.

2 Click the square to the far left of the Circles layer to display the eye icon (👁). This layer contains the circle shape you'll duplicate.

3 Make sure that the Circles layer is targeted in the Layers palette. In the document window, zoom in on the circles, leaving some room for the larger circle you'll create.

4 Using the Selection tool (↖), select the blue (outer) circle.

5 Click the Transform palette tab (or choose Window > Transform) to make the palette visible.

6 In the Transform palette, make sure that the center proxy point (⊞) is selected.

This proxy point determines that the next action you take in the Transform palette will be measured from the center of the selection rather than from one of the edges or corners. Make certain that Constrain proportion for scaling (🖉) is selected in the lower left hand corner of the control palette.

7 In the Scale X Percentage option (🖾) in the Transform palette, enter **120** and then press Alt+Enter (Windows) or Option+Return (Mac OS). A larger duplicate of the circle appears.

If you wanted to scale only the horizontal (X) dimension of the circle, you'd press only Enter or Return after typing in the value. In this case, you pressed Ctrl (Windows) or Command (Mac OS) to also make the other (Y) dimension scale proportionally, and you pressed Alt or Option to duplicate the original circle using the new scale value.

Slicing a path with the Scissors tool

Now you can simply slice off the part of the circle that you don't need.

1 Choose the Direct Selection tool ( ), and make sure that the larger circle is selected so that you can see its anchor points and path.

Note: If the larger circle still displays a bounding box after you switch to the Direct Selection tool, deselect it and then use the Direct Selection tool to select it again.

2 In the toolbox, click to select the Scissors tool ( ).

3 Using the Scissors tool, click the new circle at the anchor point on its left side. Then click the anchor point on its right side. The original path has become two separate paths and only the lower semicircle remains selected.

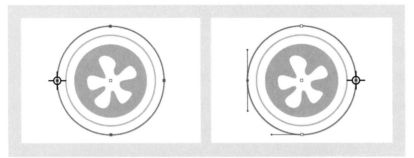

Clicking left anchor point, and right anchor point. (These icons are enlarged to show additional data.)

Note: *You don't have to click the Scissors tool on a point, but because you're creating a perfect semicircle here, the circle's anchor points are convenient places to slice.*

4 Switch to the Selection tool (⬈), and make sure that the bottom of the larger circle is selected.

5 Press the Delete key to remove the lower arc path.

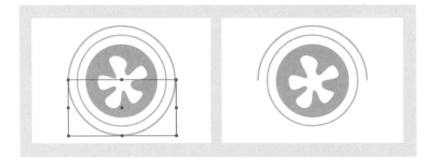

Adding an end shape to an open path

You can instantly add an end shape, such as an arrowhead, to either end of a path by using the Stroke palette. Here, you'll add a loop to the end of the semicircle you just created.

1 With the Selection tool (▶), select the semicircle.

2 Click the Stroke palette tab (or choose Window > Stroke) to make the palette visible. By default, the Stroke palette appears only partially expanded, so that only the Weight option appears.

3 Click the double arrows to the left of the word Stroke. The palette collapses further, so that only the tabs are visible. Click the double arrows again so that all the stroke options are visible.

4 In the Stroke palette, choose Circle on the Start pop-up menu. This adds a circle shape to the start of the path—the first point drawn when the path was created.

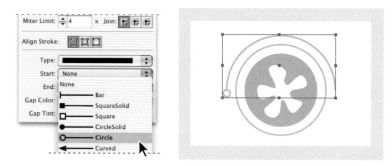

5 Deselect everything, zoom out to see the entire page, and then save the file.

💡 *To reverse the start and end of a path, use the Direct Selection tool to select a point on the path and then choose Object > Reverse Path.*

Creating a texture effect using a colorized image

In the final version of this file, you can see that the head is filled with a texture, which is actually an image placed directly inside the compound path that you'll colorize to create a duotone. You'll add the image to the compound path now.

1 In the Layers palette, click the square to the far left of the Head / eye layer to display the eye icon (👁), and make sure that the Head / eye layer is targeted.

2 Using the Selection tool (▶), select the head. Using the Selection tool selects the entire compound path that you created from the head path and eye path earlier in this lesson.

Now you'll use a keyboard shortcut for placing a file.

3 Press Ctrl+D (Windows) or Command+D (Mac OS). Double-click the file 09_c.psd in the ID_09 folder.

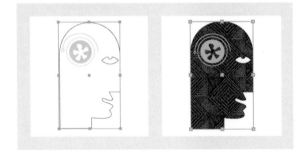

The image appears inside the head automatically, because the head was selected when you placed the image. Notice that you can still see through the eye.

Now you'll use InDesign to colorize the image, which you can do because the image was saved as a 1-bit or grayscale image.

4 In the toolbar, select the Stroke box and press the / (slash) key to apply None as the stroke color. Then press Ctrl+Shift+A (Windows) or Command+Shift+A (Mac OS) to deselect all.

5 Using the Direct Selection tool (▶), click the image inside the head. The bounding box for the texture image you placed inside the head shape is selected.

6 Select the Fill box in the toolbox, and then in the Swatches palette select TRUMATCH 50-b4. The black areas of the texture image are replaced by a dark brown color.

7 Deselecting the image, switch to the Selection tool (➤), and select the head again.

8 In the Swatches palette, select TRUMATCH 50-b4 90%. The white areas of the image are replaced by a lighter brown color, so that the textured image is more subtle and has no white or black areas.

9 Deselect everything, and save the file.

Creating and adding an inline graphic

You can add a graphic between any text characters or spaces so that the graphic flows with the text as you add or remove text. Such a graphic is called an inline graphic. You can use an ornamental font, such as a dingbat, or you can insert a graphic that you create yourself.

Using advanced settings for the Polygon tool

The Polygon tool contains controls that alter the shapes you create. You can adjust the number of points in the polygon and set the insets between points to make starlike shapes.

1 In the Layers palette, click the square to the far left of the Text layer to display the eye icon (👁), and make sure that the Text layer is targeted.

2 Choose View > Show Document Grid and then choose View > Snap to Document Grid.

3 In the document window, zoom in to the lower right area of page 1 to about 200% or higher, so that you can clearly see the smallest unit of the document grid.

4 In the toolbox, hold down the Rectangle tool (□) to see more tool options and select the Polygon tool (⬡). Then double-click the Polygon tool to open the Polygon Settings dialog box.

5 In Number of Sides, select 8, and in Star Inset, select 40%. Then click OK.

Polygon Settings

Number of Sides: 8   OK

Star Inset: 40   Cancel

6 Drag the pointer crosshairs diagonally across any one of the document grid squares to create a tiny star shape.

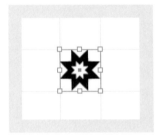

Note: It is not necessary to hold down the Shift key as you drag to constrain the shape because the Snap to Document Grid is turned on. You should still get a perfectly symmetrical star shape.

7 Choose View > Hide Document Grid and View > Snap to Document Grid to deselect that command.

Now that you've created the star, you'll simply paste it into the text to create an inline graphic.

Placing an inline graphic

1 With the polygon star still selected, choose Edit > Cut to remove the star and place it on your computer clipboard.

2 Select the Type tool (**T**), and then click an insertion point after the period at the end of the sentence at the bottom of the text that reads "…we have a class for you."

3 Choose Edit > Paste to put the graphic directly into the text where you clicked the insertion point. Turn on the document grid to verify the position by selecting View > Show Document Grid.

Depending on where the insertion point was flashing when you placed the inline graphic, the graphic might be right up against a character in the text and a bit too high. You can shift the baseline alignment for the star and add space around it, because the inline graphic behaves as if it were simply another text character.

4 With the Type tool still selected, click an insertion point just before the star and press the spacebar to add a little more space as needed before or after the star shape.

5 Using the Type tool (T), drag across the star to select it. In the Character palette, change the Baseline Shift value (A↕) until the graphic sits nicely between the lines above and below it. The sample file uses a value of –3 pt.

Note: You can also change the position of the graphic by selecting it with the Selection tool and pressing the down arrow key.

6 Switch to the Selection tool (▸) and select the star.

7 In the toolbox, select the Stroke box (⬚) and then in the Swatches palette select TRUMATCH 15-c4 to color the star outline.

8 Deselect everything, zoom out to see the entire page, and then save the file.

Reflecting objects

The back of the completed invitation (page 2) will use duplicates of objects from the front. The duplicates will be reflected so that you see them as if from behind. You will quickly duplicate the objects on page 1 and then use the Transform palette to flip them.

1 In the Layers palette, make the Hair, Circles, Head / eye, Squares, Flower, and Collar layers visible in the document, and hide all other layers including any currently visible Template layers. Make sure that all visible layers are also unlocked; that is, they do not display the crossed-out pencil icons (✗).

You can't select objects on hidden layers, so don't be concerned about the lock status of hidden layers.

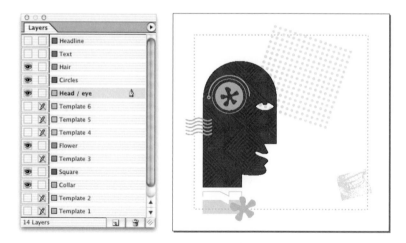

2 In the document window, zoom out so that you can see both pages of the document.

3 Choose Edit > Select All.

4 Hold down Alt (Windows) or Option (Mac OS) as you drag all of the selected objects down to page 2, positioning them on the page within the margins, just like the originals on page 1.

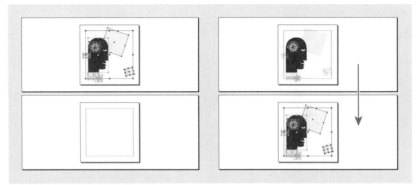

All objects selected on first spread (left), and duplicate objects dragged to the second spread (right).

Note: *If you make a mistake, choose Edit > Undo. Before you choose Select All again, be sure to activate the page 1 spread (click the first spread in the document window, not in the Pages palette). Otherwise, the Select All command will try to select objects on page 2, the last page you worked on.*

5 Make sure that all of the objects on page 2 are still selected. In the Transform palette, click the center point on the proxy (▦), and then choose Flip Horizontal from the Transform palette menu.

6 Deselect everything and save the file.

7 In the Layers palette, make the Headline and Text layers visible. You can now see the entire document you've created.

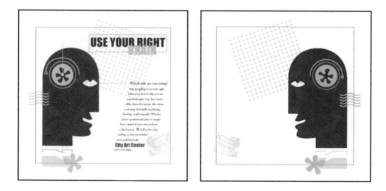

Congratulations! You've completed a design using a wide variety of drawn shapes, imported graphics, and layout effects.

On your own

In this lesson, you used the Pencil tool to draw a flower shape. You can also use the Pen tool to draw that shape. You can try recreating the flower with the Pen tool as an experiment, so that you can compare the two methods.

1 Make sure that the Snap to Document Grid command is not selected on the View menu.

2 In the Layers palette, click the eye icons (👁) for all layers. Then click the square to the far left of the Template 3 layer and the Practice layer to display the eye icons, so that they are the only visible layers. Then select the Practice layer so that it is targeted.

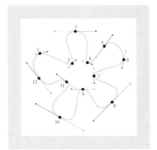

3 In the document window, scroll or zoom, if necessary, so that you can easily see all the numbers and colored direction-line guidelines on the flower template.

4 Select the Pen tool (✒). Then click and drag from point 1 to each point through point 12 to set anchor points, each time aligning the direction lines with the red lines and dots on the template layer.

5 After you draw through point 12, remember to look for the small loop next to the pointer before you click point 1 again. This ensures that your final click will close the shape. When you drag from this final anchor point, drag over the blue line and dot on the template for point 1, not the red ones.

6 Create two separate lines and join them by drawing a line between the lines using the Pencil tool and holding down the Ctrl key (Windows) or Command key (Mac OS) while drawing the line between the two paths. When drawing, try to overlap the existing lines slightly.

7 Experiment with placing different ends on lines you have created using the options available in the Stroke palette. Try the various arrows and shapes. Also try the various line styles and examine the options to create your own custom line styles, available from the Stroke palette menu.

8 Create two boxes that are slightly overlapping on the corners and experiment with the various Pathfinder options that combine separate objects in a variety of ways. Choose Window > Pathfinder to access this palette.

Review questions

1 Why is the Direct Selection tool more useful than the Selection tool when drawing or editing paths?

2 What is the key difference between smooth and corner points?

3 Which tool can change an anchor point from a corner point to a smooth point or vice versa?

4 How do you make sure that a transformation (rotating, scaling, etc.) occurs in relation to the center of an object?

Review answers

1 The Selection tool displays only the path's bounding box. The Direct Selection tool displays the path itself, and the exact location of the anchor points on it.

2 The two direction lines of a smooth point always exist at the same angle. The direction lines of a corner point (if present) usually exist at different angles, creating a corner at the anchor point.

3 You can switch between smooth and corner points using the Convert Direction Point tool (⌐). It's grouped with the Pen tool in the toolbox.

4 With the object selected, click the center of the proxy (▦) in the Transform palette.

10 | Working with Transparency

InDesign CS delivers an array of transparency features to feed your imagination and creativity. Choose combinations of settings to exploit the varied possibilities for complex and elegant interactions among overlapping layers of colors. You not only get control over opacity and color blendings using InDesign, but you can work with imported and exported files that use transparency.

In this lesson you'll learn how to do the following:

- Colorize an imported black-and-white graphic.

- Change the opacity of objects drawn in InDesign.

- Apply blending modes to overlapping objects.

- Apply feathering to soften the edges of objects.

- Adjust transparency settings for imported Adobe Photoshop files.

- Adjust transparency settings for imported Adobe Illustrator files.

- Import files with transparency set in Illustrator.

- Apply transparency settings to text.

- Apply drop shadows to text and graphics.

Getting started

The project for this lesson is a menu for a fictional restaurant, Bistro nonXista. By applying transparency into objects in a series of layers, you'll create a visual richness of color interactions right in InDesign.

To ensure that the tools and palettes function exactly as described in this lesson, delete or deactivate (by renaming) the InDesign Defaults file and the InDesign SavedData file. See "Restoring default preferences" on page 2.

1 Start Adobe InDesign.

2 Choose File > Open, and open the 10_a.indd file in the ID_10 folder, which is located within the IDCIB folder on your hard disk.

Note: If you have not already copied the resource files for this lesson onto your hard disk from the ID_10 folder from the Adobe InDesign CS Classroom in a Book CD, do so now. See "Copying the Classroom in a Book files" on page 2.

3 Choose File > Save As, name the file **10_Menu.indd**, and save it in the ID_10 folder.

The menu appears as a long, blank page because all layers are currently hidden. You'll reveal these layers one by one as you need them, so that it will be easy to focus on the specific objects and tasks that you'll do in this lesson.

4 To see what the finished project will look like, choose File > Open, and open the 10_b.indd file in the ID_10 folder, which is located within the IDCIB folder on your hard disk.

5 When you are ready to start working, you can either close the 10_b.indd file or choose Window > 10_Menu.indd to switch back to your own lesson document, leaving the sample of the finished file open for reference.

Importing and colorizing a black-and-white image

You'll begin by working with the background layer for the menu. This layer serves as a random textured background that will be visible through the objects layered above it that have transparency settings. Since there's nothing below this layer in the layer stack, you won't specify any changes for this layer's opacity.

1 In the Layers palette, select the Background layer, scrolling as necessary to find it at the bottom of the layer stack. Make sure that the two boxes to the left of the layer name show that the layer is visible (eye icon appears) and unlocked (lock icon does not appear).

2 Choose File > Place, and then locate, select, and open the 10_c.tif file in your ID_10 folder.

3 Move the loaded-graphic pointer (🖊) to the upper left corner of the page and click, so that the image fills the entire page, including any margins. After you place the graphic, it remains selected. Do not deselect.

4 With the graphic still selected, open the Swatches palette and select the Fill box (🖢). Scroll down the list of swatches to find the Lime 80% tint, and select it. The white areas of the image are now the 80% tint of the green color, but the black areas are still black. Click anywhere on the pasteboard to deselect.

5 In the toolbox, use the Direct Selection tool (🔖) to select the image again, and then select the Aqua color in the Swatches palette. The Aqua color replaces black in the original image, leaving the Lime 80% areas as they were.

Note: *Remember that the Direct Selection tool appears as a hand (🖑) when it is over a frame, but it still selects the image contents when you click.*

6 In the Layers palette, select the empty box to the left of the Background layer name to lock the layer. Leave the Background layer visible so that you can see the results of the transparency work you do above this layer.

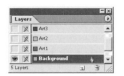

As you now know, the key to converting a black-and-white image to a two-color image is that you use the right tools to select the object. Your choice of either the Selection tool or the Direct Selection tool determines whether the swatch you specify replaces the black or the white parts of the image.

Applying transparency settings

The ability to change the opacity of an object in a single control option is just the beginning of the transparency functionality in InDesign CS. Not only can you change the opacity of fills and strokes on objects drawn or typed in InDesign and of imported images and text—including photographs—but there's more. You can also use blending modes, feathering, and drop shadows in simple procedures. You can even import objects created with existing transparency properties and compound the effect with InDesign.

In this project, you'll progress through layer by layer rather than technique by technique, so you'll get plenty of practice using the various transparency options. In this way, you'll see the interactions between transparent objects as the project builds, one layer at a time.

Changing the opacity of solid-color objects

Now that you have filled the underlying layer with color and texture, you can start adding transparency features to the layers stacked above it. You'll start with a series of simple shapes with solid fills, drawn in InDesign.

1 In the Layers palette, select the Art1 layer so that it is the active layer, and click the small boxes on the left of the layer name to unlock the layer (removing the crossed-out pencil icon (✗) and make it visible, displaying the eye icon (👁).

2 Using the Selection tool (▶), click the gold background on the right side of the page. This background is simply a rectangular frame with a solid fill, drawn in InDesign.

3 Choose Window > Transparency to open the Transparency palette.

4 For Opacity, click the arrow button to open the slider, and then drag to set the opacity at 60%. Or, you can type **60%** in the Opacity option and press Enter. Notice that you can now see the Background layer through the gold background on the Art1 layer.

5 Select the black semicircle at the top of the left side of the page, and then choose Window > Swatches to open the Swatches palette. Make sure that the Fill box is selected (■) and select Lime (not Lime 80%) to apply a fill color to the semicircle.

6 With the semicircle still selected, go to the Transparency palette and set the Opacity value at **40%**. The semicircle now appears as just a subtle variation in color against the textured background.

7 Repeat steps 5 and 6 for each of the solid circles on the Art1 layer, using the following settings:

- Left side, middle: color=Navy, Opacity=**80%**
- Left side, bottom: color=Gold, Opacity=**70%**
- Right side, top: color=Aqua, Opacity=**70%**
- Right side, middle: color=Dark Red, Opacity=**60%**
- Right side, bottom (semicircle): color=Black, Opacity=**10%**

Applying the Multiply blending mode

An Opacity setting changes a selected object by creating a color that combines the color values of the object with the objects below it. This creates the impression that the object is semi-transparent. Blending modes give you another way to create color interactions between layered objects.

In this procedure, you'll see the differences as you first change the opacity and then apply the Multiply blending mode to the same objects.

1 Using the Selection tool (↖), select the subtle green semicircle at the top of the left side of the page.

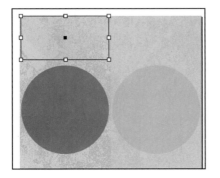

2 In the Transparency palette, open the blending mode pop-up menu (which currently shows Normal selected) and select Multiply. Notice the change in the appearance of the colors.

3 Select the black half-circle at the bottom of the right side of the page, and apply Multiply blending mode, using the same method as in step 2.

4 Choose File > Save.

For more information about the different blending modes, see "Selecting blending modes" in InDesign Help. This topic describes the results generated by each of the blending modes.

Applying feathering to the margins of an image

Another way to apply transparency to an object is to use feathering. Feathering applies a gradient transparency to the edges, softening the margins of the object. This creates a more subtle transition between the object and any underlying images.

1 If the faint black half-circle at the bottom of the right side is not still selected, use the Selection tool to select it now.

2 Choose Object > Feather to open the Feather dialog box.

3 Select the Feather check box, and then select the Preview check box so you can see the results as you adjust the settings.

4 In Feather Width, type **0.3"** (including the quotation mark to indicate inches as the unit of measurement). Leave the Corners option set as Diffused. Notice how the margins of the faint black circle are now blurred, and that the measurement units appear as "in" instead of the quotation mark. Click OK to close the dialog box.

5 Select the gold circle at the bottom of the left side of the page.

6 Using the same techniques that you used in steps 1–5 to give the black half-circle a feathered edge, apply a **0.25"** feather to the gold circle.

7 In the Layers palette, click to lock the Art1 layer and then choose File > Save.

Adjusting the transparency settings for EPS images

Up to this point in the lesson, you have applied various transparency settings to objects drawn in InDesign. You can also set opacity value, blending mode, and feathering options to Encapsulated PostScript (EPS) documents that you create in programs such as Adobe Illustrator.

1 In the Layers palette, unlock and make visible the Art2 layer.

2 In the toolbox, make sure that the Selection tool (↖) is selected.

3 On the left side of the page, click the black spiral image, which is on top of the Navy color circle, blocking your view of the lower circle. Then press Shift and click to also select the spiral that is above the red circle on the right side of the page.

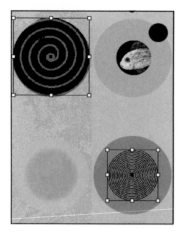

4 In the Transparency palette, select Color Dodge blending mode and set Opacity at **30%**.

5 Zoom in, if necessary, and Ctrl+click (Windows) or Command+click (Mac OS) to select the small black circle above the Navy spiral.

Note: Ctrl+click (Windows) or Command+click (Mac OS) is the keyboard shortcut you use when you want to select an object that is stacked behind another object in the layout. It is especially useful when both objects are on the same layer, as they are in this case.

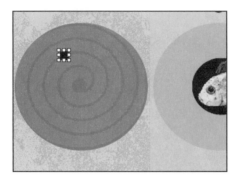

6 Set the following options for the small circle:

• In the Transparency palette, set the Opacity at **80%**.

• In the Swatches palette, select Dark Red.

7 Scroll if necessary so that you can see three more small circles in the top right area of the page, and assign the following color swatches and opacity values to them:

• Top small circle: Navy, **50%** opacity

• Middle small circle: Dark Red, **35%** opacity

• Lowest small circle: Turquoise, **50%** opacity. For this circle only, also choose Object > Feather, select the Feather check box, specify **0.21 inches** as the Feather Width, and click OK.

8 In the Layers palette, lock the Art2 layer, and then save your work.

Adjusting transparency for Photoshop images

In this procedure, you'll apply transparency to an imported Photoshop file. Although this example uses a monochromatic image, you can also apply InDesign transparency settings to complex multicolor photographs that you import from Photoshop.

1 In the Layers palette, select the Art3 layer and make it visible and unlocked. If you find it easier to see your work, you can click the eye icon (👁) to hide either the Art1 or Art2 layer or both, but leave at least one underlying layer visible so that you can see the results of the transparency interactions .

2 Using the Selection tool (↖), click the black starburst image on the upper right side of the page.

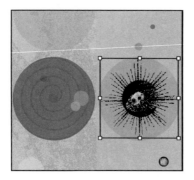

3 On the Transparency palette, type **50%** as the Opacity value.

4 Switch to the Direct Selection tool (↘), move the pointer over the starburst image so that it appears as a hand (✋), and then click once to reselect the image.

5 In the Swatches palette, select the Dark Red color swatch so that the red color replaces the black areas of the image. If you have other layers visible below the Art3 layer, you see the starburst as a muted orange color. If no other layers are visible, the starburst is red. Leave the starburst image selected, or reselect it with the Direct Selection tool now.

6 In the Transparency palette, select Screen blending mode from the pop-up list. Leave the Opacity value at 100%. Depending on which layers are visible, the starburst changes colors in various ways after you apply this change.

Importing and adjusting Illustrator files that use transparency

When you import Adobe Illustrator files into your InDesign layout, InDesign CS recognizes and preserves any transparency interactions that were applied in Illustrator. You can further adjust the transparency of the imported graphic by applying InDesign settings for opacity, blending modes, and feathering to the entire image.

1 Make sure that the Art3 layer is targeted in the Layers palette and that the Selection tool (▸) is selected in the toolbox, and then choose Edit > Deselect All.

2 Choose File > Place. Locate the 10_d.ai file in your ID_10 folder, and double-click to select it.

3 Move the loaded-graphics icon over the red circle in the middle of the right side of the page and click to place the graphic image. If necessary, drag the image so that it is approximately centered over the red circle.

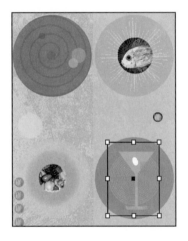

4 In the Layers palette, click any displayed eye icons for the Art2, Art1, and Background layers so that only the Art3 layer appears and you can see the transparency color interactions within the original image. Then click the boxes again to make the Art2, Art1, and Background layers visible. Notice that the white "olive" shape is completely opaque while the other shapes are partly transparent.

5 With the glasses graphic still selected, change the Opacity setting in the Transparency palette to **80%**. Notice that you can now see the black spiral behind the white olive and that the glasses are more subdued in color.

6 Still in the Transparency palette, select Color Burn as the blending mode. Now the colors and interactions of the image take on a completely different character.

7 Save your work.

Applying transparency settings to text

Changing the opacity of text is as easy as applying transparency settings to graphic objects in your layout. In this topic, you'll change the color and opacity of some words that you will add by using the InDesign Type tool.

1 Unlock and make visible the Type layer.

2 In the toolbox, select the Type tool (**T**), click to place an insertion point in the text frame "I THINK, THEREFORE I DINE," and choose Edit > Select All. If necessary, zoom in so that you can read the text easily.

3 In the Swatches palette, select [Paper].

4 Switch to the Selection tool and click to select the same text frame.

5 In the Transparency palette, select Overlay blending mode and type **70%** as the Opacity value.

Note: You cannot specify transparency options when the Type tool is active. When you switch to the Selection tool, those options are available again.

Creating a drop shadow

You can create the impression that an object is embossed or floating above the page by adding a drop shadow. Then, by selected transparency settings that apply only to the drop shadow, you can soften the shadow without changing the sharp edges of the object itself.

1 Using the Selection tool, select the large "Bistro nonXista" image in the center of the page. This graphic is an imported EPS file, created in Adobe Illustrator.

2 Choose Object > Drop Shadow.

3 In the Drop Shadow dialog box, select the following settings:

• Select the Drop Shadow check box to enable the other options.

• Select the Preview check box so that you can see the results in the document as you change the settings.

• In Mode, select Multiply.

• In Opacity, type **50%**.

• In both X Offset and Y Offset, type **0.0972 in** (or use quotation marks: **0.0972"**).

• In Blur, type **0.02 in**.

• Leave [Black] selected under Color.

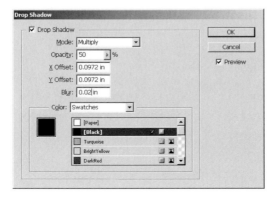

4 Click OK to close the dialog box. Then, using the Selection tool (▶), click the text frame at the bottom of the page, with five city names. (This is simply typed text created in InDesign.) If necessary, zoom in so that you can see the text easily.

5 Choose Object > Drop Shadow, and confirm the following settings:

• Select the Drop Shadow check box and the Preview check box.

• In Mode, select Normal.

• In Opacity, type **50%**.

• In both X Offset and Y Offset, type **0.03"**.

• In Blur, type **0.02"**.

• Under Color, select Swatches in the pop-up menu, and then click the Navy swatch.

6 Click OK to close the dialog box.

7 Lock all layers. Choose File > Save.

The X Offset and Y Offset values determine the horizontal and vertical lengths of the drop shadow. Positive numbers offset the shadow below and to the right of the selected object while negative values offset the shadow above and to the left .

Note: *When you export your InDesign document as an Adobe PDF, transparency is preserved when you open the file with Adobe Acrobat 5.0 or later, including the Adobe Reader. Earlier versions of Adobe Acrobat will display all objects with full opacity.*

You can install Adobe Reader 6.0 from the *Adobe InDesign CS Classroom in a Book CD* or download your free copy from the Adobe Web site.

To see your work as it will look when printed, select the Preview Mode button in the lower right corner of the toolbox.

Congratulations! You have now completed this lesson.

Like all the other lessons in this Classroom in a Book, this material serves as an introduction to the features and functions available in InDesign CS. For details and in-depth information, see Adobe InDesign CS online Help, and the Adobe Web site www.adobe.com.

On your own

Try some of the following ideas for working with InDesign transparency options:

1 Scroll to a blank area of the pasteboard and create some shapes (using the drawing tools or by importing new copies of some of the image files used in this lesson) on a new layer. Position your shapes so that they overlap each other, at least partially. Then:

• Select the topmost object in your arrangement of shapes and experiment with other blending modes, such as Luminosity, Hard Light, and Difference, by selecting them in the Transparency palette. Then select a different object and select the same blending modes to compare the results. When you have a sense of what the various modes do, select all your objects and select Normal as the blending mode.

• In the Transparency palette, change the Opacity value of some of the objects but not others. Then select different objects in your arrangement and use the Object > Send Backwards and Object > Bring Forward commands to observe different results.

• Experiment with combinations of different opacities and different blending modes applied to an object. Then do the same with other objects that partially overlap the first object to explore the enormous number of different effects you can create.

2 Double-click the page 1 icon in the Pages palette to center it in the document window. Then try clicking the eye icons for the different Art layers one at a time, to see the differences this creates in the overall effect of the project.

3 Choose Help > InDesign Help. At the top of the left pane of the Help window, click Search. Then in the Find Pages Containing box, type Creating, saving, and loading, and then click Search. After a short wait, click "Creating, saving, and loading custom flattener presets" in the lower area of the left pane to open that topic in the right pane. Then follow the procedure described there for creating a flattener style for exporting transparency pages to PDF.

Review questions

1 How do you change the color of the white areas of a black-and-white image? The black areas?

2 How can you change transparency effects without changing the Opacity value of an object?

3 What is the importance of the stacking order of layers and of objects within layers when you work with transparency?

4 Will the transparency effects you create in InDesign CS appear in a PDF that you export from InDesign?

Review answers

1 To change the white areas, select the object with the Selection tool (↖) and then select the color in the Swatches palette. To change the black areas, select the object with the Direct Selection tool (↘) and then select the color you want to use in the Swatches palette.

2 Besides selecting the object and changing the Opacity value in the Transparency palette, you can also create transparency effects by changing the blending mode, feathering the edges of the object, or adding drop shadows that have transparency settings. Blending modes determine how the base color and the blend color will be combined to produce a resulting color. For more information about blending modes, see "Selecting blending modes" in InDesign online Help.

3 The transparency of an object affects the view of objects below (behind) it in the stacking order. For example, objects below a semitransparent object can be seen behind it—like objects behind a colored plastic film. Opaque objects block the view of the area behind them in the stacking order, regardless of whether the objects behind them have reduced Opacity values, feathering, or blending modes.

4 Yes, if you open the PDF in Adobe Acrobat 5.0 or 6.0 or Adobe Reader 5.0 or 6.0. In earlier versions of Acrobat, the objects appear with all objects at 100% opacity.

11 | Creating Interactive Documents

With Adobe InDesign CS you can create interactive PDF documents including hyperlinks and movies. These can be created using existing content and the same tools you use for building your printed documents.

In this lesson you will learn how to do the following:

• Add interactive hyperlinks to your InDesign document.

• Create bookmarks that will export into an Adobe PDF.

• Use multimedia elements, including movies.

• Create buttons with actions.

Getting started

In this lesson you'll work on an interactive brochure for a flower and garden products distributor. You will add hyperlinks, movies, bookmarks and buttons to this document.

Before you begin, restore the default preferences for Adobe InDesign, using the procedure in "Restoring default preferences" on page 2.

1 Start Adobe InDesign.

2 Choose File > Open and open the 11_a.indd file in the ID_11 folder, located inside the Lessons folder within the IDCIB folder on your hard disk.

3 Choose File > Save As, rename the file **11_interactive.indd** and save it in the ID_11 folder.

4 To see what the completed PDF document will look like, open the 11_c.pdf file in the same folder, using Adobe Acrobat or Acrobat Reader. You can also locate 11_b.indd file in this same folder. This is the completed version of the InDesign document that was used to create the Adobe PDF file. When you are ready to resume working on the lesson document, you can close the 11_c.pdf file and, if necessary, the 11_b.indd file.

Note: *If you have not already copied the resource files for this lesson onto your hard disk from the ID_11 folder from the Adobe InDesign CS Classroom in a Book CD, do so now. See "Copying the Classroom in a Book files" on page 2.*

Bookmarks

A bookmark is a type of link where you click on the text and are taken to a specific destination. Bookmarks make it easier to navigate documents exported as Adobe PDF files. Bookmarks created using InDesign appear in the Bookmarks tab on the left side of the Acrobat or Adobe Reader window. You will have InDesign automatically create some bookmarks using Styles applied to text. You will then organize these bookmarks and also add your own.

1 Choose Window > Interactive > Bookmarks.

Notice the Bookmarks palette is empty, because you have not yet created any bookmarks.

2 Choose Layout > Table of Contents. Confirm that Include Paragraph Styles lists one Style to be included when assembling the Table of Contents–the Main Heading style. If necessary, select Main Heading from the Other Styles list and add it to the Include Paragraph Styles list by clicking the Add button.

3 If necessary, click to select the Main Heading style in the Include Paragraph Styles list.

Choose Catalog TOC entry style from the Entry Style drop down list. This selection determines how the Table of Contents (TOC) will be formatted.

4 If necessary, click to select Create PDF Bookmarks. This will automatically create PDF bookmarks from the text that uses the Main Heading style.

5 Click to deselect Replace Existing Table of Contents.

6 Click OK.

7 Your cursor is now "loaded" and ready to place the text for the TOC. Choose Window > Layers. If necessary, click to select the Interactive Elements layer. This will ensure that the text you are placing is located on a separate layer containing all the interactive items.

8 Move your cursor to the upper left corner of the text frame that starts just below the 12 pica mark on the vertical ruler and click to place the TOC text into the text frame.

Notice how the Bookmarks palette now includes several bookmarks that correlate to the text listed in the TOC.

9 Navigate to page 6 and with the Type tool (**T**) highlight the text "Longwood Gardens."

10 With the "Longwood Gardens" text selected, click the New Bookmark button (⊟) at the bottom of the Bookmarks palette. A new bookmark appears in the Bookmarks palette using the name of the selected text.

Note: *You can click and drag bookmarks to a new location within the palette to set the order in which the bookmarks will appear in the Adobe PDF file.*

11 Choose File > Save.

Hyperlinks

1 If necessary, use the Zoom tool (🔍) to increase your magnification on page 6 so that the text describing Longwood Gardens is visible.

2 Using the Type tool (T), highlight the text "web site."

3 Choose Window > Interactive > Hyperlinks.

4 With the text "web site" still selected, choose New Hyperlink from the Hyperlinks palette menu.

5 Make the following changes within the Destination section of the New Hyperlink window:

• For Type select URL.

• For URL enter **http://www.longwoodgardens.org**.

By specifying URL as the Type you have created a hyperlink that will take you to an Internet web site.

6 Make the following changes under the New Hyperlink Appearance.

• For Highlight select Invert.

• For Color select Blue.

These changes do not affect the function of the link, but determine how it will appear on screen and when converted to an Adobe PDF.

7 Click OK to close the New Hyperlink window.

Notice a thin line now appears around the words "web site" in the text and hyperlink is now listed in the hyperlinks palette. If necessary, deselect all text or object to make this visible by choosing Edit > Deselect All or clicking on the pasteboard.

8 Choose File > Save.

Adding a navigational button

This interactive brochure contains multiple pages. To make it easy for readers to move from one page to the next, you will create an interactive button that will automatically turn to the next page when it is clicked.

1 Navigate to Master Page B - contents page by selecting this page from the page list in the lower left corner of the document window or by double-clicking on the icon in the Pages palette.

2 If you can't see the margins of your page, choose View > Fit Page in Window. Click to select the Button tool (🔲), located in the Tool bar.

3 Move your cursor to the bottom margin of the document. In the lower right corner of the page, at approximately the 38 pica mark, click and drag to create a box that extends over to the right margin and is two picas deep. This box should be below the bottom page margin and large enough to contain the 12 point text label you will add in the next step.

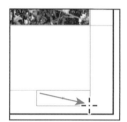

Click and drag just below the page margin.

4 Select the Type tool (**T**) and click within the button you created in the last step.

5 Enter the text **Next Page** > .

💡 *You can convert a text frame, a graphics frame, or a drawn shape to a button by selecting the object and choosing Object > Interactive > Convert to Button.*

6 Click the Selection tool (➤) and click to select the button.

7 If necessary, choose Window > Swatches to make the swatches palette visible. Click to select the fill icon (■) and then click the color **C=0, M=0, Y=100, K=0**. Then switch to the stroke icon (🔲) and choose Black.

8 With the button selected, choose Object > Interactive > Button Options.

9 In the Button Options window, change the button Name to Next Page and confirm that Visibility in PDF is set to Visible.

10 Click the Behaviors tab in the Button Options Window.

11   In the Behaviors tab, choose Mouse Up from the Event drop down list, click Go To Next Page from the Behavior Menu list, then click the Add button. Then click OK.

Note: When creating behaviors, remember to click the Add button. If you just click OK to close the dialog box, the event and behavior are not added.

12   Navigate to the second page in the document by choosing page 2 from the page drop down list in the lower left corner of the window. The button should be visible on this page and all subsequent pages. The interactive nature of the button will only be apparent when the file is exported as an Adobe PDF file.

13   Choose File > Save.

Button event types

Events determine how behaviors are activated in buttons when the document is exported to Adobe PDF. (In Acrobat, events are called triggers.)

Mouse Up–*When the mouse button is released after a click. This is the most commonly used event, because it gives the user one last chance to drag the cursor off the button and not activate the behavior.*

Mouse Down–*When the mouse button is clicked (without being released). Unless you have a specific reason for using Mouse Down, it's preferable to use Mouse Up so that users have a chance to cancel the behavior.*

Mouse Enter–*When the mouse pointer enters the button area defined by the button's bounding box.*

Mouse Exit–*When the mouse pointer exits the button area.*

On Focus–*When the button receives focus, either through a mouse action or pressing the Tab key.*

On Blur–*When the focus moves to a different button or form field.*

–From Adobe InDesign CS online Help.

Button behavior types

When you create a behavior, you specify the event that causes the behavior. (In Acrobat, behaviors are called actions.) You can assign the following behaviors to occur when the event type is activated:

Close–Closes the PDF document.

Exit–Exits the application, such as Adobe Reader, in which the PDF document is open.

Go to Anchor–Jumps to the specified bookmark or hyperlink anchor in the InDesign document you specify.

Go to [page]–Jumps to the first, last, previous, or next page in the PDF document. Select an option from the Zoom menu to determine how the page is displayed.

Go to Previous View–Jumps to the most recently viewed page in the PDF document.

Go to Next View–Jumps to a page after going to the previous view. In the same way that a Forward button is available in a Web browser only after someone clicks the Back button, this option is available only if the user has jumped to a previous view.

Go to URL–Opens the Web page of the specified URL.

Movie–Lets you play, pause, stop, or resume the selected movie. Only movies that have been added to the document appear in the Movie menu.

Open File–Launches and opens the file that you specify. If you specify a file that is not PDF, the reader needs the native application to open it successfully. Specify an absolute pathname (such as c:\docs\ sample.pdf).

Show/Hide Fields–Toggles between showing and hiding a field in a PDF document.

Sound–Lets you play, pause, stop, or resume the selected sound clip. Only sound clips that have been added to the document appear in the Sound menu.

View Zoom–Displays the page according to the zoom option you specify. You can change the page zoom level (such as Actual Size), the page layout (such as Continuous–Facing), or the rotation orientation.

–From Adobe InDesign CS online Help.

Adding a movie

You will add a movie clip to this document and then create a button to play the movie.

Note: *This section requires the use of the Quicktime movie player to view and place the movie file. If you do not already have this free player, it is available for both Windows and Macintosh computers at www.apple.com/quicktime/download.*

1 Navigate to the sixth page in the document by choosing page 6 from the page drop down list in the lower left corner of the window.

2 Choose File > Place.

3 Click to deselect the Replace Selected Item option.

4 Browse to the ID_11 folder, located inside the Lessons folder within the IDCIB folder on your hard disk.

5 Double-click to select the fountain.mov movie file. You will place this file in the lower right corner of the page.

6 Click the loaded cursor ( ) at the intersection of the gutter separating the right and left column and the ruler guide located approximately 18 picas down on the page. The movie is placed within the document.

7 Choose the Selection tool ( ) and double-click the movie you placed in the previous step. The Movie Options window opens.

8 In the Options section of the Movie Options window, select Choose Movie Frame as Poster from the poster drop down menu. In the Choose Movie Frame as Poster window, click and drag the movie timeline to approximately the middle of the movie, when the fountain becomes visible, then click OK.

9 Click OK to close the Movie Options dialog box.

10 Choose File > Save.

About movie posters

A poster is the image that represents a media clip. Each movie or sound can appear with or without a poster. If the poster in InDesign is larger than the movie, the poster is clipped to the size of the movie in the exported PDF document. For best results, use a poster that is the same size as the movie; use the Scale tool to resize the page item.

You cannot simply use a placed image as a poster. Instead, specify any of the following types of poster images in the Movie Options or Sound Options dialog box:

None–*Shows no poster for the movie or sound clip. This option is useful if you want the movie or sound clip to not be visible on the page. For example, you may want the media to be played only when you turn the page, or you may want a more complex design beneath the movie to show instead of the poster.*

Standard–*Displays a generic movie or sound poster that isn't based on the contents of the file. To use a different standard poster, save an image as StandardMoviePoster.jpg or StandardSoundPoster.jpg, and replace the existing file of the same name. (Use the system search utility to locate the existing poster files.)*

Default Poster–*Displays the poster image packaged with the movie file. If the selected movie doesn't have a frame designated as the poster, the first frame of the movie is used as the poster image.*

Choose Image as Poster–*Lets you select an image to use as the poster. Click Browse, and then double-click the image you want to use. You can select bitmap graphics, not vector graphics, for posters.*

–From Adobe InDesign CS online Help.

Adding a button with rollover and down states

To make the movie easy to view, you will add a button that will cause the movie to play. First you will create the button and set its appearance.

1 Click to select the Button tool and then Choose Window > Interactive > States. From the Appearance option in the States palette, choose Beveled.

2 Click and drag to create a new button in the bottom right corner of the left column, to the left of the movie file you placed. The button should be approximately 10 picas wide and 2 picas tall. In the Name option in the States palette, type **Play Movie** to name the button.

3 Confirm that the Up state is selected in the States palette, then choose the Type tool (T) and double-click inside of the button. Once you have a text insertion point, enter the text **Play Movie**.

4 Center the text horizontally by clicking Center (≡) from the Control palette. If necessary click the paragraph (¶) option in the Control palette to make these options visible.

5 Choose Object > Text Frame options and in the Text Frame Options window select Center from the Vertical Justification: Align drop down menu. This will center the text top-to-bottom within the button. Then click OK.

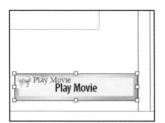

6 Click to choose the Selection tool (↖) and click once to select the button.

7 In the States palette notice the button has three different appearances, or states. The Up state is the default state of the button when it is not being clicked or when the mouse is not rolling over the button. Rollover will change how the button appears when the mouse rolls over the button, and Down will change the appearance when the button is clicked.

Note: Remember the button states affect how the button will appear when the button is exported to an Adobe PDF file, not how the button appears within Adobe InDesign.

8 Select the Rollover state from the States palette menu.

9 With the Rollover state selected, choose the Type tool (T) and double-click on the button. Insert the text **Watch Movie** so the button will read Watch Movie in its active state.

10 Repeat steps 3 and 4 to format your text accordingly to match the appearance of the text Play Movie.

11 Choose the Selection tool (↖) and then click to select the button again.

12 Click to select the Down State. With the Down state selected, choose the Type tool (T) then double-click on the button and insert the text **Enjoy Movie**, then repeating steps 3 and 4 once again to format the text accordingly.

13 Select the Selection tool (↖). In the States palette, confirm that Rollover and Down states both have a check mark to the left of the icon representing the button. This checkbox enables the state for exporting to an Adobe PDF.

Adding a play movie action to a button

Now that you have created the button you can add interactivity so that it causes the movie to play.

1 Click to choose the Selection tool (↖) and click to select the button you created in the previous section.

2 Choose Objects > Interactive > Button Options and click on the Behaviors tab.

3 In the Behaviors Tab of the Button Options select the Behavior called Movie. Confirm that the Movie selected is fountain.mov and that the Play Options are set to Play.

4 Click the Add button.

5 Click OK.

6 Choose File > Save.

Exporting the final document as an Adobe PDF

1 Choose File > Export.

2 If necessary, change the Save as Type to Adobe PDF and choose the ID_11 folder inside the IDCIB folder on your hard disk,

3 Name the file **interactive.pdf.**

4 Click Save.

5 In the Export PDF Dialog box choose eBook from the PDF Preset drop-down menu at the top of the dialog box. Then click to select Acrobat 6 from the Compatibility drop down menu.

Note: *Selecting Acrobat 6 changes the Preset to Custom, as it is a change from the default eBook settings.*

The eBook setting automatically includes Bookmarks, Hyperlinks and interactive content and makes the PDF accessible to individuals with Adobe Acrobat or Adobe Reader version 5 or later, which causes the interactive elements to be linked to the PDF file rather than embedded. Because you know that the Adobe Reader 6.0 is widely used and available, you want to embed the interactive movie to make it easy to share the complete document.

6 Under the Include section of the Export PDF window, click to select Interactive Elements and then choose Embed All from the Multimedia drop down menu.

Note: *If you are unable to select Embed All, be certain you have selected Acrobat 6 from the compatibility drop down menu, as indicated in step 5.*

7 Click to enable "View PDF After Exporting."

8 Click Export.

Congratulations. You finished the lesson.

On your own

1 Place the fountain.mov or another movie or .swf file and experiment with the options for choosing various movie posters.

2 Create a button to navigate backwards through the document and place it on the master page, adjacent to the Next Page button.

3 Place a sound file inside the InDesign document and use a button to play the sound.

4 Create additional bookmarks from other text in the lesson.

5 Export the PDF using the default eBook settings and Acrobat 5 compatibility and examine what happens to the interactive elements.

Review questions

1 How can you have InDesign automatically add Adobe PDF Bookmarks to a document?

2 What are some of the possible destinations of hyperlinks created using Adobe InDesign?

3 Can you use buttons to navigate within an InDesign file?

Review answers

1 Adobe InDesign can automatically add Adobe PDF Bookmarks to an InDesign document at the time it is converted to Adobe PDF. To do this you can first create a Table of Contents and select Create PDF, Bookmarks in the Table of Contents window. Then, when exporting to Adobe PDF choose the Include Bookmarks checkbox.

2 Adobe InDesign hyperlinks can take you to another page within an InDesign document, another InDesign document, or any valid Internet protocol address such as a web site. For more information about linking between InDesign documents see Adobe InDesign CS online Help.

3 Buttons created within an Adobe InDesign file are not used for navigating in the InDesign file. Buttons add interactivity to your documents when they are converted to Adobe PDF.

12 | **Combining Files into Books**

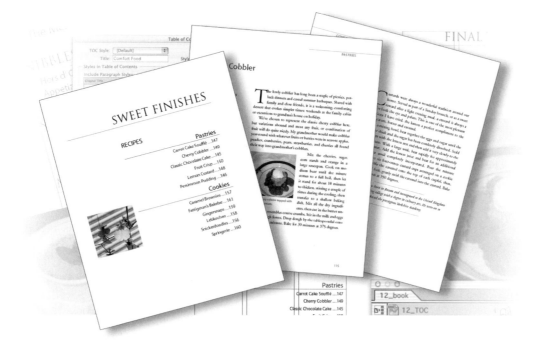

You can assemble your individual InDesign documents into multi-file books. Automatic page numbering from file to file is just the beginning—you can also create tables of contents and indexes for the entire book. Additionally, using the book features, multiple files can be printed or converted to PDF in one step.

In this lesson you'll learn how to do the following:

• Associate multiple InDesign documents into a book.

• Specify page numbering throughout a book.

• Create a Table of Contents for a book.

• Assign a file to act as the source document for defining styles.

• Update book files after changing page count, style definitions, and headings.

• Embed multi-tiered index references and specify options.

• Generate an index file and sort entries.

• Edit index references.

Getting started

In this project, you'll gather together a collection of several InDesign documents, each representing one chapter of a cookbook. Using InDesign CS, you'll assemble these chapters into a book so that you can easily create common elements, such as a table of contents, index, unified page numbering, styles, and color definitions.

To ensure that the tools and palettes function exactly as described in this lesson, delete or deactivate (by renaming) the InDesign Defaults file and the InDesign SavedData file. See "Restoring default preferences" on page 2.

Note: If you have not already copied the resource files for this lesson onto your hard disk from the ID_12 folder from the Adobe InDesign CS Classroom in a Book CD, do so now. See "Copying the Classroom in a Book files" on page 2.

Defining a book

Your project will pull together four existing chapters into a book. In InDesign, defining a book means that you specify the relationships among multiple existing files, including which files are included in the book and in what order they appear.

The sample files you'll use for this project are works in progress, so most of the pages are merely placeholders for content that would be added at some future date. Because of this, you'll see many blank or nearly blank pages if you open and scroll through the various chapters.

Your first step will involve renaming the files for this lesson.

Rename the six files for this lesson as follows:

- Rename the 12_c.indd **12_Starters.indd.**
- Rename the 12_d.indd **12_Entrees.indd.**
- Rename a copy of 12_e.indd **12_Nibbles.indd.**
- Rename a copy of 12_f.indd **12_Finishes.indd.**
- Rename a copy of 12_g.indd **12_TOC.indd.**
- Rename a copy of 12_h.indd **12_Index.indd.**

Now you can start building a book using the first four of these copied files.

Note: *If your computer alerts you that the files are locked or can not be renamed, use the following procedure to unlock the files.*

- (Windows) Right-click the file and choose Properties. Then deselect the Read-Only check box and click OK.

- (Mac OS) Select the "12_c.indd copy" file and choose File > Get Info > General Information. Then deselect the Locked check box and close the Info window.

Creating a book file

The next task is to define which InDesign files will be part of the book.

1 Start Adobe InDesign.

2 Choose File > New > Book.

3 In the New Book dialog box, type **12_Book.indb** as the filename and save the file in the ID_12 folder. The Book palette opens, but it is empty.

Note: An .indb file is not like other InDesign documents. If you double-click an .indb file in your desktop or Finder, no documents actually open, but the Book palette appears.

4 In the Book palette menu, choose Add Document, to open the Add Documents dialog box.

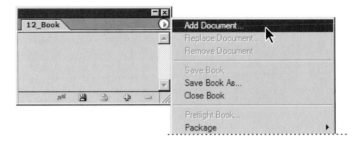

5 Open the ID_12 folder and select four of the documents you renamed: 12_Starters.indd, 12_Entrees.indd, 12_Nibbles.indd, and 12_Finishes.indd. Do not add the index or table of contents files at this time.

To select multiple files in one step, click one of the four documents and then Ctrl+click (Windows) or Command+click (Mac OS) each of the other three files. Or, you can add documents one at a time, repeating steps 4–6 for each of the four files.

6 With all four files selected, click Add (Windows) or Open (Mac OS).

The four document names now appear in the Book palette. Notice that the pages for each chapter also appear in the palette.

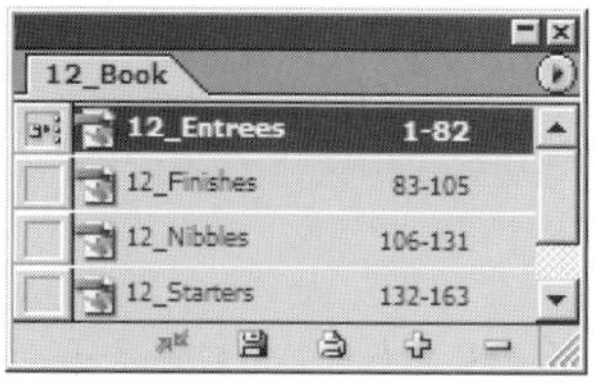

7 Examine each of the four open documents and notice the order in which the files appear. The order in your Book palette may differ from the illustration above, depending on the order in which you selected and added the files.

Setting the order and pagination

The plan for the cookbook is to organize the chapters by the order they would be served in a meal, beginning with appetizers ("Nibbles") and progressing on to desserts ("Finishes"). Your next task is to organize the chapters in the order appropriate for the book, so that the sequence and page numbers flow as needed.

1 In the Book palette, click and drag the 12_Nibbles.indd file to the top of the list. When a black bar appears just under the Book tab, release the mouse. Notice that the pagination has changed to reflect the page-count difference between this file and the file that was previously in the top position on the list.

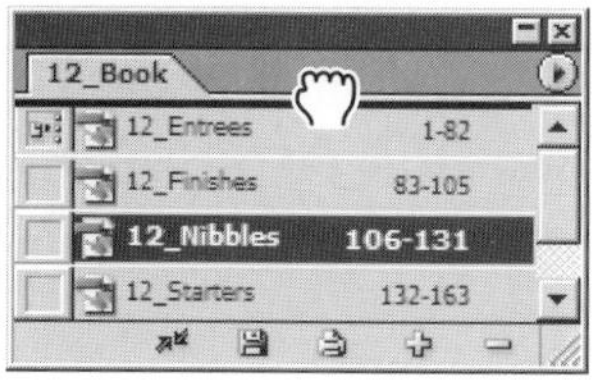

2 As necessary, drag the other files into position on the list so that they appear in the following order (from top to bottom): 12_Nibbles, 12_Starters, 12_Entrees, 12_Finishes.

Notice that some of the chapters start on odd-numbered pages. You want each chapter to start on an even numbered page so that the left page of the first spread is a photograph and the right page is the chapter title page. You'll fix that next.

3 In the Book palette menu, choose Book Page Numbering Options.

4 In the dialog box that appears, select Continue on Next Even Page, and then click OK. All chapters except the first one begin on even-numbered pages.

5 In the Book palette select the 12_Nibbles file to open the Document Page Numbering Options dialog box and then choose Document Page Numbering Options from the Book palette menu.

Note: Selecting the Document Page Number Options command in the Book palette menu will also automatically open the file.

6 Select the Start Page Numbering at option and type **2** so that the first page of the document appears on page 2. Then click OK.

```
Document Page Numbering Options
┌─ ☑ Start Section ─────────────────┐      ┌──────────┐
│  ○ Automatic Page Numbering        │      │    OK    │
│  ● Start Page Numbering at: [2│]    │      └──────────┘
│  ┌─ Page Numbering Options ──────┐  │      ┌──────────┐
│  │  Section Prefix: [        ]   │  │      │  Cancel  │
│  │         Style: [1, 2, 3, 4... ▼] │  │      └──────────┘
│  │  Section Marker: [        ]   │  │
│  │  ☐ Include Prefix when Numbering Pages │
│  └───────────────────────────────┘  │
└──────────────────────────────────────┘
```

7 Choose File > Save and then choose File > Close to close the 12_Nibbles document, but do not close the Book palette.

Working with a table of contents

A table of contents (TOC) for a book can be a separate InDesign document or it can be placed in an existing document that is part of the book. In this project you'll create both kinds: a high-level table of contents for the entire book and more detailed content lists for each chapter.

Adding the table of contents file

When you create a new file just for the book TOC, you should carefully select all the same document-setup specifications that you use in the other chapters of your book, such as the page size, paper orientation, and so forth. For this lesson, that file has already been created for you but you will add the actual content.

1 In the Book palette, choose Add Document, and then locate and double-click the 12_TOC.indd file in your ID_12 folder.

2 Drag the 12_TOC.indd file to the top of the Book palette list.

3 In the Book palette, double-click the 12_TOC.indd file name to open it in the document window. At this point, this document is a single, blank page.

4 On the Book palette menu, choose Document Page Numbering Options, or simply double-click the page number for the 12_TOC file in the Book palette list.

5 Under Style in the Document Page Numbering Options dialog box, select the lowercase roman numerals option, i, ii, iii, iv..., and then click OK.

6 Select File > Save Book from the Book palette menu.

Generating a table of contents for the book

Now you will have InDesign create the listings for you.

1 With the 12_TOC.indd file open, choose Layout > Table of Contents.

2 At the top of the dialog box, type **Comfort Food** as the Title for the table of contents and select TOC Book Title for Style. (You may need to scroll in the Style pop-up menu to find the TOC Book Title paragraph style.) The words Comfort Food will appear at the top of the table-of-contents page, formatted in the TOC Book Title paragraph style.

3 Under the Other Styles list on the right side of the dialog box, select Chapter Title, and then click the Add button to place the Chapter Title in the Include Paragraph Styles list. Repeat this process to move the Chapter Section style into the Include Paragraph Styles list.

With this selection, you designate that all paragraphs in the book that are formatted in the Chapter Title paragraph style will be listed in the table of contents.

4 Click to select Chapter Title in the list of included Paragraph Styles, then click the More Options Button.

Table of Contents	
TOC Style: [Default]	OK
Title: Comfort Food Style: TOC Book Title	Cancel
Styles in Table of Contents	Save Style...
Include Paragraph Styles: Other Styles:	More Options

```
Include Paragraph Styles:        Other Styles:
Chapter Title                    Body_first
Chapter Section                  Body_next
              << Add             Caption
              Remove >>          Index Level 1
                                 Index Level 2

Style: Chapter Section
   Entry Style: [Same style]

Options
  ☑ Create PDF Bookmarks
  ☐ Replace Existing Table of Contents
  ☐ Include Book Documen(12_Book.indb)
```

5 Under Style: Chapter Title, select the following formatting options:

• For Entry Style, select TOC Head 1 to apply that paragraph style to the listing of chapter titles in the table of contents.

• For Page Number, select No Page Number.

Note: *If you do not see these options, make sure that you clicked the More Options button.*

6 Click to select Chapter Section from the list of included paragraph styles.

7 Under Style: Chapter Section, select TOC Head 2 for Style. In the Page Number option, make sure that After Entry is selected, or select it now.

8 Under Options, select the Include Book Documents check box, and then click OK. This will generate the table of contents which you will place into the document in the next step.

9 Move the loaded-text icon to the upper left margins of page 1, and click to place the text. The TOC flows into the page, showing the four chapters and major subdivisions within each one.

10 Choose File > Save.

Note: *In this file, custom paragraph styles for the table of contents have been created for you. When you create your own documents, you can adjust and format the text and style definitions as you would for any other text frame.*

Creating a table of contents for an individual chapter

The table of contents in the front of the book is limited to broad categories. Next, you'll create a secondary table of contents for an individual chapter. This subordinate TOC will include the next level of interest: the recipe names.

1 Choose File > Open and select the 12_Finishes.indd file in your ID_12 folder. On page 143, click the Selection tool (↖) in the right side of the page to select the placeholder text frame.

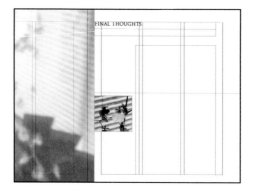

2 Choose Layout > Table of Contents, and type **Recipes** as the Title. Then for Style, select Chapter Section as the formatting style for the TOC title.

3 In the Other Styles list, double-click Chapter Section to place it in the Paragraph Styles list.

4 If necessary, click to select Chapter Section from the list of included styles. Then under Style: Chapter Section, select the following options:

• For Entry Style, select TOC Chapter Section.

• For Page Number, select No Page Number.

Now all chapter sections, such as "Pastries," "Cookies," and so forth will appear in the table of contents for the chapter but without page references. The chapter sections were identified through the use of the Chapter Section paragraph style.

5 Repeat step 3 but this time double-click Recipe Name, and then select the following style options:

• For Entry Style, select TOC Recipe Name.

• For Page Number, select After Entry.

- For Between Entry and Number, type **. . .** (space, period, space, period, space, period) to create three spaced leader dots before the page numbers in the chapter table of contents.

- Select the Sort Entries in Alphabetical Order check box.

6 In the lower left corner of the dialog box, deselect the Include Book Documents check box if it is currently selected, so that only recipes in this chapter appear in this table of contents. Then click OK.

7 Click the loaded-text icon inside the text frame you selected in step 1. Then save your file by choosing File > Save. Leave the file open

Maintaining consistency across book files

In order to create a unified look for your long publication, you can make sure that paragraph-style specifications and color definitions are consistent throughout the book. To make this easier to manage, InDesign designates one of the files as the style source document. By default, the first file that you place in the book becomes the style source. This is not necessarily the file at the top of the list in the Book palette.

You can tell which file is the style source by looking in the Book palette. A Style Source icon (▫▪) appears in the box to the left of the designated source file. This box is empty for all other book files.

Reassigning the style source

Designating a different file as the style source couldn't be easier: Here you'll make the TOC file the style source file with just one click.

• In the Book palette, click the empty box to the left of the 12_TOC file.

The style source indicator now appears in the box next to the TOC file.

Synchronizing book documents

When you synchronize documents, InDesign automatically searches all the style and swatch definitions in the selected files and compares them to the definitions in the designated style source file. When the set of definitions in a file does not match the set in the style source file, InDesign adds, removes, and edits the definitions in the selected file so that they match those in the style-source-file. After synchronizing, all documents in the book have identical sets of styles, ensuring consistency throughout the book.

Currently, the paragraph definitions for several of the paragraph styles are defined differently in the 12_TOC file and the other chapters. You'll update the definitions of each style list in each chapter in one simple process. By leaving the 12_Finishes file open to page 143 (its table of contents) you'll be able to see the changes in style.

1 Make sure that the style source icon (⊟⋮) appears next to the 12_TOC file in the Book palette, indicating that it is the designated style source file.

2 Holding down Shift and clicking, select these four files in the Book palette: 12_Nibbles, 12_Starters, 12_Entrees, and 12_Finishes. It is not necessary to select the 12_TOC file.

3 In the Book palette menu, select Synchronize Selected Documents.

Note: If all documents are selected, the option will be to "Synchronize Book" as opposed to "Selected Documents."

4 After a short delay, a message appears, telling you that synchronization was successful and that some documents may have changed. Click OK.

Notice the change in the table of contents for the 12_Finishes table of contents page: The chapter title now appears flush right instead of flush left and with 30-point type instead of 18-point type. The font for the chapter sections and recipe names has changed and the text is also aligned on the right side of the page.

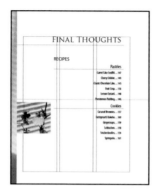

Updating the table of contents after editing

When a heading or subheading requires such changes, all TOC and cross-references must also be updated to reflect the revisions. Fortunately, updating a TOC using InDesign is a simple process.

1 If the Desserts chapter is not open, choose Window > 12_Finishes.indd to open it.

2 Using the Type tool (**T**), select the words Final Thoughts on page 143, and type **Sweet Finishes** to change the chapter title.

3 Choose File > Save.

4 Choose Window > 12_TOC.indd to make that file active, and then use the Selection tool (**k**) to select the table-of-contents text block.

5 Choose Layout > Update Table of Contents.

6 After short delay, a message appears telling you that the table of contents has been updated successfully. Click OK.

The table of contents now reflects the new chapter title for the final chapter in the book.

7 Choose File > Save, and then close the 12_TOC.indd file. Leave the "Sweet Finishes" file (12_Finishes.indd) open for more work in the next topics.

Indexing the book

Creating a good index is an art, as every reader who has tried to find a reference to a specific topic appreciates. Indexing is also a work that traditionally requires extraordinary attention to detail, with precise checking and rechecking of the entries. InDesign makes the job easier by facilitating the mechanical aspects of the process.

To create an index with InDesign, you embed index references right in the text. When you add or delete text or entire pages in the document so that the pagination changes, the index reference flows along with the text. This ensures that the updated index always shows the correct page. You can switch your view of these markers on and off as you work, but the markers themselves never appear in the printed document.

You can create indexes for individual chapters, but usually you'll want to publish just one index at the end of this book, covering the entire contents.

Creating index references

Some indexing has already been embedded in the project documents for this lesson. You'll add some index markers so you'll know how to do this yourself.

1 In the Pages palette, double-click the icon for page 146 to center that page—the "Persimmon Pudding" recipe—in the document window.

2 Choose Window > Type & Tables > Index to open the Index palette.

3 Select the Type tool (**T**) in the toolbox, and select the words Persimmon Pudding in the recipe title.

4 Press Ctrl+Alt+U (Windows) or Command+Option+U (Mac OS). The entry "Persimmon Pudding" is added to the Index palette. If necessary, scroll down the list to the letter P and click the arrow to see the new page reference. Make sure that the Reference button is selected at the top of the Index palette.

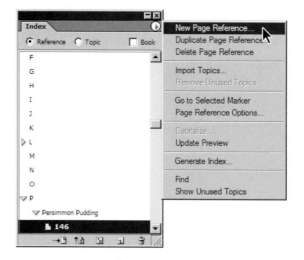

5 Choose New Page Reference on the Index palette menu to add another index reference to page 146.

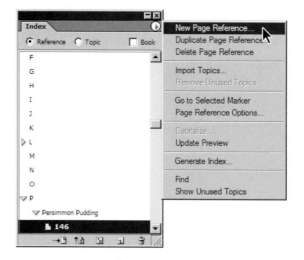

6 In the dialog box that opens, Under Topic Levels, type **puddings** in the box labeled "1."

7 In the 2 box under Topic Levels, type **persimmon**, creating a sublevel entry under puddings. Then click Add. The new listing now appears in the large box at the bottom of the dialog box, under the letter P. You may need to expand the listings to make this visible.

8 Create another new index entry by typing **fruit desserts** in level 1 and **persimmon pudding** in level 2. You will need to replace the text from the last entry. Click Add again. Then click OK (Windows) or Done (Mac OS) to close the New Page Reference dialog box.

9 In the Index palette, scroll to review your new page references in the index list. If necessary, click the arrows by letters to expand and collapse items in the index list. Click Done to close the window.

Creating index cross-references

Many indexes include cross-references to other listings within the index, especially for common synonyms for a term used in the text. In this procedure, you'll add a cross-reference directing readers who are looking in the index for entries under "sweets" to look under "desserts" instead.

1 In the 12_Finishes.indd file, choose Edit > Deselect All.

2 In the Index palette menu, choose New Cross-reference.

3 In Topic Level 1, type **sweets**.

4 In the Type pop-up menu, select See.

5 Scroll down the list in the bottom of the dialog box and find the page reference to "desserts" under the letter "D." Then drag the "desserts" index entry into the Referenced box.

6 Click Add, and then click OK.

7 Scroll down the list in the Index palette to see the new cross-reference. Then save your work.

Generating the index

Like the table of contents, you can place the index in a separate InDesign file or on pages of a file in the book that also contains other content. In this project, you'll put the index in a separate file.

1 In the Book palette, click an empty area to deselect all files, and then in the Book palette menu, choose Add Document.

2 Locate the 12_Index.indd file in your ID_12 folder and double-click to add the file to the book. If the 12_Index file is not at the bottom of the list in the Book palette, drag it to that position now.

3 In the Book palette, double-click the 12_Index file name to open the index document.

4 If the Index palette is not already open, choose Windows > Type & Tables > Index, and then select Generate Index on the Index palette menu.

5 In the Generate Index dialog box, do the following:

• In Title, delete the word Index so that the box is empty. The title Index already appears on the page, so you don't need to include it a second time.

• Select the Include Book Documents check box.

• Deselect Replace Existing Index.

• Click OK.

6 After a short pause, the pointer appears as a loaded text icon. Move it to the intersection of the left margin and the horizontal guide located at approximately 12 picas on the vertical ruler. Hold down Alt (Windows) or Option (Mac OS) and click in the first, second and third columns. This will place the index text in one column after another until you finish filling all three columns.

7 Choose File > Save.

The index combines all index references embedded in the book files into one unified index.

Always use the Index palette to enter and edit index entries. Although you can edit the index directly, like any other text frame, those changes will be lost when you regenerate the index.

Congratulations; you have completed this lesson.

For more information about refining and formatting your tables of contents and index files, see "Creating Books, Tables of Contents, and Indexes" in Adobe InDesign CS online Help.

On your own

1 Open the 12_Nibbles file and delete several pages. Save the file. Then update your book numbering by doing the following:

• In the Book palette menu, choose Repaginate.

• In the 12_Index file, on the Index palette menu, choose Generate Index. Make sure that the Replace Existing Index and the Include Book Documents check boxes are selected, and click OK.

• In the 12_TOC file, select the table-of-contents text frame and choose Layout > Update Table of Contents.

In each case, notice the changes in the page numbering on the Book palette, index references, and table-of-contents references, respectively.

2 Examine the available options when you select all the files in the Book palette and then choose the following commands (one at a time) on the Book palette menu:

• Preflight Book.

• Package Book.

• Export Book to PDF.

• Print Book.

In each case, click Cancel after you finish reviewing the dialog boxes.

3 Create an index reference for a range of pages. For example, in the 12_Starters file, select the word Salads on page 41 and choose New Page Reference on the Index palette menu. Then, under Type, select the To End of Section option to create an index reference from pages 41 to 59.

Review questions

1 What are the advantages of the book feature in InDesign CS?

2 Describe the process and the results of removing a chapter file from a book.

3 What is the best way to edit an index? Why?

Review answers

1 The book feature makes it easy to coordinate related elements in a long document that consists of multiple files. By defining documents as a book, you can automate what would otherwise be time-consuming work, including the following:

- Maintaining the proper sequence of documents.

- Updating the pagination of the entire book after adding or removing pages.

- Generating a book-wide index and table of contents with accurate page references.

- Specifying options for preflight, packaging, exporting, and printing the entire book.

2 To remove a file from a book, first select the file in the Book palette. Then, on the Book palette menu, choose Remove Document. The result of removing a chapter is that the book no longer appears in the list of files included in the Book palette. When you repaginate the book, update the index, and update the table of contents, all page references that involve pages that were below the removed file now change. Although the file is removed from the book, the file is not deleted; it is still stored on your hard disk.

3 Always update index page references in the Index palette. To do this, double-click the index reference you want to edit in the Index palette (or select it and choose Page Reference Options on the Index palette menu), and then make your changes in the dialog box and click OK. When you finish making changes to index references, open the Index file. Then, on the Index palette menu, choose Generate Index and replace the existing index for all book documents.

It is important to do your editing in the Index palette instead of simply editing the index text directly. The reason is that any edits you make directly in the index text will be lost when you regenerate the index. If you then make changes in the book pagination, you risk having many incorrect index page references. If you edit in the Index palette, all those references are automatically updated when you generate a new index to update the existing one.

13 | Printing and Print Preparation

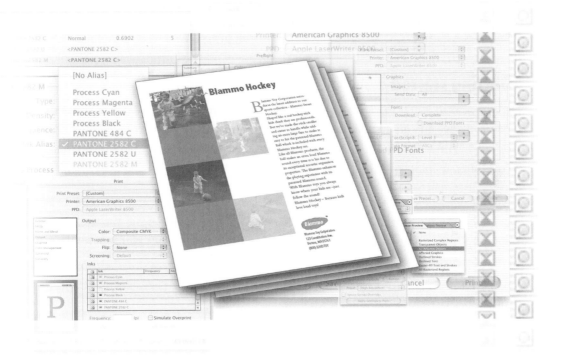

You can use Adobe InDesign's advanced printing and print preparation controls to manage your print settings, regardless of your output device. With Adobe InDesign you can easily print to your laser printer, inkjet printer, or high resolution film, or computer-to-plate imaging device.

In this lesson you will learn how to do the following:

• Confirm that an InDesign file and all its elements are ready for printing.

• Assemble all necessary files for printing or delivery to a service provider or printer.

• Print documents containing spot colors.

• Select appropriate print settings for fonts and graphics.

• Create a Print preset to automate the printing process.

Getting started

In this lesson you'll work on a single page product marketing sheet that contains full-color images and also a spot color. The document will be printed on a color inkjet or laser printer for proofing and also on a high resolution imaging device, such as a computer-to-plate or film imagesetter.

Note: Even if you don't have a printer on your computer or have access to only a black and white printer for proofing, you can still follow the steps for this lesson. You will use some default print settings that help you better understand the controls and capabilities InDesign offers for printing and imaging.

Before you begin, restore the default preferences for Adobe InDesign, using the procedure in "Restoring default preferences" on page 2.

Note: If you have not already copied the resource files for this lesson onto your hard disk from the ID_12 folder from the Adobe InDesign CS Classroom in a Book CD, do so now. See "Copying the Classroom in a Book files" on page 2.

1 Start Adobe InDesign.

2 Choose File > Open and open the 13_a.indd file in the ID_13 folder, located inside the Lessons folder within the IDCIB folder on your hard disk.

3 An alert message informs you that the document contains missing or modified links. Click Don't Fix, as you will correct this problem in the next step.

4 Choose File > Save As, rename the file **13_brochure.indd** and save it in the ID_13 folder.

Preflight

Adobe InDesign provides integrated controls for checking the availability of all files necessary for imaging a document. You can use these controls to Preflight your file and confirm that all graphics and fonts used in the file are available for printing. You can also check the colors used in the document, including those used in placed graphics.

1 Choose File > Preflight.

2 In the Preflight dialog box, review the summary panel that appears. InDesign alerts you to the following potential concerns, noted by the yellow triangle adjacent to the information:

• One image is missing.

• One image uses RGB colors.

• A duplicate spot-color may exist.

The summary section of the Preflight dialog box provides a fast overview of possible concerns in a document. For more detailed information you can click each of the six options along the left side of the dialog box.

3 Click the Fonts option to see a detailed list of fonts used in the document. You can learn about the fonts used in this job and whether they are Open Type, PostScript or True Type. You can also obtain additional information about fonts used in this job, including:

• Whether a font is OK for printing, missing or incomplete.

- If a font is protected from embedding by the font manufacturer.
- The first page on which the font is used.
- The location of the font file being used.

4   While continuing to examine the Fonts, click to select the Show Problems Only checkbox at the bottom of the Preflight dialog box. Notice how no fonts are listed, as all fonts are available for printing and there are no problems with them.

5   Click the Links and Images option along the left side of the Preflight dialog box.

Notice that information regarding all images used in the file is displayed. We only want to view possible problems.

6   Click to select Show Problems Only. Notice that two images are displayed as possible problems. One file, which is embedded, uses RGB colors. Because the document will be printed using CMYK colors, this could be a problem. The other image, blammo_logo.ai is missing and needs to be located before the document can be printed.

You will replace the Blammo logo with a revised version that includes a trademark symbol along with the logo. You will address the RGB image in the printing process.

7 Click the Repair All button. Browse to the Links folder inside the ID_13 folder, located inside the Lessons folder within the IDCIB folder on your hard disk. Double-click the blammo_logo_revised.ai

8 Click to select the blammo_logo_revised.ai then click Update.

Because the file name is different, InDesign did not automatically update the image. If the selected file had not been modified since it was originally placed, InDesign would not have required you to update the link.

Note: *The Repair All allows you to repair missing or modified links. It does not allow you to change the color space defined in a placed graphic. You can do this by opening the linked image in Photoshop and changing its color space or you can have InDesign convert the colors for printing. For more information, see Lesson 7, Importing and Linking Graphics.*

9 Click the Colors and Inks option.

Notice that the four subtractive primary colors are listed: Cyan, Magenta, Yellow and Black along with three variations of Pantone 2582. The C is for coated, M for matte and U for uncoated. Because we will not want all three of these colors to print independently, we will want to correct this at the time we print this document.

10 Click the Cancel Button.

Note: You could directly package the file as the next step in preparing your file for delivery. For this lesson we have decided to create the package as a separate step.

Package

You can use the package command to gather a copy of your InDesign document, all linked items, including graphics and text. InDesign also copies all fonts needed for printing.

1 Choose File > Package.

2 Click Continue in the dialog box that warns of possible problems discovered during Preflight.

Whenever you Package a file, InDesign automatically uses the Preflight command to confirm that all elements are available and that there are no possible problems. Because you still have not corrected the RGB image, InDesign alerts you to its presence. You will convert this image to CMYK for printing using InDesign later in this lesson.

3 In the Printing Instructions window, enter the file name and contact information, then click Continue.

Adobe InDesign uses this information to create an instructions text file that accompanies the InDesign file, links and fonts.

4 In the Package Publication dialog box, browse to locate the ID_13 folder and confirm the folder being created for the package is named 13_brochure Folder. InDesign automatically names the folder based upon the document name, which you created in the Getting Started section of this lesson.

5 Confirm that the following are selected:

• Copy Fonts.

• Copy Linked Graphics.

• Update Graphic Links In Package.

6 Click the Package button.

7 Read the Font Alert message that informs you about the various licensing restrictions that may affect your ability to copy fonts, then click OK.

8 Switch to your operating system and navigate to the 13_brochure Folder in the ID_13 folder, located inside the Lessons folder within the IDCIB folder on your hard disk.

Notice that Adobe InDesign created a duplicate version of your document and also copied all fonts, graphics and other linked files necessary for high resolution printing. Because you selected the Update Graphics Links In Package, the InDesign file now links to the graphics located in the package folder. This makes the document easier for a printer or service provider to manage, and also makes the package file ideal for archiving.

Separation preview

If your documents need to be color separated for commercial printing, you can use the Separations Preview palette to gain a better understanding of how each portion of the document will print.

1 Choose Window > Output Preview > Separations.

2 Click to select Separations from the View drop-down menu in the Separations Preview palette.

3 Click the eye icon (👁) adjacent to each of the Pantone 2582 colors to disable each color.

Notice how certain objects, images and text disappear as you click to disable viewing each color separation. Each of these objects has a different variation of the Pantone color associated with it. You will correct this later using the Ink Manager feature.

4 Click Off from the View drop-down menu in the Separations Preview palette to enable viewing of all colors.

Transparency flattener preview

The images in this brochure have been adjusted using the transparency feature. You use the Transparency Flattener to determine how the transparency will impact the final printed version.

1 Choose Window > Output Preview > Flattener.

2 Choose All Affected Objects from the Highlight drop-down menu in the Flattener Preview palette.

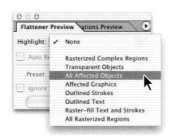

3 Choose High Resolution from the Preset drop-down menu. This is the setting you will use later in this lesson when imaging this file.

Notice how a red highlight appears over some of the objects on the page. These are the objects that will be impacted by the transparency that has been used in this document. You can use this highlight to help identify areas of your page that may be unintentionally affected by transparency and can adjust your transparency settings accordingly.

4   Choose None from the highlight menu in the Flattener Preview palette.

About flattening transparent artwork

Whenever you print from InDesign or export to a format other than Adobe PDF 1.4 (Acrobat 5.0) or PDF 1.5 (Acrobat 6.0), InDesign performs a process called flattening. Flattening cuts apart transparent art to represent overlapping areas as discrete pieces that are either vector objects or rasterized areas. As artwork becomes more complex (mixing images, vectors, type, spot colors, overprinting, and so on), so does the flattening and its results.

For your convenience, InDesign includes three predefined transparency flattener presets. The settings are designed to match the quality and speed of the flattening with the appropriate resolution for rasterized transparent areas, depending on the document's intended use.

***Low Resolution**–Use for quick proofs that will be printed on black-and-white desktop printers, and for documents that will be published on the Web or exported to SVG.*

***Medium Resolution**–Use for desktop proofs and print-on-demand documents that will be printed on PostScript color printers.*

***High Resolution**–Use for final press output, and for high-quality proofs such as separations-based color proofs.*

–From Adobe InDesign CS online Help.

Printing a laser or inkjet proof

1 Choose File > Print.

2 From the Printer drop-down list, choose your inkjet or laser printer.

Notice how Adobe InDesign automatically selects the PPD that was associated with this printer at the time you installed the printer.

Note: *If you do not have a printer connected to your computer or computer network, choose PostScript File from the Printer list and choose Device Independent from the PPD list.*

3 Click the Setup option on the left side of the Print window and choose the following options:

• Letter Paper Size.

• Scale to Fit.

• Centered Page Position.

Note: *If you selected PostScript File as opposed to an actual printer along wtih the Device Independent PPD you will not be able to apply scaling or adjust the positioning of where the file will image.*

4 Click the Marks and Bleeds option on the left side of the Print window and click to enable the following options:

• Crop Marks.

• Color Bars.

• Page Information.

This document does not have items that extend off the edge of the page, so it is not necessary for us to change the Bleed Settings.

5 Click the Output option on the left side of the Print window. Confirm that Color is set to Composite CMYK in the Color drop-down menu. This will take any RGB images, such as the placed RGB photograph, and convert them to CMYK at the time it is printed. It will not change the original, placed graphic. Spot colors will still be included in the output.

Note: *You can have InDesign maintain the existing colors used in a job by choosing Composite Leave Unchanged in the Color drop-down menu. Additionally, if you are a printer or service provider and need to print color separations from Adobe InDesign, choose Separations or In-RIP separations based upon the workflow that you use.*

6 Click the Ink Manager button in the lower right corner of the Print Window.

You can use the Ink Manager to convert spot colors to Pantone colors, and to manage duplicate spot colors. You will address both of these issues.

7 In the Ink Manager window, click the spot icon (◉) to the left of the Pantone 484 color swatch. It changes to a CMYK icon (⊠). This color will now print as a CMYK breakdown as opposed to printing on its own, separate color plate.

8 In the Ink Manager window, click the Pantone 2582 U color swatch and then select Pantone 2582 C from the Ink Alias drop-down menu. The Ink Alias tells Adobe InDesign to print this color if you are printing color separations.

By applying an Ink Alias, all objects with this color will now print on the same separation as its Alias color. Rather than getting two separate color separations you will get one. Repeat this process to select Pantone 2582 M and choose Pantone 2582 C. Now all three duplicate Pantone colors will print on the same separation. Click OK.

9 Click the Graphics option on the left side of the Print window. Confirm that Optimized Subsampling is selected from the Send Data drop-down menu.

When Optimized Subsampling is selected, InDesign sends only the image data necessary for the printer you have selected in the Print window. To have the entire high resolution image information sent to the printer, which may take longer to image, select All from the Send Data drop-down menu.

10 If necessary, select Complete under the Font Download drop-down menu.

Determining how graphics print

When you are exporting or printing documents that contain complex graphics (for example, high-resolution images, EPS graphics, PDF pages, or transparent effects), it will often be necessary to change resolution and rasterization settings in order to obtain the best output results.

Choose from the following options in the Graphics section of the Print dialog box to specify how graphics are handled during output.

Send Data–Controls how much image data in placed bitmap images to send to the printer or file.

All–sends full-resolution data, which is appropriate for any high-resolution printing, or for printing grayscale or color images with high contrast, as in black-and-white text with one spot color. This option requires the most disk space.

Optimized Subsampling–Sends just enough image data to print the graphic at the best possible resolution for the output device. (A high-resolution printer will use more data than a low-resolution desktop model.) Select this option when you're working with high resolution images but printing proofs to a desktop printer.

Note: InDesign does not subsample EPS or PDF graphics, even when Optimized Subsampling is selected.

Proxy (72 dpi)–Sends screen-resolution versions of placed bitmap images, thereby reducing printing time.

None–Temporarily removes all graphics when you print and replaces them with graphics frames with crossbars, thereby reducing printing time. The graphics frames are the same dimensions as the imported graphics, so you can still check sizes and positioning. Suppressing the printing of imported graphics is useful when you want to distribute text proofs to editors or proofreaders. Printing without graphics is also helpful when you're trying to isolate the cause of a printing problem.

-From Adobe InDesign CS online Help

Setting options for fonts

Printer-resident fonts are fonts stored in a printer's memory or on a hard drive connected to the printer. Type 1 and TrueType fonts can be stored either on the printer or on your computer; bitmap fonts are stored only on your computer. InDesign downloads fonts as needed, provided they are installed on your computer's hard disk.

Choose from the following options in the Graphics section of the Print dialog box to control how fonts are downloaded to the printer.

***None**–Includes a reference to the font in the PostScript file, which tells the RIP or a postprocessor where the font should be included. This option is appropriate if the fonts reside in the printer. TrueType fonts are named according to the PostScript name in the font; however, not all applications can interpret these names. To ensure that TrueType fonts are interpreted correctly, use one of the other font downloading options.*

***Complete**–Downloads all fonts required for the document at the beginning of the print job. InDesign automatically subsets fonts that contain more than the maximum number of glyphs (characters) specified in the Preferences dialog box.*

***Subset**–Downloads only the characters (glyphs) used in the document. Glyphs are downloaded once per page. This option typically results in faster and smaller PostScript files when used with single-page documents, or short documents without much text.*

***Download PPD Fonts**–Downloads all fonts used in the document, even if those fonts reside in the printer. Use this option to ensure that InDesign uses the font outlines on your computer for printing common fonts, such as Helvetica, Times, and so on. Using this option can resolve problems with font versions, such as mismatched character sets between your computer and printer or outline variances in trapping. However, unless you commonly use extended character sets, you don't need to use this option for desktop draft printing.*

–From Adobe InDesign CS online Help

11 Click the Advanced Tab and set the Transparency Flattener Preset to High Resolution from drop-down menu.

You can choose the appropriate transparency flattener preset for your needs. The preset determines the quality of placed artwork or images that include transparency. The preset also impacts the quality of objects with transparency applied to them using InDesign's transparency feature, including objects with drop shadows or feathering.

12 Click the Save Preset button and name the preset **Proof** and click OK.

Creating a Print preset saves these settings so you do not need to individually set every option each time you print to the same device. You can create multiple presets to meet various quality needs of individual printers you may use.

13 Click Print.

If you are creating a PostScript file, click Save and browse to the ID_13 folder, located inside the Lessons folder within the IDCIB folder on your hard disk. The PostScript file could be provided to your service provider, commercial printer or converted to an Adobe PDF using Adobe Acrobat Distiller. If you do not have Adobe Acrobat Distiller, you can delete the PostScript file after you have completed this lesson.

You can use absolute page numbering when working with documents that are broken into sections. For example, to print the third page of a document you can input +3 in the Page Range section of the print dialog box. You can also use section names. For more information see Specifying Which Pages to Print in the Adobe InDesign online Help.

On your own

1 Create a new Print preset by choosing File > Print presets > Define. Use the resulting dialog boxes to create presets to use for oversize printing or for printing to various color or black and white printers you may use.

2 Open the 13_brochure.indd file and explore how each color separation can be enabled or disabled using the Color Separation Preview. Switch to viewing the Ink Limit preview using the same palette. See how the total ink settings used in creating CMYK colors affects how various images will print.

3 Using the 13_brochure.indd file, Choose File > Print. Then click the Output option on the left side of the Print window and examine the different choices for printing color documents.

4 Choose Ink Manager from the Swatches palette menu and experiment with using add ink alias for spot colors and with converting spot colors to process.

Review questions

1 What elements does InDesign gather when it packages a file?

2 What items does InDesign look for when using the preflight command?

3 If you want to print the highest quality version of a scanned image on a lower resolution laser printer or proofer, what options can you select?

Review answers

1 Adobe InDesign gathers a copy of the InDesign document along with copies of all fonts used in the document and copies of all graphics used in the original document. The original items remain undisturbed.

2 You can confirm that all items necessary for high-resolution printing are available by choosing File > Preflight. This command looks to confirm that all fonts used in the document or inside placed graphics are available. InDesign also looks for linked graphic files and even linked text files to confirm that they have not been modified since they were initially imported.

3 InDesign sends only the image data necessary to an output device as its default setting. If you want to send the entire set of image data, even if it may take longer to print, you can choose All from the Send Data drop-down menu in the Graphics options of the Print window.

14 | Exporting to PDF

With Adobe InDesign you can quickly convert your document into the popular and widely accepted Adobe PDF file format. You can also convert pages and documents into HTML, allowing your InDesign documents to serve as the foundation for information posted to the Internet or your organization's intranet.

In this lesson, you'll learn to do the following:

• Convert your InDesign documents to Adobe PDF.

• Apply security settings to Adobe PDF files created from InDesign.

• Apply appropriate quality settings when converting to Adobe PDF.

• Create and apply PDF presets to standardize PDF creation.

Getting started

In this lesson you'll take an existing Adobe InDesign document and convert to an Adobe PDF document suitable for posting on a web site and another version that would be appropriate for delivery to a commercial printer for offset printing.

This lesson involves procedures that use Adobe Acrobat Professional 6.0. If you do not use Adobe Acrobat 6.0 you can still create the Adobe PDF files from Adobe InDesign CS, but you will view your completed document using the Adobe Reader software as opposed to Adobe Acrobat 6.

1 Start Adobe InDesign.

2 Choose File > Open, and open the 14_a.indd file in the ID_14 folder located inside the Lessons folder within the IDCIB folder on your hard disk.

Note: If you have not already copied the resource files for this lesson onto your hard disk from the ID_14 folder from the Adobe InDesign CS Classroom in a Book CD, do so now. See "Copying the Classroom in a Book files" on page 2.

3 To see what the finished document will look like, open the 14_b.pdf file using either Adobe Acrobat or the free Adobe Reader. If you prefer, you can leave this document open as you work to act as a guide and to help you better understand the PDF features used in this lesson. When you're ready to resume working on the lesson document, switch to the 14_a.indd document using Adobe InDesign.

4 Choose File > Save As and rename the file **desserts.indd.**

About Adobe PDF and Adobe InDesign CS

While many of your professional design colleagues may be using Adobe InDesign, you may want to share your work as an electronic file with others who do not have this software. The Adobe Portable Document Format (PDF) lets you share documents with users who may not have the same software you used to create a document.

Adobe PDF files can be viewed using either Adobe Acrobat software or the free Adobe Reader, of which 500 Million copies have been distributed. With Adobe PDF files you can be assured that your document will retain its fidelity to the original design, while allowing you to easily restrict access to viewing, editing or printing the file through the Adobe PDF integrated security features.

Adobe InDesign lets you create PDF files directly through its built-in PDF export feature. If you use Adobe Acrobat 6, you can also create PDF files using the Adobe PDF printer. The PDF export feature is integrated into Adobe InDesign CS and allows for added functionality when creating PDF files. The PDF export functionality is not dependent upon the installation of Adobe Acrobat. For more information about the Adobe PDF file format or Adobe Acrobat software visit www.adobe.com/products/acrobat.

Selecting PDF quality

When converting this document to Adobe PDF you will want to determine the appropriate quality settings so that it can be efficiently posted on a web site and also so that a separate version of the PDF can be sent to a commercial printer.

Create PDF for emailing or web posting

You will want to create the smallest possible file when converting this InDesign document to an Adobe PDF file. You can then easily send the file by email for review, or post it to a web site. By keeping the file size small you can ensure it will download more quickly.

1 Choose File > Export.

2 If necessary, change the Save as Type to Adobe PDF and choose the ID_14 folder inside the IDCIB folder on your hard disk.

3 Name the file **desserts_screen.pdf**.

4 Click Save.

5 In the Export PDF Dialog box choose Screen from the PDF Preset drop-down menu at the top of the dialog box.

Notice in the General tab the following items have a checkbox selected when you choose the Screen PDF preset. For more information about how they are created see Lesson 11 *"Creating Interactive Documents."*

• Bookmarks.

• Hyperlinks.

• Interactive Elements.

Additionally, eBook tags also becomes checked, under the include section. This makes it easier for your document to be reflowed for viewing on a handheld computer, converted to HTML or even read by a screen reading device by users with visual impairments. For more information on adding eBook tags to Adobe PDF files, see *Adobe InDesign CS online Help.*

6 Click View PDF After Exporting.

7 Click Export.

Viewing the PDF created from Adobe InDesign CS

1 If necessary, open Adobe Acrobat 6 or Adobe Reader 6 and choose
File > Open and locate the flowers_screen.pdf. Because you selected View PDF file after
Exporting, you should not need to open the file separately if you are continuing on from
the previous step.

2 Move your cursor over the text Persimmon Pudding on the first page. Notice the
cursor changes to an interactive pointer ( ). Click once to follow the link to this recipe.
The InDesign Table of Contents was automatically converted to hyperlinks when the
document was converted to an Adobe PDF file.

*Use InDesign's automatic Table of Contents feature to have hyperlinks automatically
built into your PDF file. You can also add hyperlinks manually. For more information see
lesson 11, Creating Interactive Documents.*

3 Return to the first page of the desserts_screen.pdf.

4 Select the Zoom In tool ( ) and click and drag a box around the picture of the
piece of cake and the base of the spoon. Notice the clarity of the artwork in this file.
Adobe InDesign maintains high quality, resolution independent vector artwork when
exporting to PDF, such as this Adobe Illustrator graphic.

5 Take the Hand tool ( ) and drag the document window over to the right. Notice that the type also remains high quality, even though you selected Screen settings.

6 Choose View > Fit Page.

7 Move your mouse over the internet web address www.sweetfinishesmagazine.com. With your mouse over the link, hold down the Shift key. Notice the cursor becomes a pointer with a W adjacent to the hand. Click to open the link in your Web browser.

Note: Holding down the Shift key causes Adobe Acrobat to open the link in your Web browser. If you click without holding down the Shift key the web link will open within Acrobat as a PDF page. You can choose additional options relating to how the web link will be opened by right-clicking (Windows) or Ctrl+clicking (Mac OS) the link.

8 Choose File > Close.

9 Return to InDesign.

About Tagged PDF Files Exported from Adobe InDesign CS

When you apply structure tags to a document for PDF export, the tags do not control which content is exported to PDF, as is the case with XML export. Instead, the structure tags give Acrobat more information about the document's structural contents. By applying Acrobat structure tags to your document before exporting to PDF, you can do the following:

• *Map InDesign paragraph style names to Acrobat tagged Adobe PDF paragraph styles to create a reflowable PDF file for viewing on handheld devices and other media.*

• *Mark and hide printing artifacts, text, and images so that they won't appear when reflowed in Acrobat. For example, if you tag a page item as Artifact, the page item will not be displayed in Acrobat Reflow view.*

• *Add alternative text to figures so that the text can be read aloud to the visually impaired with screen-reading software.*

• *Replace graphic letters, such as ornate drop-caps, with readable letters.*

• *Provide a title for a set of articles, or group stories and figures into articles.*

• *Order stories and figures to establish a reading order.*

–From Adobe InDesign CS online Help.

Creating a PDF file with layers

Note: This exercise creates an Adobe PDF file using layers that can be accessed using Adobe Acrobat 6.0 Professional. If you do not use Adobe Acrobat Professional, you can still create and view the PDF file using the free Adobe Reader. However, you will not be able to work with the layers in the PDF file you create.

1 If necessary, choose File > Open to select the desserts.indd file that you renamed in the Getting Started portion of this lesson.

2 Choose Window > Layers. Notice the two layers used in this document. These layers can be maintained in the exported PDF file so that they are available to be enabled or disabled by the viewer using Adobe Acrobat 6 Professional.

3 Choose File > Export.

4 If necessary, change the Save as Type to Adobe PDF and choose the ID_14 folder inside the IDCIB folder on your hard disk.

5 Name the file **desserts_layered.pdf**.

6 Click Save.

7 In the Export PDF Dialog box choose Acrobat 6 Layered from the PDF Preset drop-down menu at the top of the dialog box.

Notice in the General tab, the Create Acrobat Layers option becomes available and is selected.

8 Click the "View PDF After Exporting" and also click to select "Visible Guides and Baseline Grids" checkbox.

9 Click Export.

Viewing a layered PDF using Adobe Acrobat Professional 6.0

1 Start Adobe Acrobat 6 or Adobe Reader 6.

2 Choose File > Open and open the file desserts_layered.pdf you created in the last exercise unless it is already open.

3 Click the Layers palette on the left side of the document window.

Note: This palette is only available on the professional version of Adobe Acrobat 6.0. You can still view the PDF file with the standard version or the free Adobe Reader, but you can not manipulate layers without the Professional version of the software.

4 Click the eye icon (👁) to disable the viewing and printing of the Graphics layer. Click the eye icon again to make this layer visible.

5 Click to select the Graphics layer then select Options > Layer Properties from the layers palette menu. Click to select Never Prints from the Print drop-down menu for the Graphics layer. Click OK. With this you can review and proof the text of a document without waiting for graphics to print. Click OK.

6 Choose File > Save.

7 Choose File > Close.

Setting PDF quality settings using predefined PDF presets

A PDF preset is a predefined set of PDF options that you can use for creating Adobe PDF files. The settings in these presets are designed to balance file size with quality, depending on how the Adobe PDF file is to be used. You can also create new presets with custom settings.

Check your InDesign Adobe PDF settings periodically using the Summary area of the Export PDF dialog box. InDesign uses the last set of Adobe PDF settings defined or selected. The settings do not automatically revert to the default settings. You can choose from the following sets of predefined Adobe PDF presets:

eBook–Creates Adobe PDF files that will be read primarily on-screen—on desktop or laptop computers or eBook readers, for example. This set of options balances file size against image resolution to produce a relatively small, self-contained file; compresses all information; converts all colors to RGB, or to Monitor RGB (if color management is enabled); and embeds subsets of all fonts used in the file (except the Base 14 fonts). Adobe PDF files created with the eBook options are compatible with Acrobat 5.0 and later, and Adobe Acrobat eBook Reader 2.2 and later.

Screen–Creates compact Adobe PDF files that will be displayed on the World Wide Web or an intranet, or that will be distributed through an e-mail system for on-screen viewing. This set of options uses compression, downsampling, and a relatively low resolution to create an Adobe PDF file that is as small as possible; converts all colors to RGB, or to Monitor RGB (if color management is enabled); embeds subsets of all fonts used in the file (except the Base 14 fonts); maintains compatibility with Acrobat 4.0 and later; and optimizes files for byte serving.

Print–Creates Adobe PDF files that are intended for desktop printers, digital copiers, and CD-ROM publishing; you can also send them to clients as publishing proofs. In this set of options, file size is still important, but it is not the only objective. This set of options uses compression and downsampling to keep a file size down; leaves colors unchanged; embeds subsets of all fonts used in the file; and prints at medium resolution to create a reasonably accurate rendition of the original document.

Press–Creates Adobe PDF files that will be printed to imagesetters or platesetters as high quality final output. In this case, file size is not a consideration. The objective is to maintain all of the information in an Adobe PDF file that a commercial printer or service provider will need to print the document correctly. This set of options converts color to CMYK; embeds all fonts used in the file; prints at a higher resolution; and uses other settings to preserve the maximum amount of information contained in the original document.

PDF/X-1a–Converts the document content to a PDF/X-1a–compliant representation. Graphical content is converted to a compliant equivalent, if possible, or a warning appears. PDF/X-1a, an ISO (International Organization for Standardization) standard for graphic content exchange, requires that all fonts are embedded, that appropriate PDF boxes are specified, and that color appears as either CMYK or spot colors. PDF files that meet PDF/X-1a requirements are targeted to a specific output condition (for example, web offset printing according to SWOP). PDF/X-1a files are intended to be used by applications that support PDF/X.

PDF/X-3–Converts the document content to a PDF/X-3 compliant representation. Graphical content is converted to a compliant equivalent, if possible, or a warning appears. Like PDF/X-1a, PDF/X-3 is an ISO standard for graphic content exchange.

The main difference is that PDF/X-3 supports device-independent color. PDF/X-3 files are intended to be used by applications that support PDF/X.

Note: For both PDF/X-1a and PDF/X-3, you can modify only those export options that conform to the selected standard. For example, for PDF/X-1a, the Color option is unavailable. For both PDF/X standards, the Compatibility setting in the General panel is Acrobat 4 (PDF 1.3). Any change to the Compatibility setting changes the Standard setting to None.

Acrobat 6 Layered–Creates a PDF file in which all InDesign layers, including hidden layers, are saved as Acrobat layers. This allows Adobe Acrobat 6.0 users to generate multiple versions of a document from a single file.

–From Adobe InDesign CS online Help

Creating & applying a PDF preset

With Adobe InDesign CS you can quickly create a set of preferences describing the settings you use when creating Adobe PDF files. These settings, called presets, can then be used any time you convert a document to PDF. Adobe InDesign ships with a number of default presets, such as the Acrobat 6 Layered preset and the Screen preset, both of which you used in the previous steps. In this exercise you will create your own preset that will include some more detailed PDF export options.

1 If necessary, open Adobe InDesign CS.

2 Choose File > PDF Export Presets > Define.

3 In the PDF Exports Presets dialog box click once to select the Press preset and then click the New button.

Selecting an existing preset before clicking New uses the preset as the foundation for the new preset.

4 In the New PDF Export Preset window, name the preset **Press Quality with Bleed** then click to enable the View PDF after Exporting checkbox.

5 Click the Marks and Bleeds section on the left of the dialog box and make the following changes:

6 In the Marks Section, click to enable the following:

• Crop marks.

• Registration marks.

• Color Bars.

• Page Information.

7 In the Bleeds Section set the bleed to .125 for the Top then click the Make all settings the same button.

Click the Make all settings the same button.

8 Click OK then click the OK button in the PDF presets dialog box.

Using your PDF preset and applying security to an Adobe PDF

You will create a PDF file that would be appropriate to hand off to many commercial printers.

Note: The settings we have specified are a good set of general guidelines to follow, but may not be appropriate for the needs of every commercial printer or service provider. Be certain to discuss the quality settings, marks and bleed dimensions with your service provider or commercial printer before sending them an Adobe PDF file.

1 If necessary open the desserts.indd file located inside the Lessons folder within the IDCIB folder on your hard disk. If you are continuing on from the previous sections of this lesson, you may already have this file open.

2 Choose File > Export.

3 If necessary change the Save as Type to Adobe PDF and choose the ID_14 folder inside the IDCIB folder on your hard disk as the location to save the file.

4 Name the file desserts_final.pdf.

5 Click Save.

6 In the Export PDF Dialog box choose Press Quality with Bleed from the PDF Preset drop-down menu at the top of the dialog box.

Click the Marks and Bleeds section on the left of the dialog box and notice that the settings you created as a part of the preset are automatically applied to this PDF.

7 Click the Export Button.

8 Open Adobe Acrobat 6.0 or Adobe Reader 6.0.

9 Choose File > Open and open the desserts_final.pdf, if necessary.

10 Choose View > Fit Page. Notice how the pages include the marks and page information that was specified in the preset.

11 Click the Last Page button (▶❙) to navigate to the last page in the document.

Notice how the page includes portions of the picture that extend beyond the edge of the trim marks. This extra portion of the picture, known as bleed, allows for edge-to-edge printing without having any white area show around the edge of the picture. The extra area will be cut off at the marks, after it is printed.

12 Choose File > Close.

Note: *You can view this additional page information in Adobe Reader 6.0 and Adobe Acrobat 6.0. But your commercial printer or service provider would use Adobe Acrobat 6.0 Professional because it includes extra tools for checking, correcting and printing high resolution color separations.*

Congratulations, you have completed this lesson.

For more information about creating Adobe PDF documents from Adobe InDesign CS see the Adobe InDesign online Help files. For more information about Adobe PDF visit www.adobe.com.

On Your own

You have security features available in the Export settings that can limit access to select PDF functions such as viewing, saving and printing.

1 Open the desserts.indd file.

2 Choose File > Export, naming the file **secure.pdf**.

3 Click Save.

In the Security section of the Export PDF dialog box, experiment with the Document Open Password and the Permissions passwords to create secure Adobe PDF files.

Export text only for use in word processing applications by choosing Rich Text Format in the Export type pull-down menu.

1 Open the desserts.indd file and select the Text tool.

2 Click within the text frame on the first page.

3 Choose File > Export.

4 Choose Rich Text Format from the Save as type.

5 Name the file **Copy.rtf** and click Save.

6 Open the resulting file using your word processing software.

Review questions

1 Why would you convert and InDesign document to an Adobe PDF file?

2 Are all Adobe PDF files created from Adobe InDesign CS the same?

3 What settings should you use when sending an Adobe PDF file to a commercial printer or service provider?

Review answers

1 Adobe PDF files are perfect for sharing your InDesign documents with a variety of users.

• You can share your InDesign documents with your professional colleagues and use the commenting and collaboration tools to conduct an electronic review, mark-up or approval of the document.

• You can share the document on-line as a PDF posted on an Internet Web site. This allows users to see the exact design you had created, because the PDF will include all necessary graphics along with the font information.

• You can send your InDesign document as a PDF to a commercial printer or service provider for high resolution output.

2 Adobe PDF files created from Adobe InDesign vary in both their file size, included attributes and even their quality. The settings, which are most easily controlled by the PDF Presets determine what information is included in the PDF file.

3 When exporting an Adobe InDesign document to an Adobe PDF file you should be certain to ask your printer, publication or service provider about the settings they prefer to have you use. In general, the Press quality settings will provide the high quality information necessary for commercial printing. However, if the document includes bleed information or you need to include any marks, such as crop and registration marks, these are not enabled by default and must be turned-on manually before exporting the file.

15 | Ensuring Consistent Color

When your document must meet color standards set by clients and designers, viewing and editing color consistently becomes critical, all the way from scanning source images to creating final output. A color management system reconciles color differences among devices so that you can be reasonably certain of the colors your system ultimately produces.

In this lesson, you'll learn how to do the following:

• Specify a color management engine.

• Specify default source ICC profiles.

• Assign ICC profiles in InDesign.

• Embed ICC profiles in graphics created in other Adobe programs.

Note: *This lesson is designed for users who work with InDesign in environments that also involve Adobe Illustrator (version 9 or later) and Adobe Photoshop (version 5.0 or later). If you do not have those programs installed on your computer, you will skip some of these step-by-step instructions for color-managing graphics from Illustrator and Photoshop.*

Getting started

Color management is important in environments where you must evaluate image color reliably in the context of your final output. Color correction is a different issue that involves images with tonal or color-balance problems, and is usually handled in the original graphics application, such as Photoshop.

In this lesson, you'll set up color management for an advertisement for a fictitious chocolate company called Tifflins Truffles. The ad will run in a variety of publications, so getting consistent and predictable color is your goal. You will set up the color management system using a CMYK press-oriented workflow, build the document using graphics from other Adobe products, and specify ICC profiles for individual graphics to ensure color integrity.

Do you need color management?

Use the following guidelines to determine whether or not you need color management:

• Color accuracy in your working environment isn't required if you rely completely on prepress service providers and commercial printers for all your color work.

• Color management is recommended for maintaining color accuracy in monitor display, the ability to soft-proof colors, and color consistency in large workgroups.

• Color management is recommended if you reuse color graphics for print and online media, use various kinds of devices within a single medium (such as different printing presses), or print to different domestic and international presses.

If you decide to use color management, consult with your production partners—such as graphic artists and prepress service providers—to ensure that all aspects of your color management workflow integrate with theirs.

–From Adobe InDesign CS online Help

See also "About color management" in Adobe InDesign online Help.

1 Start Adobe InDesign. Choose File > Open, and open the 15_a.indd file in the ID_15 folder, located inside the Lessons folder within the IDCIB folder on your hard disk.

Notice that the brown colors and images look muddy and lack clarity, and the overall color is saturated. This is because you have not enabled color management.

2 Choose File > Save As, rename the file 15_truffles.indd, and save it in the ID_15 folder.

3 If you want to see what the finished document will look like, open the 15_b.indd file in the ID_15 folder. The ad consists of graphics created in InDesign and other Adobe applications. You will color-manage those graphics to achieve consistent color output from InDesign.

Note: *Although color management is turned on for this document, the colors may still lack clarity because you have not yet set up color management for your computer or set a Preferences setting for displaying all available high-resolution image data.*

A. InDesign object. *B.* Photoshop PSD file. *C.* Legacy (archived) CMYK file.
D. Illustrator file exported as a bitmap.

4 When you're ready to resume work on the lesson document, choose its name from the Window menu.

Color management: An overview

Devices and graphics have different color gamuts. Although all color gamuts overlap, they don't match exactly, which is why some colors on your monitor can't be reproduced in print or online. The colors that can't be reproduced in print are called out-of-gamut colors because they are outside the spectrum of printable colors. For example, you can create a large percentage of colors in the visible spectrum using programs such as InDesign, Photoshop, and Illustrator, but you can reproduce only a subset of those colors on a desktop printer. The printer has a smaller color space or gamut (the range of colors that can be displayed or printed) than the application that created the color.

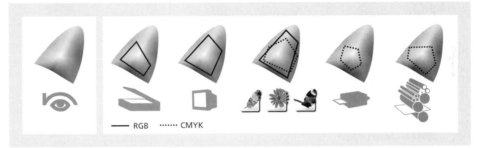

Visible spectrum containing millions of colors (far left) compared with color gamuts of various devices and graphics.

To compensate for these differences and to ensure the closest match between on-screen colors and printed colors, applications use a color management system (CMS). Using a color management engine, the CMS translates colors from the color space of one device into a device-independent color space, such as CIE (Commission Internationale d'Éclairage) LAB. From the device-independent color space, the CMS fits that color information to another device's color space by a process called color mapping, or gamut mapping. The CMS makes any adjustments necessary to represent the color consistently among devices.

A CMS uses three components to map colors across devices:

• A device-independent (or reference) color space.

• ICC profiles that define the color characteristics of different devices and graphics.

• A color management engine that translates colors from one device's color space to another.

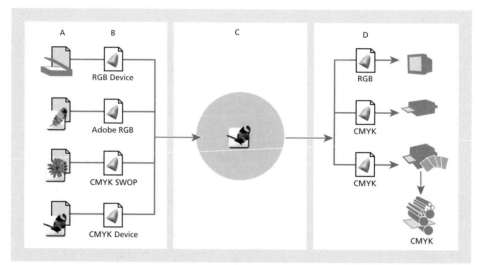

A. *Scanners and software applications create color documents.* **B.** *ICC source profiles describe document color spaces.* **C.** *A color management engine uses ICC source profiles to map document colors to a device-independent color space through supporting applications.* **D.** *The color management engine maps document colors from the device-independent color space to output-device color spaces using destination profiles.*

About the device-independent color space

To successfully compare gamuts and make adjustments, a color management system must use a reference color space—an objective way of defining color. Most CMSs use the CIE (Commission Internationale d'Éclairage) LAB color model, which exists independently of any device and is big enough to reproduce any color visible to the human eye. For this reason, CIE LAB is considered device-independent.

About ICC profiles

An ICC profile describes how a particular device or standard reproduces color using a cross-platform standard defined by the International Color Consortium (ICC). ICC profiles ensure that images appear correctly in any ICC-compliant applications and on color devices. This is accomplished by embedding the profile information in the original file or assigning the profile in your application.

At a minimum, you must have one source profile for the device (such as a scanner or digital camera) or standard (such as SWOP or Adobe RGB) used to create the color, and one destination profile for the device (such as monitor or contract proofing) or standard (SWOP or TOYO, for example) that you will use to reproduce the color.

About color management engines

Sometimes called the color matching module (CMM), the color management engine interprets ICC profiles. Acting as a translator, the color management engine converts the out-of-gamut colors from the source device to the range of colors that can be produced by the destination device. The color management engine may be included with the CMS or may be a separate part of the operating system.

Translating to a gamut—particularly a smaller gamut—usually involves a compromise, so multiple translation methods are available. For example, a color-translation method that preserves correct relationships among colors in a photograph will usually alter the colors in a logo. Color Management engines provide a choice of translation methods, known as rendering intents, so that you can apply a method appropriate to the intended use of a color graphic. Examples of common rendering intents include Perceptual (Images) for preserving color relationships the way the eye does, Saturation (Graphics) for preserving vivid colors at the expense of color accuracy, and Relative and Absolute Colorimetric for preserving color accuracy at the expense of color relationships.

Components of a CMYK press-oriented workflow

In a CMYK workflow, you work with CMYK images prepared for a specific printing press or proofing device, or legacy (archived) CMYK images. You generate a source profile based on your press or contract-proofing standard and embed it into the CMYK images or assign the profile in InDesign. The profile enables consistent CMYK printing at other color-managed sites, such as when printing a widely distributed magazine on presses in many different cities. Because you use color management, the reliability and consistency of color display improves across all your workstations. For final printed output, you select a printer profile in the Print dialog box that describes your contract-proofing standard or your printing press.

Setting up color management in InDesign

No mechanical device can produce the full range of color visible to the human eye: no monitor, film, printer, copier, or printing press. Each device has a specific capability, so that different devices make different kinds of compromises in reproducing color images. The unique color-rendering abilities of a specific output device are known collectively as its gamut or color space.

InDesign and other graphics applications, such as Adobe Photoshop, Adobe Illustrator, and others, use color numbers to describe the color of each pixel in an image. The color numbers correspond to the color model, such as the familiar RGB values for red, green, and blue or the CMYK values for cyan, magenta, yellow, and black.

Color management is simply the designation of a consistent way of translating the color numbers for each pixel from the source (the document or image stored on your computer) to the output device (such as your monitor, color printer, or high-resolution printing press, each with its own specific gamut).

In an ICC workflow—that is, one that follows the conventions of the International Color Consortium (ICC)—you specify a color management engine and a color profile. The color management engine is the software feature or module that does the work of reading and translating colors between different color spaces. A color profile is the description of how the color numbers map to the color space (capabilities) of output devices.

Specifying the Adobe ACE engine

Different companies have developed various ways to manage color. To provide you with a choice, you use a color management system to designate a color management engine that represents the approach you want to use. Remember that the color management engine translates colors from the source. InDesign CS now offers the Adobe ACE engine as one of your choices. This engine uses the same architecture as in Photoshop and Illustrator, so that your color management choices are integrated across these Adobe graphics applications.

1 Choose Edit > Color Settings.

The color management engine and other settings you choose in the Color Settings dialog box are saved with InDesign and apply to all InDesign documents you work on in the future.

2 Select the Enable Color Management check box.

By default, color management for the document is turned off, because successful color management requires that you set it up properly before depending on it.

3 Under Conversion Options in the lower part of the dialog box, select Adobe (ACE) in the Engine pop-up menu.

4 For Intent, select Perceptual from the pop-up menu. Later in this lesson, you'll explore the Intent options in more detail.

5 Leave the dialog box open so you can use it in the next section.

Choose Adobe ACE unless your prepress service provider recommends another engine. Use the same engine throughout your workflow in Photoshop, Illustrator, Acrobat and InDesign.

Setting up default working spaces

To complete the application-wide color management setup, you'll choose profiles for the devices you will use to reproduce the color, including your monitor, composite proofing device, and final separations standard. InDesign refers to these preset profiles as working spaces. These working spaces are also available in other Adobe graphics applications, including Illustrator and Photoshop. Once you designate the same working space in all three applications, then you've automatically set up consistent color for illustration, digital images, and document layouts.

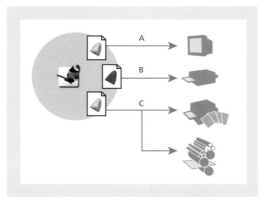

A. Monitor profile. B. Composite profile. C. Separations profile (which can be an output device or press standard, such as SWOP or TOYO).

First, you'll select a monitor profile. If the Color Settings dialog box is not still open from the previous procedure, reopen it now.

1 Under Working Spaces, for CMYK select U.S Web Coated (SWOP) v2.

In a later section, you'll set the on-screen display of images to full resolution so that InDesign can color-manage all available image data.

2 Move the dialog box out of your way and study the colors in the ad.

Notice the heavy use of brown. You'll see a noticeable difference in the browns when you apply color management by closing the dialog box in the next step.

3 Click OK.

4 Choose View > Proof Colors. This will show soft-proof colors on your monitor. Depending upon your viewing conditions, this can give you a more accurate preview of how your image will print.

Several colors change in the ad, but most noticeably the browns; they appear to have more detail. It's important to note that although the images look better than they did when you opened the document, the images themselves have not been altered—only the display of the images has changed. Specifically, what you see now represents the color characteristics of the following devices:

• The program or scanner that saved the image, using the source profile embedded in the image.

• The final output device for the document, using the destination profile you set up earlier in the lesson.

Note: *If you turn on color management after you open a document, color management settings apply only to the current document. For color management to become the InDesign default, turn it on when no documents are open.*

It's easy to see that the success of color management ultimately depends on the accuracy of your profiles.

Assigning source profiles

Source profiles describe the color space InDesign uses when you create colors in InDesign and apply them to objects, or when you import an RGB, CMYK, or LAB color graphic that wasn't saved with an embedded profile. When you import an image with embedded profiles, InDesign will color-manage the image using the embedded profiles rather than the profiles you choose here, unless you override the embedded profiles for an individual image.

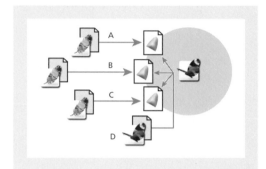

A. LAB profile. B. RGB profile. C. CMYK profile.
D. InDesign document applying a profile that matches the color model of each image that lacks a profile.

1 Choose Edit > Assign Profiles.

2 In both the RGB Profile and CMYK Profile areas of the dialog box, select the Assign Current Working Space options which should be to Adobe RGB (1998) U. S. Web Coated (SWAP) v2, as shown.

Notice that the text following the words "working space" contains the same working-space information that you entered in the Color Settings dialog box. With these settings, the Adobe ACE engine won't unnecessarily convert colors for which you've already specified a profile.

3 Leave the dialog box open so you can use it in the next section.

Specifying the rendering intent

The rendering intent determines how the color management engine converts colors, based on the source and destination profiles you specify in InDesign. You'll specify the color-translation method for the InDesign color management engine to apply to the graphics in the advertisement.

1 In the lower area of the Assign Profiles dialog box, leave Relative Colorimetric selected for the Solid Color Intent option. This option preserves individual colors at the expense of color relationships, so it's appropriate for business logos and other such graphics.

2 Make sure that Use Color Settings Intent is selected in both the Default Image Intent and After-Blending Intent options. These options are appropriate for this photo-intensive page spread.

3 Click OK to close the Assign Profiles dialog box, and then save your work.

Using full-resolution display with color management

When you use image-display resolutions lower than High Quality so that screen redraw is faster, image-color display is also made faster by displaying their colors less precisely. Image colors display most precisely when you view images at the fullest resolution (in addition to turning on color management).

1 Choose Edit > Preferences > Display Performance.

2 For Default View Settings, select High Quality on the pop-up menu, and then click OK.

It's especially important to view color-managed images at full resolution when you work with duotones.

When color management is on, image display is set to full resolution, and you use accurate profiles that are applied properly, you see the best possible color representation that your monitor is capable of showing.

Note: *To save disk space, the sample files for this lesson are 150 pixels per inch (ppi), so the colors are not as precise as they would be using a higher resolution.*

Color-managing imported graphics in InDesign

When you import a graphic, you can control its color management in your document. If you know that an imported graphic contains an accurate embedded profile with an appropriate rendering intent, you just import it and continue working. InDesign will read and apply the embedded profile to the graphic, integrating it into the CMS for the document. If an imported bitmap image does not include an embedded profile, InDesign applies the default source profile (CMYK, RGB, or LAB) to the image.

InDesign also applies a default source profile to InDesign-drawn objects. You can assign a different profile within InDesign—using Edit > Assign Profiles to open the Assign Profiles dialog box—or open the graphic in the original application and embed the profile there.

The ad already includes two images that were saved without embedded profiles. You'll integrate those images into the document CMS using two different methods: assigning a profile within InDesign and opening the original image so that you can embed the profile. Later in the lesson, you'll import two additional graphics and practice two methods of assigning a profile before you place them in the ad.

Assigning a profile after importing an image

When you import images that were saved without embedded profiles into InDesign, InDesign applies its default source profile to the image. If an imported image was not created in the default color space, you should assign the profile that describes the image's original color space.

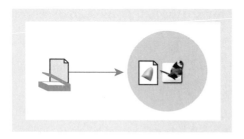

InDesign applies its default source profile to any bitmap image without embedded profiles.

You'll work with an image that was imported into InDesign before you turned on color management. First, you'll confirm the default profile InDesign is using to color-manage the image. Then, within InDesign, you'll assign a new profile because the image's original color space is different from the default color space.

1 Using the Selection tool (↖), select the plate of truffles on the left side of the ad.

2 Choose Object > Image Color Settings.

Notice that the Enable Color Management check box is selected and that Use Document Default is selected for Profile. InDesign enables color management for each imported image and assigns the default source profile you set up earlier in this lesson. You can disable color management for individual images using the Image Color Settings dialog box. You can also assign a new profile here. Because you are assigning the profile within InDesign, the change will apply only to the selected image in this document.

3 For Profile, choose U. S. Sheetfed Coated v2 to match the image's original color space. This profile represents the color-lookup tables used by the scanner operator who originally scanned this as a CMYK image.

4 Leave the Rendering Intent set as Use Document Image Intent, and click OK. The colors deepen noticeably.

InDesign will color-manage the image using the newly assigned profile.

Embedding a profile in a Photoshop TIFF image

As a general rule, you should embed ICC profiles in files before importing the files into another document that uses color management. That way, images with embedded profiles will more likely appear as intended in InDesign or other color-managed programs without requiring any additional work.

In this section, you'll work with a previously imported, color bitmap image that does not contain an embedded profile.

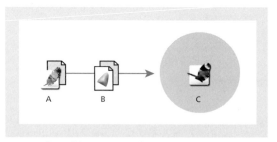

A. Image's working CMYK color space. B. Image with embedded ICC profile. C. InDesign uses embedded profile.

Note: *If you don't have Photoshop installed on your system, you can use the Photoshop files provided in the lesson folder. The steps indicate when to do so.*

Setting up color management in Photoshop

First, you'll define the working color spaces (used for viewing and editing) for the image's RGB and CMYK color modes.

1 Start Photoshop, and choose Edit > Color Settings (Mac OS: Photoshop > Color Settings).

2 For Settings, select U.S. Prepress Defaults on the pop-up menu.

3 For the CMYK option under Working Spaces, select U.S. Web Coated (SWOP) v2, if it is not already selected, so that the embedded profile matches the default separations profile you specified in InDesign CS.

4 Leave the other settings as they are, and click OK.

Embedding the profile

Now that you have specified the working color spaces for the Photoshop image, you'll embed the specified profile.

1 From Photophop Choose File > Open and select 15_d.psd inside the ID_15 Folder.

2 In Photoshop, if the Missing Profile dialog box appears, select Assign Working CMYK. Notice that it is already set to U.S. Web Coated (SWOP) v2, which is the profile you selected in the previous procedure, "Setting up color management in Photoshop." Click OK. If you do not receive a Missing Profile warning, choose Image > Mode > Convert to Profile and choose US Web Coated (SWOP) v2 as the Destination Profile and click OK.

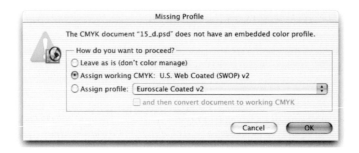

3 To embed the profile, choose File > Save As. Select your ID_15 folder in your IDCIB folder, and then choose TIFF from the Format drop down menu. Type **15_dprof.tif** for File Name. Make sure that the ICC Profile: U.S. Web Coated (SWOP) v2 check box (Windows) or the Embed Color Profile check box (Mac OS) is selected, and click Save (Windows) or OK (MacOS).

4 In the TIFF Options dialog box, click OK to accept the default.

5 Close the image, exit Photoshop and return to InDesign.

Updating the image within InDesign

Now that you've embedded the ICC profile in the Photoshop file, you can update the image in InDesign. InDesign will color-manage the image using the embedded profile.

1 In InDesign, select the large chocolate image.

2 Do one of the following:

• If you followed Photoshop instructions in the previous sections, click the Relink button (⬛→⬛) at the bottom of the Links palette. Click Browse and locate the 15_dprof.tif file you just saved in the ID_15 folder. Double-click the file.

Note: When relinking to a file using a different file format, you need to select All Files under the Files of Type drop down menu when browsing for the file on the Windows operating system.

• If you don't have Photoshop or skipped the previous two sections, click the Relink button (⬛→) at the bottom of the Links palette. Click Browse and locate 15_dprof.psd in the Final folder. Double-click the file.

Note: You may need to select All Files for Files of Type.

3 To confirm that the embedded profile is being used, open the Links palette menu (choose Window > Links if the Links palette is not visible), and choose Link Information. In the Link Information dialog box, make sure that the Profile says U.S. Web Coated (SWOP) v2, and then click Done.

A quick way to check profiles for all graphics in a document is by using the Preflight feature to view document components.

Now that you have fixed existing graphics in the document, you will finish the ad by importing two additional graphics and setting options as you import.

Assigning a profile while importing a graphic

If you know that a color-managed image uses a color space that is different from the color space described by the default source profile, you can assign a profile to it while you're importing the image into InDesign. In this section, you'll import a legacy (archived) CMYK image scanned without a profile, and assign a profile before you place it in the ad.

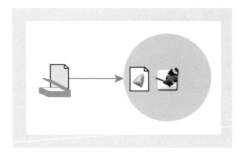

You can assign a profile while you import an image.

1 In InDesign, choose View > Show Frame Edges to show the outline of the frame for the graphic you're about to place—and the outlines for all the graphics frames in the ad.

2 If necessary, adjust your view so that you can easily see the frames in the lower right area of the spread. Using the Selection tool (⬆), select the topmost of these three frames.

3 Choose File > Place to open the Place dialog box, and do the following:

• Open ID_15 folder in the IDCIB folder and select the 15_e.psd file.

• Select the Show Import Options check box, so that you'll have an opportunity to specify a profile.

• Click Open.

4 In the Image Import Options dialog box, select the color tab on the right side of the dialog box.

5 Make sure that Enable Color Management is selected. Then select the following options:

• For Profile, select U.S. Sheetfed Coated v2 to match the image's original color space.

Note: If you selected a different profile in "Assigning a profile after importing an image," select the same profile here.

• For Rendering Intent, select Perceptual (Images).

• Click OK.

The image appears in the selected frame. InDesign will color-manage the image using the profile you assigned.

Embedding a profile in an Illustrator graphic

In this lesson, you'll set up Illustrator (version 9 or later) so that its color-management settings match InDesign. You'll then save a color-managed Illustrator graphic and place it in an InDesign document.

InDesign can color-manage vector graphics created in Illustrator 9 or later when you save them in formats that embed profiles, such as PDF or TIFF. In this lesson, you'll save a file as PDF and then place the graphic in InDesign.

Note: If you don't have Illustrator 9 or later installed on your system, you can read the information in the next two sections, and then skip to step 2 in "Placing a color-managed Illustrator file into InDesign" on page 504 to use the Illustrator file provided in the ID_15 folder.

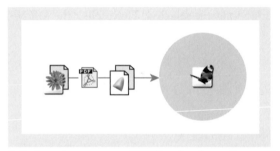

InDesign color-manages a PDF file using the profiles saved with the PDF version of the file.

Setting up color management in Illustrator

Now you'll set up color management in Illustrator so that it matches color management settings in InDesign. This ensures that the colors are consistent from Illustrator to InDesign on-screen and in print. Setting up color management in Illustrator also enables you to embed an ICC profile in an exported version of the Illustrator file. When you place the exported Illustrator file in the InDesign layout, InDesign color-manages the logo using the embedded profile.

1 Start Adobe Illustrator, and choose Edit > Color Settings.

2 In the Color Settings dialog box, select U.S. Prepress Defaults, and then select the Advanced Mode check box to expand the dialog box so that you see more options.

3 Under Working Spaces, for RGB select sRGB IEC61966-2.1. Leave CMYK set for U.S. Web Coated (SWOP) v2.

4 Review the conversion options and make sure that the Adobe (ACE) engine, and Relative Colorimetric intent are selected.

5 Click OK.

You have finished setting up color management in Illustrator.

Embedding a profile in a graphic from Illustrator

You can embed an ICC profile in files that you create in Illustrator and export in PDF or bitmap (.bmp) formats. Then, InDesign can use the profile to color-manage the graphic. In this task, you'll export a file to PDF format, and then place the graphic in an InDesign document.

1 In Illustrator, choose File > Open. Locate and double-click the 15_f.ai file in the ID_15 folder inside the IDCIB folder on your hard disk.

2 When the Missing Profile dialog box opens, select Assign current working space: U.S. Web Coated (SWOP) v2, and click OK.

3 Choose File > Save As.

4 Name the file **15_Logo.pdf**, and choose Adobe PDF from the Save as Type (Windows) or Format (Mac OS) menu. Make sure that the ID_15 folder is targeted, and then click Save to close the Save As dialog box and the Adobe PDF Format Options dialog box will appear next.

5 Make sure that the PDF compression options are appropriate for your final print production, by clicking the drop-down that says General.

6 For Compatibility, choose Acrobat 5.0, if it is not already selected and match the settings shown below. This setting ensures that the profile is saved with the PDF file. Then click OK.

7 Close the file and quit Illustrator.

Placing a color-managed Illustrator file into InDesign

Now that you have created a PDF file of the Illustrator document, you'll place it in InDesign.

1 In InDesign, select the remaining empty frame in the bottom right area of the ad.

2 Do one of the following:

• If you followed Illustrator instructions in the previous sections, choose File > Place and select the 15_Logo.pdf file that you created. Make sure that Show Import Options is checked when you place the graphic.

• If you don't have Illustrator or skipped the previous two sections, choose File > Place and select the 15_Logo.pdf file in the Final folder in the ID_15 folder, located inside the Lessons folder within the IDCIB folder on your hard disk. Make sure that Show Import Options is selected before you click Open.

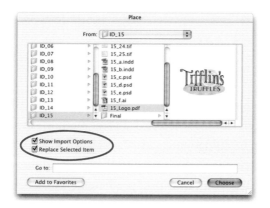

3 In the Place PDF dialog box, for Crop To, choose Bounding Box. This option places only the logo's bounding box—the minimum area that encloses the logo.

4 Make sure that Transparent Background is selected, so that you can see any text or graphics behind the bounding box, and then click OK.

The logo appears in the selected frame. InDesign will color-manage the PDF file using the embedded profile.

5 Save the file.

In this lesson, you have learned how to set up color management across three Adobe applications—an admirable achievement. You have learned several methods for incorporating graphics so that they can be color-managed when placed in InDesign documents. Because you described your color environment to the other Adobe applications whose graphics you imported, you can expect predictable, consistent color for those graphics across the applications.

At this time, you could either hand off the native InDesign file with all the linked files, or export the InDesign file as PDF, embedding the ICC profiles you assigned. If you create a PDF file of the document, the colors in the ad will look the same across all publications that use the ad, regardless of the color-management settings used by the publication's layout application. Other users can preview and proof your color-managed files more accurately and repurpose them for different print conditions when that is useful, or when it is a requirement of your project.

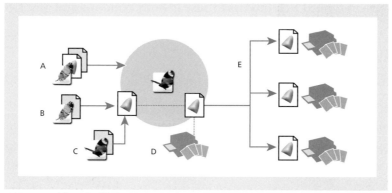

A. *Image with embedded CMYK profile.* **B.** *Image with CMYK profile assigned in InDesign.* **C.** *InDesign document using a CMYK profile based on a separation profile.* **D.** *Separation profile.* **E.** *Different separation profiles when targeting different presses.*

Other information resources for color management

You can find additional information on color management on the Web and in print. Here are a few resources that are available as of the date of publication of this book:

• At the Adobe Web site (www.adobe.com), search for color management.

• At the Apple Web site (www.apple.com), search for ColorSync.

• At your local library or bookstore, look for Real World Color Management (ISBN 0201773406).

Review questions

1 What does the color management engine do?

2 What do source profiles describe?

3 What are three ways to attach an ICC profile to a graphic so that InDesign can color-manage the graphic?

4 Why would you embed an ICC profile in a graphic?

5 Which file formats embed ICC profiles for use in both Windows and Mac OS?

Review answers

1 The color management engine translates colors from the color space of one device to another device's color space by a process called color mapping.

2 Source profiles selected in the Assign Profiles dialog box describe the color space InDesign assigns to objects you create using the drawing tools, or when you import an RGB, CMYK, or LAB color graphic that wasn't saved with an embedded profile.

3 You can embed the profile in the original file, assign a profile within InDesign, or use the default profile you specified when you set up color management in InDesign.

4 Embedding an ICC profile ensures that the graphic displays correctly in any application that uses ICC-compliant color management. The application that uses the graphic honors the embedded profile rather than applying a default one.

5 A growing number of formats can contain an embedded ICC profile, but the most widely supported formats to use with embedded ICC profiles at this time are bitmap image formats such as Photoshop (PSD), TIFF, and JPEG.

Working with Version Cue

If you own Adobe® Creative Suite Standard or Premium, you can take advantage of Adobe Version Cue™, an integrated workflow feature designed to help you be more productive, by saving you—and others you work with—valuable time.

With Version Cue, you can easily create, manage, and find, different versions of your project files. If you collaborate with others, you and your team members can share project files in a multi-user environment that protects content from being accidentally overwritten. You can also maintain descriptive comments with each file version, search embedded file information to quickly locate files, and work with robust file-management features while working directly within each application.

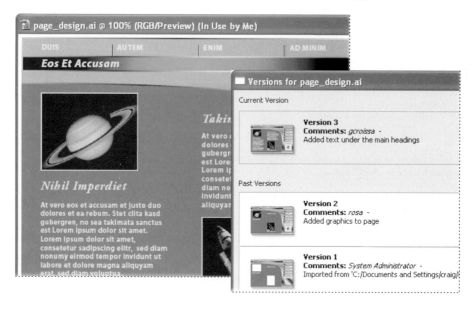

Note: The Version Cue workspace is a feature of Adobe Creative Suite. If you purchased Adobe GoLive CS, Adobe Illustrator CS, Adobe InCopy CS, Adobe InDesign CS, or Adobe Photoshop CS separately, and don't own Adobe Creative Suite, you can use the Version Cue feature in your Adobe CS application only if an owner of Adobe Creative Suite gives you network access to their Version Cue workspace.

Following are the steps you need to take before you begin working with Version Cue, and how to use Version Cue.

1 Set up the Version Cue workspace.

You and others in your workgroup need access to a Version Cue workspace in order to work with the Version Cue feature. When you fully install Adobe Creative Suite, a Version Cue workspace automatically installs on your computer. Depending upon each project's needs, you may choose to work with other Version Cue workspaces located on your colleagues' computers, or on a server.

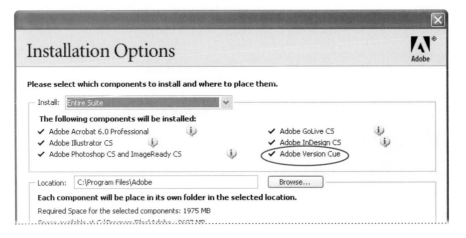

For projects and file versions that you don't need to share with others, or if you work on a laptop that isn't always connected to a network, it's easiest to use the Version Cue workspace located on your own computer. When you change your mind, Version Cue lets you immediately share any Version Cue project with other users. If you mostly intend to collaborate with others, make sure that a Version Cue workspace is located on a computer that everyone can access on a network, and that the collaborative projects are kept in that workspace. For installation instructions, see "How To Install" on the Adobe Creative Suite CD.

2 Turn on the Version Cue workspace.

Before you can begin working with the Version Cue feature, you need to turn on the Version Cue workspace. Open the Adobe Version Cue preferences from Control Panel (Windows) or System Preferences (Mac OS) on the computer where the Version Cue workspace is located, and choose On from the Version Cue pop-up menu. To allow others to see and access the workspace over the network, choose This Workspace is Visible to Others from the Workspace Access menu, or, to keep it private, choose This Workspace is Private, and then click OK.

3 Enable the Version Cue preference in Adobe InDesign CS.

In InDesign CS, choose Edit > Preferences > File Handling (Windows) or InDesign > Preferences > File Handling (Mac OS). Select Enable Version Cue, and click OK. Restart InDesign.

4 Create a Version Cue project for each set of related files.

Now you're ready to create a Version Cue project, which is used to organize related files. For example, to begin with, you can create a Version Cue project for files you want to keep private, and another project for those files you want to share with others. Choose File > Open and click the Version Cue button; the Open dialog box then switches to display tabs, buttons, and menus for working with Version Cue projects. Double-click a Version Cue workspace to open it, and then choose New Project from the Project Tools menu. Enter a project name, information about the project (optional), and select Share This Project With Others if you want to give other users access to your project. Click OK.

5 Add files to the Version Cue project.

To add an existing file or new file to the Version Cue project, choose File > Save As. Then click the Version Cue button, open your Version Cue project and its Documents folder, enter comments for this version in the Version Comments text box, and click Save.

If you have several files to add to a Version Cue project, you can add the files to the project's Documents folder inside the My Documents/Version Cue (Windows) or Documents/Version Cue (Mac OS) folder on your computer. Then choose File > Open, click the Version Cue button, open your Version Cue project, and then choose Synchronize from the Tools menu.

6 Create file versions.

After you've saved a file to a Version Cue project, you can begin creating versions of the file and adding comments to it by choosing File > Save A Version.

File versioning with Version Cue ensures that no one overwrites the work of anyone else in a Version Cue project, but also prevents users from locking out others who need to work on the same file. You can use versioning to seamlessly retain multiple states of a single file as you work on it, in case you need to restore the file to a previous version. You can also use versioning to quickly compare file versions with team members or with a client before selecting a final version.

7 Review all versions of a file.

After you've created several versions of a file, you can choose File > Versions to view thumbnails of all versions of the file, alongside comments and dates for each, and then open, manage, or delete the versions.

8 Collaborate on a Version Cue project.

When you want to work with other users on one of your Version Cue projects, you can instantly give them access to your Version Cue project. Choose File > Open, click the Version Cue button, and then open the Version Cue workspace that contains the Version Cue project you want to share. Select the project in the dialog box, and then choose Share Project from the Project Tools menu.

To access your Version Cue project, other computers need to be on the same subnetwork as the computer where the Version Cue workspace is installed. Computers outside the subnetwork can access the workspace by choosing Connect To from the Version Cue Tools menu and entering the Version Cue Client URL (IP address).

9 Locate files by searching embedded metadata.

Adobe Creative Suite lets users enter a wide variety of information in the File Info dialog box. This information gets embedded into a document as XMP metadata. For example, the metadata might contain a document's title, copyright, keywords, description, properties, author, and origin. Also, any comments you add to each file version are included in the file's metadata. With Version Cue you can quickly locate a file by searching the embedded metadata of all files in a Version Cue project, including Version Cue comments. You can also view a subset of metadata to quickly check the status of a file, its last comment, version date, and who is editing it.

Choose File > Open, click the Version Cue button, open the Version Cue workspace that contains the project you want to search, and then select the project. Select the Search tab and enter any text that may be embedded in the metadata of the file you want to locate or search by filename.

10 Perform advanced tasks with the Advanced Version Cue Workspace Administration utility.

You can choose to set up a simple collaboration where you share a Version Cue project with anyone using a Creative Suite application, or you can set up a more controlled environment in which users have to log in before accessing your project. Using the Version Cue Workgroup Administration utility, you can set up user IDs and define their project privileges, remove file locks, edit Version Cue Workspace preferences, and perform other project and workspace maintenance.

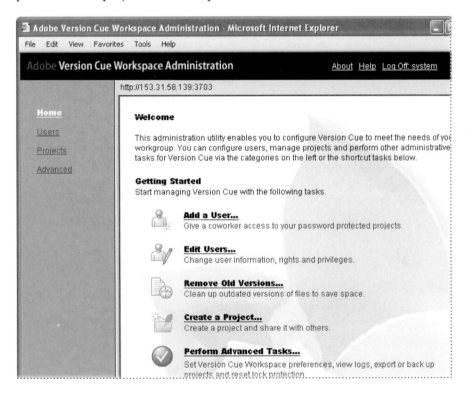

To display the Version Cue Workspace Administration utility log-in page, open the Adobe Version Cue preferences from the Control Panel (Windows) or System Preferences (Mac OS) on the computer where the Version Cue workspace is located, and click Advanced Administration.

Index

Production Notes

The Adobe InDesign CS Classroom in a Book was created electronically using Adobe InDesign. Art was produced using Adobe InDesign, Adobe Illustrator, and Adobe Photoshop. Proofing was completed using Adobe Acrobat 6 Professional using Adobe PDF files.

References to company names and telephone numbers in the lessons are for demonstration purposes only and are not intended to refer to or imply endorsement of any actual organization or person.

Typefaces used

Adobe Caslon Pro, Adobe Garamond Pro, Minion Pro, Myriad Pro and Trajan Pro are used throughout the lessons.

Update team credits

The following individuals contributed to the development of new and updated lessons for this edition of the Adobe InDesign Classroom in a Book:

Project coordinator, technical writer: Christopher G. Smith

Production: AGI Training: Luis Mendes

Proofreading: Jay Donahue, Cathy Auclair

Testing: AGI Training: Carl S. Leinbach, Larry Happy, Jeremy Osborn and Greg Heald

Designers: Thanks to Andrew Faulkner (Lessons 2 and 3), Craig Hoeschen (Lesson 12), Thom Feild (Lessons 8 and 9), and Jennifer M. Smith (Lessons 11 and 13)

Images

Photographic images and illustrations are provided in low-resolution formats and are intended for instructional use only. Illustrations of the Adobe InDesign user interface vary from chapter to chapter, representing Windows XP and Mac OS X.

Photography credits

Training and inspiration from Adobe Press

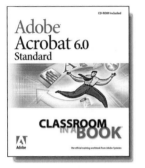

Classroom in a Book

The easiest, most comprehensive way to master Adobe software! *Classroom in a Book* is the bestselling series of practical software training workbooks. Developed with the support of product experts at Adobe Systems, these books offer complete, self-paced lessons designed to fit your busy schedule.

Each book includes a CD-ROM with customized files to guide you through the lessons and special projects.

Real World Series

Get industrial-strength production techniques from these comprehensive, "under-the-hood" reference books. Written by nationally recognized leaders in digital graphics, Web, and new media, these books offer timesaving tips, professional techniques, and detailed insight into how the software works. Covering basic through advanced skill levels, these books are ideal for print and Web graphics pros.

Idea Kits

The how-to books with a twist: Each features projects and templates that will jump-start your creativity, jog your imagination, and help you make the most of your Adobe software—fast! All the files you'll need are included on the accompanying disk, ready to be customized with your own artwork. You'll get fast, beautiful results without the learning curve.

Other Classics

Adobe Press books are the best way to go beyond the basics of your favorite Adobe application. Gain valuable insight and inspiration from well-known artists and respected instructors. Titles such as *The Complete Manual of Typography*, *Adobe Master Class: Design Invitational*, *Creating Acrobat Forms*, *Adobe Photoshop Web Design*, and *Photoshop One-Click Wow!* will put you on the fast track to mastery in no time.

The fastest, easiest, most comprehensive way to master Adobe Software

Visit www.adobepress.com for these titles and more!

Adobe Certification

What is an ACE?

An Adobe Certified Expert (ACE) is an individual who has passed an Adobe Product Proficiency Exam for a specified Adobe software product. Adobe Certified Experts are eligible to promote themselves to clients or employers as highly skilled, expert level users of Adobe Software. ACE certification is a recognized standard for excellence in Adobe software knowledge.

ACE Benefits

When you become an ACE, you enjoy these special benefits:

- Professional recognition.

- An ACE program certificate.

- Use of the Adobe Certified Expert program logo.

What is an ACTP?

An Adobe Certified Training Provider (ACTP) is a Training professional or organization that has met the ACTP program requirements. Adobe promotes ACTPs to customers who need training on Adobe software.

ACTP Benefits

- Professional recognition.

- An ACTP program certificate.

- Use of the Adobe Certified Training Provider program logo.

- Listing in the Partner Finder on Adobe.com.

- Access to beta software releases when available.

- Classroom in a Book in Adobe Acrobat PDF.

- Marketing materials.

- Co-marketing opportunities.